The Sociology Student Writer's Manual and Reader's Guide

Seventh Edition

William A. Johnson, Jr.
University of Central Oklahoma

Gregory M. Scott
University of Central Oklahoma Emeritus

Stephen M. Garrison
University of Central Oklahoma

ROWMAN & LITTLEFIELD

Lanham • Boulder • New York • London

Executive Editor: *Nancy Roberts*
Associate Editor: *Molly White*
Senior Marketing Manager: *Deborah Hudson*
Interior Designer: *Ilze Lemesis*
Cover Designer: *Sally Rinehart*

Credits and acknowledgments for material borrowed from other sources, and reproduced with permission, appear on the appropriate page within the text.

Published by Rowman & Littlefield
A wholly owned subsidiary of The Rowman & Littlefield Publishing Group, Inc.
4501 Forbes Boulevard, Suite 200, Lanham, Maryland 20706
www.rowman.com

Unit A, Whitacre Mews, 26-34 Stannary Street, London SE11 4AB, United Kingdom

British Library Cataloguing in Publication Information Available

Library of Congress Cataloging-in-Publication Data Available
  ISBN: 978-1-4422-6695-7 (cloth : alk. paper)
  ISBN: 978-1-4422-6696-4 (pbk. : alk. paper)
  ISBN: 978-1-4422-6697-1 (electronic)

∞™ The paper used in this publication meets the minimum requirements of American National Standard for Information Sciences—Permanence of Paper for Printed Library Materials, ANSI/NISO Z39.48-1992.

Printed in the United States of America

CONTENTS

TO THE STUDENT

WELCOME TO A COMMUNITY OF SKILLED OBSERVERS

One of the most successful books on counseling psychology is *The Skilled Helper* by Gerard Egan (10th Edition, Brooks Cole 2013). The title's elegant simplicity immediately directs students' attention to the essence of what they, if also successful, are to become. We have written this book to help you become a particular sort of skilled *observer*. Practitioners of all the social and physical sciences are, most essentially, skilled observers. They carefully and systematically observe behavior, accurately record their observations, and then describe how they have conducted their research and the implications of what they have discovered. Underlying all these activities, most fundamentally, is the skill of writing. Much in the way a funnel directs liquid to its intended container, writing refines and directs your thoughts into clear, capable, professional literary "vessels" through which you communicate with the community of scholars. And so this book invites and empowers you to join the particular community of skilled *observers* known as sociologists.

The larger community of skilled observers can claim its birth as 350 BCE, when Aristotle began his *Politics* with the words "Observation shows us . . ." Although some ancient Greeks and others have made careful and systematic observations, much discussion of society had centered on exercises in logic. Aristotle created a new comprehensive system with skilled observations at its heart.

The discipline of sociology as known today began in 1838 when a French philosopher Auguste Comte (1798–1857) invented its name—from the Latin socius, meaning "companion with others," and the Greek logos, meaning "the study of reason." A child of the Age of Enlightenment, Comte subscribed to its ideals of progress, political and economic freedom, individualism, the scientific method, and a profound belief in the ability of human beings to solve social problems. Highly influenced by the French Revolution and the tremendous changes it brought to European societies, Comte sought to help restore order and tranquility to French society. He believed that sociology should be recognized as the science of society, beneath which all other sciences should be placed. He had tremendous faith in science as a means to solve such social problems as war, revolution, crime, and poverty, and rejected theological and philosophical approaches (although traces of them remained in his work). With the founding of *The American Sociological Association* (ASA) in 1905, sociology formally assumed its place among contemporary social sciences.

Today, sociologists study a wide variety of topics, perhaps best illustrated by ASA's list of current organized sections of the discipline: (http://www.asanet.org/sections/list.cfm):

APSA Organized Sections:

Aging and the Life Course
Alcohol, Drugs, and Tobacco
Altruism, Morality and Social Solidarity
Animals and Society
Asia and Asian America
Body and Embodiment

Children and Youth
Collective Behavior & Social Movements
Communication, Information
Technologies and Media Sociology
Community and Urban Sociology
Comparative and Historical Sociology

Consumers and Consumption
Crime, Law, and Deviance
Culture
Development
Disability and Society
Economic Sociology
Education
Emotions
Environment and Technology
Ethnomethodology and Conversation
  Analysis
Evolution, Biology, and Society
Family
Global and Transnational Sociology
History of Sociology
Human Rights International Migration
Inequality, Poverty and Mobility
Labor and Labor Movements
Latina/o Sociology
Law
Marxist Sociology

Mathematical Sociology
Medical Sociology
Mental Health
Methodology
Organizations, Occupations, and Work
Peace, War, and Social Conflict
Political Economy of the World-System
Political Sociology
Population
Race, Gender, and Class
Racial and Ethnic Minorities
Rationality and Society
Religion
Science, Knowledge, and Technology
Sex and Gender
Sexualities
Social Psychology
Sociological Practice and Public Sociology
Teaching and Learning
Theory

Along with the thousands of professional sociologists in colleges and research institutions around the country there are many famous people who were sociology majors in college. The ASA provides the following list of some of them on their website (http://www.asanet.org/students/famous.cfm):

Politics:

Wellington Webb, mayor of Denver
Brett Schundler, mayor of Jersey City
Annette Strauss, former mayor of Dallas
Rev. Martin Luther King, Jr.
Roy Wilkins, former head of NAACP
Rev. Jesse Jackson
Rev. Ralph Abernathy
Shirley Chisholm, former
  Congresswoman from NY
Maxine Waters, Congresswoman from LA
Barbara Mikulski, U.S. Senator from
  Maryland
Tim Holden, Congressman from
  Pennsylvania
Cardinal TheordoreMcCarrick,
  Archbishop of Washington, DC

Saul Alinsky, father of community
  organizing
Saul Bellow, novelist
Ronald Reagan (double major in
  sociology and economics)
Emily Balch, 1946 Nobel Peace Prize
  winner (a social worker and social
  reformer)
Francis Perkins, social reformer and
  former Secretary of Labor
Richard Barajas, Chief Justice, Texas
  Supreme Court
Michelle Obama, wife of Barack Obama

Arts:

Saul Bellow, novelist
Regis Philbin, TV host
Dan Aykroyd, actor/Blues Brother
Robin Williams, actor/comedian
Paul Shaffer, bandleader on *David Letterman Show* (and before that, *Saturday Night Live*)

Dinah Shore, singer
Ruth Westheimer, the "sex doctor"
Kalpen Suresh Modi, White House Liaison for Arts and Humanities

Sports:

Alonzo Mourning, Miami Heat
Bryant Stith, Boston Celtics
Brian Jordan, Atlanta Braves
Joe Theisman, NFL quarterback

Eric Bjornson, Dallas Cowboys
Bobby Taylor, Eagles cornerback
Ahmad Rashad, Sportscaster

Perhaps you, too, by becoming a sociology major, may find yourself on this list. And that is why we encourage you to start writing with energy and enthusiasm. Sociology develops its understanding of all propositions through writing. Ideas do not crystallize until they are set forth on paper or in an electronic form. This manual was written to help and encourage you to make your own unique contribution to society's understanding of how we live together, and to join the marvelous pursuit of the branch of knowledge known as sociology. We wish you all success!

William A. Johnson, Jr.
Greg Scott
Steve Garrison

TO THE TEACHER

WHAT'S NEW IN THE SEVENTH EDITION?

While at times today's world appears to be an uninterrupted stream of reinvention, some things change slowly, if at all. That is why this book's primary value to you, the teacher, has remained the same for more than two decades. This book helps in dealing with three problems commonly faced by teachers of sociology:

1. Students increasingly need *specific directions* to produce a good paper.
2. Sociologists, as always, want to *teach sociology, not English.*
3. Students do not yet understand how and why to avoid plagiarism.

How many times have you assigned papers in your sociology classes and found yourself teaching the basics of writing—not only in terms of content but form and grammar as well? This text, which may either accompany the primary text you assign in any class or stand on its own, allows you to assign one of the types of papers described in Parts 2 and 3, with the knowledge that virtually everything the student needs to know, from grammar to sources of information to reference style, is in Part 1 of this one volume.

What's New in *The Sociology Student Writer's Manual and Reader's Guide, Seventh Edition*

Every chapter and its section has been updated and revised, many substantially.

The following chapter sections are *entirely new* in this edition:

1.1 Read Analytically
1.2 Read News Media as Societal Influence
1.3 Read News Like a Sociologist
1.4 Read to Respond to Social Issues
4.1 Welcome to the American Sociology Association (ASA)
4.2 How to Locate Dissertations and Other Sociology Information Sources
4.3 How to Locate Studies by Think Tanks
4.4 Welcome to the Library of Congress
4.5 How to Find Government Statistics
4.6 How to Find Studies by Government Agencies
5.1 Introductory Observation: Social Life
5.2 Introductory Observation: Race and Ethnicity
9.1 Advanced Observation: Cultural Analysis
9.2 Advanced Observation: Socialization
9.3 Advanced Observation: Inequality
9.4 Advanced Observation: Ethnicity and Race

The following writing assignments are *entirely new* in this edition:

Read & Write: Analyze a Presidential Address
Read & Write: Compare the Slants of Front Pages
Read & Write: Critique a Lead News Article
Read & Write: Respond to an Editorial

Read & Write: Proofread for the President
Read & Write: Explain the Data in This Table
Read & Write: Create a Scholarly Bibliography
Read & Write: Properly Summarize an Article from *Rolling Stone* or *The Economist*
Read & Write: Write an Email to an ASA Section Chair
Read & Write: Collect Six Dissertation Abstracts on a Topic of Interest
Read & Write: Collect Six Think Tank Studies on a Topic of Interest
Read & Write: Listen to a Webcast Presented by the American Folklife Center
Read & Write: Analyze Statistics on a Current Topic
Read & Write: Evaluate a Recent Qualitative Article from a Sociology Journal
Read & Write: Evaluate Three Qualitative Sociology Articles
Read & Write: Compare Cultures of Aging in Two Nations
Read & Write: Analyze the Effects of Social Media on Personal and Cultural Socialization
Read & Write: Describe the Extent and Effects of Increasing Economic Inequality in the United States
Read & Write: Describe Current Trends in Ethnic and Race Relations
Read & Write: Interview Fellow Students
Read & Write: Conduct a Focus Group on a Topic of Interest

We hope you find *The Sociology Student Writer's Manual and Reader's Guide, Seventh Edition* to be helpful to your students and you and we wish you all success.

William A. Johnson, Jr.
Greg Scott
Steve Garrison

READING AND WRITING FOR INTRODUCTORY SOCIOLOGY COURSES

1 Read and Write to Understand Society

2 Read and Write Effectively

3 Practice the Craft of Scholarship

4 Become Familiar with Government and Private Information Sources

5 Introduction to Skilled Observations

1

READ AND WRITE TO UNDERSTAND SOCIETY

1.1 READ ANALYTICALLY

Getting Started

It doesn't matter how good a reader you are right now, how much you enjoy reading, how often you read, what sorts of texts you like or avoid, how fast you read, or how effective your level of retention is. The fact is that the remainder of your academic career—the remainder, in fact, of your life—would be made richer if you were better at reading than you are now. This book attempts to make you a better reader—first, by offering you tips for improvement and suggestions aimed at enhancing your enjoyment and understanding of any text, and second, by supplying you with exercises to improve your reading in the specific discipline of sociology.

But why do we need improvement in writing? It's such a basic skill, something we all learned to do in grade school. Right?

Well, sort of. Our grade school teachers taught us the basics: how to distinguish words in the characters on a page and how to pace ourselves through a sentence or a paragraph to arrive at a coherent meaning. Without these fundamental skills, we couldn't read at all. That's what secondary school focuses on: giving us the basics.

The problem is that there is more to reading than just those first few steps. If there weren't, then we would all be able to read any text pretty much as well as anybody else. It goes without saying, however, that all of us read at different levels of comprehension with varying degrees of enjoyment, depending on what we're reading. We are all different people, each with his or her own preferences, his or her own unique set of experiences that resonate with certain stimuli and less so with others.

Think of all the different worlds you inhabit, your favorite pastimes, hobbies, sports, and school subjects. Each is its own world, with its own set of rules and traditions, modes of behavior and thought, and its own language. Do you remember the first time you watched a professional basketball game on television? The action on the court was no doubt dizzying, but so was the conversation by which the sportscasters and commentators explained each play as it happened. What's a "pick and roll"?

A "double double"—or, for that matter, a "triple double"? Why do some penalties allow for a free throw or two, while some don't? Basketball is a world with its own rules, its own ways of thinking and speaking. How long did it take you to become comfortable in this world—to become an *insider*?

To read well in virtually any subject, particularly in any school subject or profession, it is essential that you acknowledge to yourself, as you begin to read, that you are entering a new world, one inhabited by insiders and one that can be difficult to understand for people who aren't insiders.

Difficult, but not impossible.

It is possible for us to learn how to tailor our reading skills to texts in different disciplines, including those for which we do not have a natural affinity or a set of closely related personal experiences. It requires energy and imagination and, above all, a shift in attitude.

Whether you are reading a textbook chapter, a newspaper or magazine article, an essay in a journal, a book, or a blog, here are some tips to help you master the text.

Read with Patience

Different texts require varying degrees of patience from the reader. When you read a text written in an unfamiliar discipline, be sure you are reading carefully to allow the material—and the world from which it comes—to sink in. Reading with patience means performing certain prereading activities that can help you in mastering the text. Some of these activities are discussed below.

Reading with patience requires making sure to give yourself plenty of time to read the text. If it's a homework assignment, don't start reading the night before it's due. The sense of urgency—if not panic—that attends a rushed reading assignment can drive the material right out of your head before you can master it. Reading with patience also means eliminating distractions—the television blaring in the next room or the MP3 player driving songs through those earbuds you're wearing. Too many people in the apartment? Go find a coffee house with only a few customers or hit the library and find a comfortable chair in the reading room. Would a snack help or hurt your ability to immerse yourself in the text?

To read with patience means arranging your environment to enhance the clarity of your reading experience. The optimal environment is different for each person. What if you actually find television noise or earphone music helpful to your reading? If so, use it, but be honest with yourself about the effect of external stimuli on your reading. The point is to do whatever you can to *reduce your resistance to reading*.

Clarify Your Goals Before You Begin to Read

What is it *exactly* that you hope reading this text will do for you? Are you merely looking for a few facts to shore up a point you are making in a paper? Are you cramming for a test? Are you working to establish a general understanding of a particular topic, or the contours and details of a many-sided argument? Or are you simply reading to amuse yourself? Whatever the reasons that sent you to the text, remind yourself of them from time to time as you read, comparing what you are finding in the text to whatever you are hoping to find. Be ready to revise your goals depending on what you learn from the text. If, for example, you begin reading an article in the *New Republic* examining Republican Congressional opposition to funding gun violence studies, would you become interested in examining the National Rifle Association's (NRA's) campaign contributions to members of Congress?

Explore the Text's Format

Reconnoiter before diving in. You need to remember that the writer, whoever it is, wants you to understand his or her writing and has used a variety of devices to help you. If the text has headings and subheadings, read through them first, to see if they give you a sense of the author's direction and purpose. Note any distinctions among the headings, some of which might use larger type or bold print to underscore their organizational importance. Understanding the relationship among headings can help you determine the shape of the text's argument.

Are there illustrations? Graphs? Charts? Photographs or drawings? If so, a quick study of them will enhance your understanding of the text's goals and its potential usefulness to you.

Keep in Mind the Writer's Goals

Read carefully the first paragraph or first page of the text looking for the writer's main idea and strategy for presenting it. Even if you don't find a specific thesis statement—a sentence or two explaining clearly the purpose of the text—most writers will find a way to signal what it is they hope their text accomplishes. Often the thesis is in the title, as it was for a December 30, 2015, *New York Times* article by Noam Scheiber and Patricia Cohen with the following, rather long-winded title: "For the Wealthiest, a Private Tax System That Saves Them Billions: The Very Richest Are Able to Quietly Shape Tax Policy That Will Allow Them to Shield Billions in Income." Note how the first paragraph of this article neatly answers the question implied in the title, namely, "How do these billionaires shape tax policy to suit them?"

> WASHINGTON—The hedge fund magnates Daniel S. Loeb, Louis Moore Bacon and Steven A. Cohen have much in common. They have managed billions of dollars in capital, earning vast fortunes. They have invested large sums in art—and millions more in political candidates. Moreover, each has exploited an esoteric tax loophole that saved them millions in taxes. The trick? Route the money to Bermuda and back.[1]

Remember, too, that there is always another goal the writer hopes to achieve: *he or she is writing to change you* by inviting you to step a little further, and at a slightly different angle than before, into the world of the text, whatever that might be: politics, cuisine, sports, fashion design, music, animal physiology, higher mathematics, or film history. The text is the writer's way of asking you to pass through a doorway

---

[1] Noam Scheiber and Patricia Cohen. 2015. "For the Wealthiest, a Private Tax System That Saves Them Billions: The Very Richest Are Able to Quietly Shape Tax Policy that will Allow Them to Shield Billions in Income." *New York Times*, 29 December. Retrieved March 25, 2016 (http://www.nytimes.com/2015/12/30/business/economy/for-the-wealthiest-private-tax-system-saves-them-billions.html).

into an environment with which you may not be familiar but which, the writer is convinced, offers you a worthwhile experience. As you read and understand the text, you are becoming more of an insider in that particular environment, broadening the way you look at the world.

Take Notes

Jot down notes based on your early explorations of text features. Your assessment of critical features—headings, illustrations, and the introduction—has no doubt set up expectations in your mind about the direction and content of the text. Quickly listing down those expectations and then comparing them with what you find as you actually read the text can help in setting the text material in high relief in your mind.

Note-taking Strategies   Your goal in taking down notes is to help you remember those elements in the text that your reading tells you will be useful to you. Two prominent strategies for effective note-taking are:

(1) restating the material from the text in your own language and
(2) phrasing notes in a way that establishes a dialogue with the text's writer.

Translate noteworthy material into your language. Any method of note-taking that requires rewriting the text in your own words requires you to engage the text at its most basic level, that of its language. To restate the text, you must understand it. Merely recopying the text's words doesn't require the level of engagement that restating does.

Similarly, underlining or highlighting text is usually not a very effective way to "own" what it is saying. It's just too easy. You often find yourself highlighting so many lines that the marking loses its effectiveness. Also, by highlighting the text, you do not run the material through your own language-making processes, which means you don't participate in the making of meaning as significantly as you must.

Engage in a give-and-take with the author. Besides recasting the wording of the text into your own language in your notes, you can also enhance your understanding by adopting a note format that actually establishes a dialogue with the author.

Ask questions. Rather than simply finding equivalents for key words or phrases in the text, consider phrasing your notes in the form of a question or a criticism aimed at the writer's argument. This sort of give-and-take helps you in clarifying and controlling the range of expectations that occur to you as you read. This is a good way to sharpen your thinking about the text. For example, after reading the *New York Times* article quoted above, you might write:

Why do the wealthiest citizens enjoy special tax privileges that most U.S. citizens don't? Why can't ordinary citizens do what the wealthy do? Why does the general public let the wealthy get away with not paying their fair share of taxes?

It takes very little time to formulate useful questions about the material in almost any text. Never forget the six basic questions: *who, what, when, where, how,* and *why.* Practice using these questions in the exploratory stages of your reading until asking them becomes almost a reflex as you read.

Once you have examined the obvious features of a text and formulated some basic questions, you're ready to read.

Observe How Sentence Structure Aids Understanding

Pay attention to the little words. As we thread our way through the pages of any text, our movement is actually directed by little words, mostly prepositions and conjunctions. These little words don't actually add facts or narrative information but act as traffic signals, preparing us for a shift in emphasis or direction. Phrases such as "furthermore," "however," "on the contrary," and "nevertheless" reinforce our interpretation of a preceding passage and prepare us to understand how the next passage will fit along with it. There are words that *add* the meaning of the coming passage to the last one: "also," "and," "furthermore," "not only . . . but also," "too." And there are phrases that *contrast* the preceding passage with the coming one: "but," "despite," "nevertheless," "instead of," "rather than," "yet." The phrase "of course" indicates that the next fact follows obviously from the last one, as does the word "obviously." Phrases such as "if," "provided," and "unless" indicate that the truth contained in the passage you've just read may be changed by what the next passage adds to the argument.

You know such little words so well that it's easy to overlook their usefulness as markers. Don't. They are extremely important to your reading, shoring up your confidence line-by-line and preparing your mind for the next passage.

Pay attention to the rhythms of the sentences. Often, writers invite you to anticipate the way a sentence moves, perhaps by repeating a word, a phrase, or a syntactical structure, setting up a rhythmic expectation in your mind that, when satisfied, adds greatly to your grasp of the passage's meaning.

In his brief address commemorating the establishment of a military cemetery at the Gettysburg Battlefield, Abraham Lincoln uses the repetition of a syntactical pattern to stop the forward motion of his speech and to shift its focus from the audience's participation in the ceremony to the sacrifice that has occasioned the need for the graveyard:

> But, in a larger sense, we cannot dedicate—we cannot consecrate—we cannot hallow—this ground. The brave men, living and dead, who struggled here, have consecrated it, far above our poor power to add or detract.[2]

As You Read, Be Aware of Other Language Tools

Your writer will employ a range of devices designed to make you feel comfortable in the world of the text. Look for them and allow them to do their work.

- An *analogy* is a comparison between two things that are similar in some important way. Expect to find your writer composing analogies in which some element of the world of the text—unfamiliar to a noninsider—is compared with some element more common to everyday life. Here's an example, from Elizabeth Kübler-Ross:

[2] Abraham Lincoln. [1863] N.d. "The Gettysburg Address." Abraham Lincoln Online. Retrieved March 25, 2016 (http://www.abrahamlincolnonline.org/lincoln/speeches/ gettysburg.htm).

"People are like stained-glass windows. They sparkle and shine when the sun is out, but when the darkness sets in, their true beauty is revealed only if there is a light from within."[3]

Analogies can be helpful in clarifying concepts that are employed to explain social institutions and behavior. To what extent, for example, is it correct to call America a "melting pot"? To answer this question you must do considerable research and clarify many concepts and definitions along the way.

- *Concrete details*—those that evoke and engage the senses—can often do more to communicate meaning and intent than the most elaborate abstract description. A powerful example is the campaign ad that Lyndon Johnson ran, just once, on television in his 1964 presidential race against Republican Senator Barry Goldwater. Instead of offering a spoken appeal for voters to reject what Johnson's campaign was painting as Goldwater's dangerously warlike attitude toward the Soviet Union, the ad simply shows a little girl standing in a field pulling petals off a flower and counting them as they fall, until the girl's soft voice is suddenly replaced by a man's echoing harshly the countdown to a rocket launch and the image of the girl's face is replaced by that of an exploding nuclear bomb.[4]

Test Your Recollection

It is easy to forget material right after you've learned it, so as you read you'll need to stop occasionally and recollect to yourself the material you have just acquired. Recite it *in your own language* to ensure that you have truly assimilated the content. This recollection is an important part of the reading process, but it can be dangerous, in that if you stop to recollect too often you can lose your sense of forward motion through the text. So, no matter how often you find yourself stopping to recollect material, and it may happen frequently in a difficult text, try not to stop for long. Remember that the very next sentence may unravel the difficulty that has induced you to make a momentary stop. *Keep going.*

Reread

The single most effective strategy for mastering a text is to reread it. The first time through you are finding your way, and the text's concepts, facts, and lines of argument are forming themselves in your mind as you read, which means you have difficulty anticipating the text's direction. To use an analogy, reading a challenging text for the first time is like driving down a twisting country road at night, one you have never traveled before, with only your car's headlights to guide you.

---

[3] Elizabeth Kübler-Ross. N.d. "Quotes." Elizabeth Kübler-Ross Foundation. Retrieved March 25, 2016 (http://www.ekrfoundation.org/quotes/).

[4] Drew Babb. 2014. "LBJ's 1964 Attack Ad 'Daisy' Leaves a Legacy for Modern Campaigns." *Washington Post*, 5 September. Retrieved February 23, 2016 (https:// www.washingtonpost.com/opinions/lbjs-1964-attack-ad-daisy-leaves-a-legacy-for-modern-campaigns/2014/09/05/d00e66b0-33b4-11e4-9e92-0899b306bbea_story.html).

But once you've experienced that road, you will be able to navigate it again more confidently, anticipating its tricky turns. The same thing happens when you reread a text. Having been there before, you now know where the argument is going and can see more clearly not only what the writer is trying to say but also his or her motives for saying it.

Rereading as an aid to understanding a text is most effective once you have gotten through the *entire* text. Only then will you have experienced the entire shape of the writer's argument and can commit your full attention to clarifying passages that were difficult during your first run-through.

Pacing Is Vital

How can you possibly pay attention to all the reading tips just discussed and get any sense at all out of the text they are trying to help you understand? Practice. Learning how to improve your reading effectiveness takes time. Try one or two of the suggestions often enough to incorporate them into your reading routine, and then move on to others. The more reading you do, the better you'll get at it, and the wider and more interesting your world will become.

Read&Write 1.1 Analyze a Presidential Address

Here is a brief address from Barack Obama made during in the last year of his presidency. Read through it and then read it again, looking for the strategies discussed above for enhancing reader involvement.

Remarks of President Barack Obama
Weekly Address
The White House
January 1, 2016

Happy New Year, everybody. I am fired up for the year that stretches out before us. That's because of what we've accomplished together over the past seven.

Seven years ago, our businesses were losing 800,000 jobs a month. They've now created jobs for 69 straight months, driving the unemployment rate from a high of 10% down to 5%.

Seven years ago, too many Americans went without health insurance. We've now covered more than 17 million people, dropping the rate of the uninsured below 10% for the very first time.

Seven years ago, we were addicted to foreign oil. Now our oil imports have plummeted, our clean energy industry is booming, and America is a global leader in the fight against climate change.

Seven years ago, there were only two states in America with marriage equality. And now there are 50.

All of this progress is because of you. And we've got so much more to do. So my New Year's resolution is to move forward on our unfinished business as much as I can. And I'll be more frequently asking for your help. That's what this American project is all about.

That's especially true for one piece of unfinished business, that's our epidemic of gun violence.

Last month, we remembered the third anniversary of Newtown. This Friday, I'll be thinking about my friend Gabby Giffords, five years into her recovery from the shooting in Tucson. And all across America, survivors of gun violence and those who lost a child, a parent, a spouse to gun violence are forced to mark such awful anniversaries every single day.

And yet Congress still hasn't done anything to prevent what happened to them from happening to other families. Three years ago, a bipartisan, commonsense bill would have required background checks for virtually everyone who buys a gun. Keep in mind, this policy was supported by some 90% of the American people. It was supported by a majority of NRA households. But the gun lobby mobilized against it. And the Senate blocked it.

Since then, tens of thousands of our fellow Americans have been mowed down by gun violence. Tens of thousands. Each time, we're told that commonsense reforms like background checks might not have stopped the last massacre, or the one before that, so we shouldn't do anything.

We know that we can't stop every act of violence. But what if we tried to stop even one? What if Congress did something—anything—to protect our kids from gun violence?

A few months ago, I directed my team at the White House to look into any new actions I can take to help reduce gun violence. And on Monday, I'll meet with our Attorney General, Loretta Lynch, to discuss our options. Because I get too many letters from parents, and teachers, and kids, to sit around and do nothing. I get letters from responsible gun owners who grieve with us every time these tragedies happen; who share my belief that the Second Amendment guarantees a right to bear arms; and who share my belief we can protect that right while keeping an irresponsible, dangerous few from inflicting harm on a massive scale.[5]

---

[5] Barack Obama. 2016. "Weekly Address: Making America Safer for Our Children." The White House, 1 January. Retrieved February 23, 2016 (https://www.whitehouse.gov/the-press-office/2016/01/01/weekly-address-making-america-safer-our-children).

1.2   READ NEWS MEDIA AS
SOCIETAL INFLUENCE

Sociology: Helping You Perceive and Evaluate Influence in Society

A central focus of sociology is the study of the mechanisms of influence: political, economic, cultural, and social. One of most important mechanisms of influence on the planet is what we commonly call the news. Without a free-flowing supply of news in a country, freedom, democracy, and security are unavailable, and personal vitality and fulfillment for most people are severely impaired. Even with a free flow of news, those who control that flow have enormous influence.

Influence Is Deciding Who Shows up on the Radar Screen and the Size of Their Blip   Control of the news means controlling what people know and what they don't know. It means controlling who makes the local, national, and international radar screen and who does not. A local news story about a child dying of cancer can produce an immediate inflow of assistance that many other families in similar situations must go without. In some areas of the world making the radar screen is a matter of life and death for millions of people. At any particular time, tens of thousands of people worldwide face war, disease, famine, and natural disasters. Some get a lot of help, some get moderate assistance, and some get virtually none at all. What determines who gets what?

Politics always plays a role, but publicity can be equally important. "The pen is mightier than the sword," wrote Edward Bulwer-Lytton in his play *Richelieu; Or the Conspiracy* in 1839.[6] Here are three historical examples of the power of the press . . .

. . . to save lives:

One of the most notable and successful efforts to save lives by exploiting the media radar screen was conducted by Mohandas Gandhi (1869–1948). Having developed techniques of nonviolent resistance to racial oppression in South Africa in the 1890s, Gandhi went to India during World War I and began organizing peaceful demonstrations against the British occupation there. His first task was to liberate India from the British without a violent Civil War. Through several prison terms, large-scale protest marches and well-orchestrated trips to London to see top officials, Gandhi attracted press attention wherever he went. When Civil War between Hindus and Muslims began to threaten India after World War II, Gandhi walked hundreds of miles through villages of both religions. In so doing Gandhi not only succeeded in averting a war of independence, saving hundreds of thousands of lives, he also averted a Civil War saving hundreds of thousands more. His deep commitment to justice and nonviolence and his superior management of publicity helped him save more lives than anyone else in history.

---

[6] Edward Bulwer-Lytton. 1839. *Richelieu: Or, the Conspiracy, a Plan in Five Acts.* II, ii, p. 39. New York: Samuel French, [186–?]. *Making of America*. Ann Arbor University of Michigan Library, 2005. Retrieved February 23, 2016 (http://name.umdl.umich.edu/AAX 3994.0001.001).

... to defeat racism:

Sometimes lives are saved when the words and actions of certain people are denied making the media radar screen. Atop Magnetic Mountain, overlooking the rolling verdant hills of Eureka Springs, Arkansas, stands a 65.5-foot-tall statue of Jesus, beckoning visitors to *The Great Passion Play*, a dramatic depiction of the last week of Jesus's life. The play and statue are monuments to the energies of evangelist and political organizer Gerald L. K. Smith (1898–1976). A powerful speaker who attracted sizeable crowds, Smith was a Christian nationalist and white supremacist. Virulently anti-Semitic, Smith founded the America First Party in 1946. A firm believer that the Jews killed Jesus and that they have been a primary source of evil ever since, after World War II Smith preached against Jews at every opportunity while defending Nazis. The Holocaust, in which several million Jews were killed in Nazi death camps, was a fresh memory in the late 1940s and early 1950s. The world over, Jews knew they had to energetically combat anti-Semitism wherever they encountered it, so Smith naturally became a prime concern for the Jewish Anti-Defamation League (ADL) and the American Jewish Committee (AJC). Jewish leaders adopted a tactic of "dynamic silence." They asked newspaper editors to first consider the extent to which their coverage was helping Smith draw so much attention. Then they asked the editors to consider whether Smith's hatred-filled rants deserved the free publicity they were getting. They proposed that if the papers stopped covering Smith's rallies, his movement would dry up along with his publicity. The editors agreed and stopped coverage, and Smith's momentum declined. Although Smith continued work on his statue and passion play, his movement never recovered.

... to make policy, not always for the better:

Finally, sometimes the radar screen is purposely distorted in the interest of particular news media. By the late 1880s, Cuba was a prosperous Spanish colony whose sugar plantations sweetened American muffins, piña coladas, and Coca-Colas. But American-owned Hawaiian plantations became sufficiently powerful to gain import-tax advantages from Congress. Its main market for its primary product gone, Cuba's economy collapsed. Penniless and hungry, the plantation workers revolted. Spain responded by sending troops who rounded up thousands of protestors and herded them into *concentrado* camps, a name borrowed by the Nazis for use in the Holocaust. A decade of unrest followed, which unfortunately was useful to newspaper czar William Randolph Hearst, who wanted to create news to outsell his competition, and to Assistant Secretary of the Navy (later President) Theodore Roosevelt, who wanted to increase America's image as a world power. Pumping up false charges against Spain of cruelty (in what became known as *yellow journalism*), and blaming Spain for the sinking of the American battleship USS *Maine* in Havana Harbor, America declared war on Spain in 1898 and wrested control of Spanish territories in the Caribbean and the Pacific.

Read&Write 1.2 Compare the Slants of Front Pages

A "slant" is a repeated emphasis of one viewpoint as opposed to another, or of one type of content as opposed to another. This writing exercise is relatively simple. The online versions of major newspapers contain much more content than printed versions because web pages provide more space for links to many more articles than appear on printed front pages.

When you visit the home pages of the online versions of the *New York Times* (nytimes.com) and the *Wall Street Journal* (wsj.com), note that you will find a link that says "Today's Paper" immediately under the names of the two newspapers.

Start by visiting the home pages of both of these papers, and select the "Today's Paper" link on both of them. Here you will find the most recent news that is featured in their print editions. Copy into a Word file the titles of the half dozen or so bold print articles you find on each page. In a page or two, describe what you infer about the character and aims of each paper from the article titles in each newspaper. How do the priorities of the two papers differ? What are the social, economic, and political implications of that difference? Is there an obvious political slant to the articles selected? To what do you attribute the slant(s) you find, if any.

1.3   READ NEWS LIKE A SOCIOLOGIST

Because sociologists spend a lot of their time reading newspapers, it is vital for them to know how to read skillfully—how to understand and evaluate newspaper material accurately and quickly. Learning how to do so requires the mastery of certain reading techniques that people may not typically apply to the reading of their local paper. This chapter offers tips that can help you read a newspaper like a sociologist.

Understand the Task

Besides entertainment and advertising, the content of any newspaper includes news and opinions, and because these two categories can be easily and even intentionally confused, and because accurately differentiating them is essential, let's take a quick look at them.

News is composed of two types of data: information and analysis.

- *Information* is composed of facts, specifically, accounts of events and background. The title of an account of an event could be "Conservative Christians Hold 'City on a Hill' Conference." A background statement could be "This is the third time this year that Conservative Christians have met in Washington, DC."

- *Analysis* is comprised of interpretations of the information rendered in the news story. After observing the goings-on at the "City on a Hill" conference, the reporter interprets what he or she has witnessed there: "A primary purpose of the conference seems to have been to encourage Conservative Christians to develop a new strategy to restrict abortions."

Opinions are evaluations of the information reported in newspapers and are composed of editorials, op-ed pieces (opinion pieces written by named authors who are not on the newspaper's staff), opinion columns, blogs, and other contributions such as transcripts of interviews. An opinion concerning the "City on a Hill" conference, published in one of the newspaper's editorials, might read, "Once again conservatives seek to consolidate their weakening power by angering a variety of social constituencies." Clearly, the line between analysis and opinion is a thin one.

A Conundrum   On a daily basis, renowned newspapers such as the *New York Times* and the *Wall Street Journal* attempt to clearly identify and separate news from opinion. Their integrity and credibility depend on their success. Their articles are clearly identifiable as news or opinion, and usually their news articles have a high degree of objectivity. Opinion is opinion and is persuasive to the extent it seems reasonable or appeals to a certain prejudice. Intelligent readers rarely confuse opinion with news.

But "news" suffers from a congenital defect. No matter how objective a reporter tries to be, perfection is intrinsically beyond reach. Philosopher Karl Popper (1902–1994) was fond of starting courses with a simple command to his students: "Observe." He would stand quietly and wait until a student broke the tension with the question "Observe what?" "Precisely," was Popper's retort. His point was that no observation is purely objective and value-free. The moment we try to observe, we necessarily choose what to observe, and that choice is always full of values.

When editors assign stories, their selections are affected by not only their experienced sense of importance but also their perceptions of the prospective author and their estimate of what sells as well. Therefore, although "objective reporting" is the hallmark of a good newspaper, good reporters understand and exploit the tension between "news" and "opinion," allowing, at least to some extent, their quest for relevance to temper their thirst for facts.

Read the Front Page

Daily newspapers are much like highway maps, providing thousands of bits of information, which together form a coherent web that can be imagined as a compact image of life on this planet, or on part of it, on any particular day. The newspaper's front page is the symbol key to that map. Start reading your newspaper by noting both what is included on the front page and what is not. Here is your front page analytical checklist.

Content   What gets premium front-page coverage tells you what the newspaper's priorities and biases are. Here are the front-page stories of the *New York Times* on December 15, 2015:

- Top News All Los Angeles Public Schools Closed After Bomb Threat
- Jurors in Freddie Gray Case Say They Are Deadlocked
- U.S. Prosecutors Expected to Charge Two Venezuelans
- Experts Were Wrong About Where Health Care Costs Less
- Do Areas that Spend Less on Medicare Also Spend Less on Health Care Overall?
- Curing Hepatitis C, in an Experiment the Size of Egypt
- Where the Candidates Stand on 2016's Biggest Issues
- How Trump Could Win, and Why He Probably Won't
- Setting Sights on Cruz, and Pondering a Tricky Target in Trump
- Trump to Meet Donor Sheldon Adelson Before Debate
- A Refugee Crisis, a Greek Debt Showdown, Russian Aggression and Terrorism in the Streets: How 2015 Has Threatened the E.U.
- Towers of Secrecy: A "Starship" and a Shell Company Stir Resentment

- In the Booming, High-end Market of Los Angeles, One House Stands Out.
- New Scrutiny of New York Prison Diversion Programs: Some Aid to Afghans Ends Up Helping Taliban, U.S. Says
- International Atomic Agency Ends Iran Inquiry
- Fabled Nazi Gold Train Looks Like a Fable
- New York City Homelessness Chief Is Leaving
- "Shamed and Victimized for Life": Rape in India

By contrast, here are the articles on the cover of the *New York Post* for December 15, 2015:

- Catching Fish: Brilliant Beckham Lifts Giants
- Sleazy Riders: Subway Sex Crimes Skyrocket
- Cosby Sues Seven Accusers

And here are the front-page stories of the *Wall Street Journal* on December 15, 2015:

- Fed Poised to Mark The End of an Era
- Stocks Rise Ahead of Fed Decision
- L.A. Officials Defend Decision to Close Schools After Threat
- E.U. Officials Settle on Privacy Law
- Second-Tier Hopefuls Face Off in GOP Debate
- Republican Presidential Candidates Are Gathering in Las Vegas on Tuesday Night for the Fifth Night of Presidential Debates. Here Is Our Live Blog of the Event
- Analysis: Seven Insights About the Republican Field
- The Inevitable Cruz–Rubio Collision
- Trump Supporters in Nevada Struggle With Caucus Process
- Poll Finds National Security Now a Top Concern
- U.N. Experts Say Iran Missile Firing Violated Sanctions
- Iran's Firing of a Medium-Range Ballistic Missile in October Violated U.N. Sanctions Banning the Islamic Republic from Launches Capable of Delivering Nuclear Weapons, U.N. Experts Said in a New Report
- IAEA Board Agrees to Close File on Iran's Past Nuclear Activities
- Jurors in Baltimore Police Officer Trial Say They Are Deadlocked
- Jurors in the First Baltimore Police Officer Trial in Connection with the Death of Freddie Gray Last April Told the Judge Tuesday Afternoon They Were Deadlocked. The Judge Told Them to Continue Deliberations
- U.S. Boosts Online Scrutiny
- U.S. Graduation Rate Rises
- Meet Your Child's New Partner
- Ousted Cheniere Energy CEO in Line for Big Payout

What assumptions about the character of each newspaper can you make by comparing the contents of their front pages?

Layout   The position on the front page indicates the editor's estimate of the importance of the article. A banner headline is big-time news. Traditionally, newspapers are in the habit of placing the lead article in the upper right corner of the front page because when they are displayed on old-style newsstands the papers are folded in the middle and arrayed so that the upper right part of the paper is visible. The second most important story appears on the upper left. The bigger the title font, the more important the article.

Everything about the front page of a newspaper is done on purpose. Did you ever notice that when you enter Walgreen's to pick up a prescription, the pharmacy is in the rear of the store? Try getting to the pharmacy without being distracted, if ever so slightly, by the candies, cosmetics, cuticle clippers, coffee cups, crayons, and birthday cards. The front page of a typical newspaper is organized a bit like the aisles in Walgreen, offering something for everyone.

Structure of an Article   Every article in a newspaper has three jobs to do:

1. Get your attention.
2. Tell you the story's bottom line.
3. Tell a convincing story in a very short time.

To meet these goals, the news articles must follow a standard format known as the *inverted pyramid*. While literary stories start with small details and build to a climax at the end, news articles do the opposite. The article title is the "bottom line." It tells you the punchline of the story right up front. Details follow in descending order with the most important ones appearing first. Background and incidentals come last.

Read&Write 1.3   Critique a Lead News Article

Read the following article from the *Washington Post*, a highly respected newspaper, and examine, in a response of approximately 500 words, the hierarchy of flow within it. Is it an inverted pyramid? Explain.

Actor Sean Penn Secretly Interviewed Mexico's 'El Chapo' in Hideout
The Washington Post
By Joshua Partlow, January 10 at 12:15 AM

CULIACAN, Mexico—The Joaquín "El Chapo" Guzmán story could hardly have seemed more unbelievable, with its multiple prison breaks, endless sewers and tunnels, outlandish sums of money, and feverish manhunts. And then Sean Penn entered the story.

While Guzmán was the world's most-wanted fugitive, dodging Mexican military operations and U.S. Drug Enforcement Administration surveillance, he was secretly meeting with the Hollywood movie star in an undisclosed Mexican hideout and has now provided what appears to be the first public interview of his drug-running career, published Saturday by *Rolling Stone*.

Among the revelations in the article, Guzmán, who was captured Friday morning in his home state of Sinaloa, bragged to Penn about his prowess in the drug trade.

"I supply more heroin, methamphetamine, cocaine and marijuana than anybody else in the world," Guzmán said. "I have a fleet of submarines, airplanes, trucks and boats."

The Associated Press reported that a Mexican law enforcement official said the Penn meeting helped authorities locate Guzmán in Durango state in October.

Escaped Mexican drug lord 'El Chapo' recaptured

The leader of the Sinaloa cartel, who had been locked up in what has been described as the country's most impenetrable prison, was recaptured in western Mexico after a shootout that left five dead.

Penn provides a lengthy account of how he met the elusive criminal. Penn tried to protect his communications using burner phones and encryption and anonymous email addresses. The meeting was brokered by the Mexican actress Kate del Castillo and took place at an undisclosed location in the Mexican mountains.

Penn reportedly spent seven hours with Guzmán and then did follow-up interviews by phone and video, including one posted on the *Rolling Stone* website of Guzmán in a paisley blue shirt speaking in front of a chain-link fence.

Guzmán, who in the past has denied participation in the drug trade and portrayed himself as a peasant farmer, spoke unapologetically and serenely about his lucrative trade.

Where he grew up, in the mountains of Sinaloa state, "the only way to have money to buy food, to survive, is to grow poppy, marijuana," he said, and he began at a young age.

"It's a reality that drugs destroy. Unfortunately, as I said, where I grew up there was no other way and there still isn't a way to survive, no way to work in our economy to be able to make a living."

Despite the deadly wars his Sinaloa cartel has fought with other gangs and authorities, Guzmán described himself as not a violent person.

"Look, all I do is defend myself, nothing more," he said. "But do I start trouble? Never."

The interview with Penn may have helped authorities finally recapture Guzmán, who was arrested on Friday after a military raid on a house in the coastal city of Los Mochis. Guzmán fled in a sewer and carjacked a getaway vehicle but was stopped on the highway.

Mexico's attorney general, Arely Gómez González said on Friday night that authorities zeroed in on Guzmán after movie producers and actresses made contact with him.

Penn met with Guzmán in early October, just before a military operation targeting Guzman in a ranch in the town of Pueblo Nuevo in Durango. Mexican authorities said Guzmán got away because a helicopter didn't want to fire at him because he was fleeing with two women and a girl.

Guzmán wrote to Penn that eight helicopters pursued him and the "marines dispersed throughout the farms. The families had to escape and abandon their homes with the fear of being killed. We still don't know how many dead in total."

Guzmán said his injuries were "not like they said. I only hurt my leg a little bit."

A senior Mexican official, who could not confirm whether Penn's interview contributed to Guzmán's arrest, described the interview with Penn as "an act of propaganda" that contributed to Guzmán's outsized myth.

"Nothing that appears in the interview changes that he is a criminal who has assassinated many people and trafficked in drugs that resulted in the deaths of many people," the official said.

The Penn interview was the latest twist in the wild "El Chapo" saga that included his dramatic arrest on Friday.

In the pre-dawn darkness, Mexican marines quietly surrounded a little white house in Los Mochis where the druglord was staying.

But the elusive Guzmán—who had escaped twice from federal prison—did it again. He vanished down an escape hatch and into the sewer. It wasn't until he popped up four blocks away, stole a car, and sped out of town that Mexican authorities finally captured him on the highway and ended six months of national humiliation for letting the world's top drug lord escape.

Guzmán was later flown to Mexico City and returned to Altiplano prison, the facility he escaped from in July.

Guzmán's capture was celebrated by law enforcement officials in Washington because Guzmán runs a drug-trafficking network with vast international reach that has been dumping tons of cocaine and heroin into U.S. cities for years. But more than that, it represented a massive vindication, at least symbolically, for a Mexican government that has often seemed incapable of alleviating the brutal drug war violence that has left some 100,000 dead in the past decade.

After two prison escapes, many expect the Mexican government to extradite Guzmán to the United States. The Mexican attorney general's office said in a statement Saturday that extradition procedures would begin. But that could take weeks or months, as the accusations against Guzmán must be reviewed and a judge needs to recommend a course of action.

"There are a series of things that could take months," one official said.

Joshua Partlow is the *Post*'s bureau chief in Mexico. He has served previously as the bureau chief in Kabul and as a correspondent in Brazil and Iraq.[7]

Reading News Reports

To accurately read a newspaper article you have a lot of work to do. Happily, as time goes on you become familiar with the publications, the journalists, their sources and other matters, but it takes practice. Here is a news article appraisal checklist:

- *Reputation.* What does the reading public think of the newspaper? What does the quality of the front page tell you? Earlier in this chapter you were invited to compare front pages from the *New York Times* and the *New York Post*. Which of these two newspapers would you rather cite as a source for information in your own term paper?

- *Author.* What are the credentials and reputation of the author of the news story? Does he or she have the background to accurately report the news? A newspaper's website normally provides the credentials of its reporters.

---

[7] Joshua Partlow. 2016. "Actor Sean Penn Secretly Interviewed Mexico's 'El Chapo' in Hideout." *Washington Post*, 10 January. Retrieved February 23, 2016 (https://www.washingtonpost.com/world/actor-sean-penn-secretly-interviewed-el-chapo-in-hideout-before-capture/2016/01/09/4cce48db-1dc5-40b2-9b21-aa412c87e7bc_story.html).

- *Information Sources.* What sources of information does the author use? Are they credible? Are they recognized individuals or institutions? Is the information source appropriate for the article's topic? Is the topic timely and is the information it provides up to date? Does the author include multiple sources to support his or her statements?
- *Writing Quality.* Is the article well-written? Is it clear and cogent? Does it use a lot of jargon? Can you understand it? Does it employ many adverbs? In general, adjectives and adverbs tend to be "opinion-words" rather than "news-words." Why, for example, is the adverb in the following sentence questionable? "Morgan *willfully* ran over my bicycle in the driveway."
- *Quantity of Information.* Is the article sufficiently comprehensive to substantiate its thesis? Does it answer the proverbial questions *Who? What? When? Where? and Why?*
- *Unsupported Assumptions.* Beware of statements like this: "Statistics prove that children in traditional two parent households are happier than children in other households." What statistics? Does the article identify them?
- *Balance.* If you are reading a *news* article about a controversial subject, the article should include information from more than one side of an argument. Also, a well-written *opinion* article will normally identify the content of opposing views, even if only to discredit them.

1.4 READ TO RESPOND TO SOCIAL ISSUES

Reading Opinion Articles: A Tale of Two Journalists

Conservative author and commentator David Brooks and liberal economist Paul Krugman have both been op-ed columnists for the *New York Times* for more than a decade. In July 2015 each wrote a *Times* column on recent proposals to raise the minimum wage.

In his article "The Minimum Wage Muddle" (July 24, 2015), David Brooks, in a typical conservative fashion, reveals once again his distrust in government intervention in the economy in general and proposals to raise the minimum wage in particular. Brooks states, "Some economists have reported that there is no longer any evidence that raising wages will cost jobs."[8] Brooks may well have had in mind a *New York Times* article by Paul Krugman, titled "Liberals and Wages" (July 17, 2012), which states, "There's just no evidence that raising the minimum wage costs jobs, at least when the starting point is as low as it is in modern America."[9] Both Brooks and Krugman cite multiple studies as evidence for their arguments opposing (Brooks) and supporting (Krugman) minimum wages.

---

[8] David Brooks. 2015. "The Minimum-Wage Muddle." *New York Times,* July 24. Retrieved March 7, 2016 (http://www. nytimes.com/2015/07/24/opinion/david-brooks-the-minimum-wage-muddle .html).

[9] Paul Krugman. 2015. "Liberals and Wages." *New York Times,* July 17. Retrieved March 7, 2016 (http:// www.nytimes. com/2015/07/17/opinion/paul-krugman-liberals-and-wages.html).

If you open the *New York Times* website and read both articles (select the "Columnists" link in the "Opinion Pages" section), you will find that each columnist focuses on different, if overlapping, slices of the effects of raising the minimum wage. Each article provides an interesting, well-supported education in certain aspects of the issue, one that inspires many studies before the political debate subsides.

But here we can learn an important lesson. What is the central point, the *thesis* of each article? From Brooks we have a bold and unsupported further assertion: "Raising the minimum wage will produce winners among job holders from all backgrounds, but it will disproportionately punish those with the lowest skills, who are least likely to be able to justify higher employment costs."

We have already quoted Krugman's thesis that there is no evidence suggesting that raising the minimum wage will cost jobs, "at least when the starting point is as low as it is in modern America." Krugman continues his argument with an unsupported conclusion, asserting that the market for labor isn't like the market for, say, wheat, because workers are people. And because they're people, there are important benefits, even to the employer, from paying them more, such as better morale, lower turnover, and increased productivity. These benefits, says Krugman, largely offset the direct effect of higher labor costs, so that raising the minimum wage needn't cost jobs after all.

At this point it is evident that if you want to adequately examine the arguments of each columnist, you must read their articles and examine the evidence they provide. But the important lesson here is the relative authority of the authors on the subjects they are discussing. Consider the two columnists' credentials.

According to his biography on the *New York Times* website, David Brooks also appears on *PBS NewsHour*, NPR's *All Things Considered*, and NBC's *Meet the Press*. He has authored three books: *Bobos in Paradise: The New Upper Class and How They Got There* (New York: Simon & Schuster, 2000), *On Paradise Drive: How We Live Now (And Always Have) in the Future Tense* (New York: Simon & Schuster, 2004), and *The Social Animal: The Hidden Sources of Love, Character, and Achievement* (New York: Random House, 2011), a "No. 1 *New York Times* best seller." He also teaches at Yale University.

Paul Krugman is Professor of Economics and International Affairs at Princeton University. He has taught at Yale, Stanford, and MIT, and has authored or edited 27 books and 200 academic and professional papers. A founder of "new trade theory," a substantial revision of international trade theory, he has received the American Economic Association's John Bates Clark Medal (1991) and the Nobel Prize in Economics (2008).

Which author is better qualified to draw general conclusions about effects of the minimum wage from his research? Paul Krugman, the economist, is far better qualified to draw conclusions, and owing to the enormous amount of research he has done in economics, he is far more credible *on this topic*. If you read numerous columns by David Brooks, you may well conclude that they are well written, entertaining, and contain much well-documented support for his theses. But if you read closely, you will find that he often oversteps the bounds of his professional credibility. This does not mean that Krugman is obviously correct on this particular issue. But it strongly suggests that if you want to test Krugman's assertions, you must find an equivalent authority: a solid conservative economist.

Sociologists are predisposed to be suspicious of journalism, rolling their eyes at factual errors and inaccuracies. A healthy skepticism is part of their job. But they understand that, while they have the luxury of digging deep over a substantial period of time, a journalist must often get a story and get it straight within a matter of hours. And when all is said and done, the academicians do not hesitate to affirm that nothing is as essential to the vitality of democracy as a vigorous, capable, and dedicated news media.

Read&Write 1.4 Respond to an Editorial

Perhaps at this point you are ready to launch into the real world of public discussion of national issues. One way to do so is to respond to an editorial. It is probably best to start with the newspaper in your hometown. Most, if not all, newspapers provide detailed information on how to submit such a letter. To write a letter to the editor of the *Washington Post*, for example, follow the link in the "Opinion" section entitled "How to Contact the Newsroom":

http://help.washingtonpost.com/link/portal/15067/15080/ArticleFolder/80/ How-to-Contact-the-Newsroom

Be sure to ask your instructor before submitting your letter. Newspapers can be very selective about the letters they accept for publication, and you may be up against a lot of competition. You instructor will be able to provide some suggestions that will increase your chances of success. Follow the paper's directions exactly.

Good luck!

2

READ AND WRITE
EFFECTIVELY

Writing is a way of ordering your experience. Think about it. No matter what you are writing—a paper for your American government class, a short story, a limerick, a grocery list—you are putting pieces of your world together in new ways and making yourself freshly conscious of those pieces. This is one of the reasons why writing is so hard. From the infinite welter of data that your mind continually processes and locks in your memory, you are selecting only certain items significant to the task at hand, relating them to other items, and phrasing them with a new coherence. You are mapping a part of your universe that has hitherto been unknown territory. You are gaining a little more control over the processes by which you interact with the world around you.

This is why the act of writing, no matter what its result, is never insignificant. It is always *communication*—if not with another human being, then with yourself. It is a way of making a fresh connection with your world.

Writing, therefore, is also one of the best ways to learn. This statement may sound odd at first. If you are an unpracticed writer, you may share a common notion that the only purpose of writing is to express what you already know or think. According to this view, any learning that you as a writer might have experienced has already occurred by the time your pen meets the paper; your task is thus to inform and even surprise the reader. But, if you are a practiced writer, you know that at any moment as you write, you are capable of surprising yourself. And it is that surprise that you look for: the shock of seeing what happens in your own mind when you drop an old, established opinion into a batch of new facts or bump into a cherished belief from a different angle. Writing synthesizes new understanding for the writer. E. M. Forster's famous question "How do I know what I think until I see what I say?"[1] is one that all of us could ask. We make meaning as we write, jolting ourselves by little, surprising discoveries into a larger and more interesting universe.

---

[1] E. M. Forster. [1927] 1956. *Aspects of the Novel*, 101. New York: Harvest.

A SIMULTANEOUS TANGLE
OF ACTIVITIES

One reason that writing is difficult is that it is not actually a single activity, but a process having several activities that can overlap, with two or more activities sometimes operating simultaneously as you labor to organize and phrase your thoughts. (We will discuss these activities later in this chapter.) The writing process tends to be sloppy for everyone, an often-frustrating search for meaning and for the best way to articulate that meaning.

Although the search may be Frustrating though that search may sometimes be, it need not be futile. Remember this: the writing process uses skills that we all have. The ability to write, in other words, is not some magical competence bestowed on the rare, fortunate individual. We are all capable of phrasing thoughts clearly and in a well-organized fashion. But learning how to do so takes practice.

One sure way to improve your writing is to write.

One of the toughest but most important jobs in writing is to maintain enthusiasm for your writing project. Such commitment may sometimes be hard to achieve, given the difficulties that are inherent in the writing process and that can be made worse when the project is unappealing at first glance. How, for example, can you be enthusiastic about writing a paper analyzing campaign financing for the 1998 Congressional elections, when you have never once thought about campaign finances and can see no use in doing so now?

Sometimes unpracticed student writers fail to assume responsibility for keeping themselves interested in their writing. No matter how hard it may seem at first to drum up interest in your topic, you have to do it—that is, if you want to write a paper you can be proud of, one that contributes useful material and a fresh point of view to the topic. One thing is guaranteed: if you are bored with your writing, your reader too will be bored. So what can you do to keep your interest and energy level high?

Challenge yourself. Think of the paper not as an assignment but as a piece of writing that has a point to make. To get this point across persuasively is the real reason you are writing, and not because a teacher has assigned you a project. If someone were to ask you why you are writing your paper and your immediate, unthinking response is, "Because I've been given a writing assignment," or "Because I want a good grade," or some other non-answer along these lines, your paper may be in trouble.

If, on the other hand, your first impulse is to explain the challenge of your main point—"I'm writing to show how campaign finance reform will benefit every taxpayer in America"—then you are thinking usefully about your topic.

Maintain Self-Confidence

Having confidence in your ability to write well about your topic is essential for good writing. This does not mean that you will always know what the result of a particular writing activity will be. In fact, you have to cultivate your ability to tolerate a high degree of uncertainty while weighing evidence, testing hypotheses, and experimenting with organizational strategies and wording. Be ready for temporary confusion and for seeming dead ends, and remember that every writer faces these obstacles. It is out of your struggle to combine fact with fact, to buttress conjecture with evidence, that order will arise.

Do not be intimidated by the amount and quality of work that others have already done in your field of inquiry. The array of opinion and evidence that confronts you in the literature can be confusing. But remember that no important topic is ever exhausted. There are always gaps—questions that have not been satisfactorily explored in either the published research or the prevailing popular opinion. It is in these gaps that you establish your own authority, your own sense of control.

Remember that the various stages of the writing process reinforce each other. Establishing a solid motivation strengthens your sense of confidence about the project, which in turn influences how successfully you organize and write. If you start out well, use good work habits, and allow ample time for the various activities to coalesce, you should produce a paper that reflects your best work, one that your audience will find both readable and useful.

2.1   GET INTO THE FLOW OF WRITING

The Nature of the Process

As you engage in the writing process, you are doing many things at once. While planning, you are, no doubt, defining the audience for your paper at the same time that you are thinking about its purpose. As you draft the paper, you may organize your next sentence while revising the one you have just written. Different parts of the writing process overlap, and much of the difficulty of writing occurs because so many things happen at once. Through practice—in other words, through *writing*—it is possible to learn to control those parts of the process that can in fact be controlled and to encourage those mysterious, less controllable activities.

No two people write exactly the same way. It is important to recognize the routines—modes of thought as well as individual exercises—that help you negotiate the process successfully. It is also important to give yourself as much time as possible to complete the process. Procrastination is one of the greatest enemies of writers. It saps confidence, undermines energy, and destroys concentration. Writing regularly and following a well-planned schedule as closely as possible often make the difference between a successful paper and an embarrassment.

Although the various parts of the writing process are interwoven, there is naturally a general order in the work of writing. You have to start somewhere! What follows is a description of the various stages of the writing process—planning, drafting, revising, editing, and proofreading—along with suggestions on how to approach each most successfully.

Plan   Planning includes all activities that lead to the writing of the first draft of a paper. The particular activities in this stage differ from person to person. Some writers, for instance, prefer to compile a formal outline before writing the draft. Others perform brief writing exercises to jump-start their imaginations. Some draw diagrams; some doodle. Later, we will look at a few starting strategies, and you can determine which may help you.

Now, however, let us discuss certain early choices that all writers must make during the planning stage. These choices concern *topic, purpose, and audience,* elements that make up the writing context, or the terms under which we all write. Every time you write, even if you are only writing a diary entry or a note to the milkman, these elements are present. You may not give conscious consideration to all of them in each piece of your writing, but it is extremely important to think carefully about them when writing a sociology paper. Some or all of these defining elements may be dictated by your assignment, yet you will always have a degree of control over them.

Select a Topic   No matter how restrictive an assignment may seem, there is no reason to feel trapped by it. Within any assigned subject, you can find a range of topics to explore. What you are looking for is a topic that engages your own interest. Let your curiosity be your guide. If, for example, you are assigned the subject of campaign finances, then find some issues concerning the topic that interests you. (For example, how influential are campaign finances in the average state senate race? What would be the repercussions of limiting financial contributions from special interest groups?) Any good topic comes with a set of questions; you may well find that your interest increases if you simply begin asking questions. One strong recommendation: ask your questions *on paper.* Like most mental activities, the process of exploring your way through a topic is transformed when you write down your thoughts as they arise, instead of letting them fly through your mind unrecorded. Remember the words of Louis Agassiz: "A pen is often the best of eyes."[2]

Although it is vital to be interested in your topic, you do not have to know much about it at the outset of your investigation. In fact, having too heartfelt a commitment to a topic can be an impediment to writing about it; emotions can get in the way of objectivity. It is often better to choose a topic that has piqued your interest yet remained something of a mystery to you—a topic discussed in one of your classes, perhaps, or mentioned on television or in a conversation with friends.

Narrow the Topic   The task of narrowing your topic offers you a tremendous opportunity to establish a measure of control over the writing project. It is up to you to hone your topic to just the right shape and size to suit both your own interests and the requirements of the assignment. Do a good job of it, and you will go a long way toward guaranteeing yourself sufficient motivation and confidence for the tasks ahead. However, if you do not do it well, somewhere along the way you may find yourself directionless and out of energy.

Generally, the first topics that come to your mind will be too large for you to handle in your research paper. For example, the subject of a national income security policy has recently generated a tremendous number of news reports. Yet despite all the attention, there is still plenty of room for you to investigate the topic on a level that has real meaning for you and that does not merely recapitulate the published research. What about an analysis of how one of the proposed income security policies might affect insurance costs in a locally owned company?

---

[2] Catherine Owens Pearce. 1958. *A Scientist of Two Worlds: Louis Agassiz,* 106. Philadelphia: Lippincott.

The problem with most topics is not that they are too narrow or have been completely explored, but rather that they are so rich that it is often difficult to choose the most useful way to address them. Take some time to narrow your topic. Think through the possibilities that occur to you and, as always, jot down your thoughts.

Students in an undergraduate course on political theory were told to write an essay of 2,500 words on one of the following issues. Next to each general topic is an example of how students narrowed it into a manageable paper topic.

General Topic	Narrowed Topic
Inequality	Changes in income inequality since 1990
Racism	Trends in public school integration since 2000
Gender	Women attaining positions as corporate executives
Entertainment	Changing portrayals of violence in movies

Without doing research, see how you can narrow the following general topics:

Example

General Topic	The Amish as Community Builders
Narrowed topics	The Benefits of Solidarity in Amish Communities
	Pressures to Conform to Religious Norms in Amish Communities
	Maintaining Traditions in Amish Communities

General Topics

Aging	Consumers
Illegal Drugs	Crime
Solidarity	Education
Children	Family
Social Media	Mental Health
Social Movements	Religion

Find a Thesis   As you plan your writing, be on the lookout for an idea that can serve as your thesis. A *thesis* is not a fact, which can be immediately verified by data, but an assertion worth discussing, an argument with more than one possible conclusion. Your thesis sentence reveals not only the argument you have chosen but also your orientation toward it and the conclusion that your paper will attempt to prove.

In looking for a thesis, you are doing many jobs at once:

1. You are limiting the amount and kind of material that you must cover, thus making them manageable.
2. You are increasing your own interest in the narrowing field of study.

3. You are working to establish your paper's purpose, the reason you are writing about your topic. (If the only reason you can see for writing is to earn a good grade, then you probably won't!)

4. You are establishing your notion of who your audience is and what sort of approach to the subject might best catch its interest.

In short, you are gaining control over your writing context. Therefore, it is good to come up with a thesis early on, a *working thesis*, which will probably change as your thinking deepens but will allow you to establish a measure of order in the planning stage.

The Thesis Sentence   The introduction of your paper will contain a sentence that expresses the task that you intend to accomplish. This *thesis sentence* communicates your main idea, the one you are going to prove, defend, or illustrate. It sets up an expectation in the reader's mind that it is your job to satisfy. But, in the planning stage, a thesis sentence is more than just the statement that informs your reader of your goal: it is a valuable tool to help you narrow your focus and confirm in your own mind your paper's purpose.

Developing a Thesis   Students in a class on public policy analysis were assigned a 20-page paper on a problem currently being faced by the municipal authorities in their own city. The choice of the problem was left to the students. One, Richard Cory, decided to investigate the problem posed by the large number of abandoned buildings in a downtown neighborhood through which he drove on his way to the university. His first working thesis was as follows:

Abandoned houses result in negative social effects to the city.

The problem with this thesis, as Richard found out, was that it was not an idea that could be argued, but rather a fact that could be easily corroborated by the sources he began to consult. As he read reports from such groups as the Urban Land Institute and the City Planning Commission, and talked with representatives from the Community Planning Department, he began to get interested in the dilemma his city faced in responding to the problem of abandoned buildings. Richard's second working thesis was as follows:

Removal of abandoned buildings is a major problem facing the city.

While his second thesis narrowed the topic somewhat and gave Richard an opportunity to use material from his research, there was still no real comment attached to it. It still stated a bare fact, easily proved. At this point, Richard became interested in the even narrower topic of how building removal should best be handled. He found that the major issue was funding and that different civic groups favored different methods of accomplishing this. As Richard explored the arguments for and against the various funding plans, he began to feel that one of them might be best for the city. As a result, Richard developed his third working thesis:

Assessing a demolition fee on each property offers a viable solution to the city's building removal problem.

Note how this thesis narrows the focus of Richard's paper even further than the other two had, while also presenting an arguable hypothesis. It tells Richard what he has to do in his paper, just as it tells his readers what to expect.

At some time during your preliminary thinking on a topic, you should consult a library to see how much published work on your issue exists. This search has at least two benefits:

1. It acquaints you with a body of writing that will become very important in the research phase of your paper.
2. It gives you a sense of how your topic is generally addressed by the community of scholars you are joining. Is the topic as important as you think it is? Has there been so much research on the subject as to make your inquiry, in its present formulation, irrelevant?

While determining your topic, remember that one goal of your sociology writing in college is always to enhance your own understanding of the political process, to build an accurate model of the way politics works. Let this goal help you to direct your research into areas that you know are important to your knowledge of the discipline.

Define a Purpose   There are many ways to classify the purposes of writing, but in general most writing is undertaken either to inform or to persuade an audience. The goal of informative, or expository, writing is simply to impart information about a particular subject, whereas the aim of persuasive writing is to convince your reader of your point of view on an issue. The distinction between expository and persuasive writing is not hard and fast, and most writing in sociology has elements of both types. Most effective writing, however, is clearly focused on either exposition or persuasion. Position papers (arguments for adopting particular policies), for example, are designed to persuade, whereas policy analysis papers (Chapter 9) are meant to inform. When you begin writing, consciously select a primary approach of exposition or persuasion, and then set out to achieve that goal.

Read & Write 2.1   Explain or Persuade?

Can you tell from the titles of these two papers, both on the same topic, which is an expository paper and which is a persuasive paper?

1. Social Services Funding in the Second Obama Administration
2. How the Second Obama Administration Increased Social Services Funding

Again taking up the subject of campaign finances, let us assume that you must write a paper explaining how finances were managed in the 2016 Republican presidential campaign. If you are writing an expository paper, your task could be to describe as coherently and impartially as possible the methods by which the Republicans administered their campaign funds. If, however, you are attempting to convince your readers that the 2016 Republican campaign finances were criminally mismanaged by an elected official, you are writing to persuade, and your strategy will be radically different. Persuasive writing seeks to influence the opinions of its audience toward its subject.

Learn what you want to say By the time you write your final draft, you must have a very sound notion of the point you wish to argue. If, as you write that final draft, someone were to ask you to state your thesis, you should be able to give a satisfactory answer with a minimum of delay and no prompting. If, on the other hand, you have to hedge your answer because you cannot easily express your thesis, you may not yet be ready to write a final draft. You may have to write a draft or two or engage in various prewriting activities to form a secure understanding of your task.

EXERCISE Knowing What You Want to Say

Two writers have been asked to state the thesis of their papers. Which one better understands the writing task?

Writer 1: "My paper is about tax reform for the middle class."

Writer 2: "My paper argues that tax reform for the middle class would be unfair to the upper and lower classes, who would then have to share more responsibility for the cost of government."

Watch out for bias! There is no such thing as pure objectivity. You are not a machine. No matter how hard you may try to produce an objective paper, the fact is that every choice you make as you write is influenced to some extent by your personal beliefs and opinions. What you tell your readers is truth, in other words, is influenced, sometimes without your knowledge, by a multitude of factors: your environment, upbringing, and education; your attitude toward your audience; your political affiliation; your race and gender; your career goals; and your ambitions for the paper you are writing. The influence of such factors can be very subtle, and it is something you must work to identify in your own writing and in the writing of others in order not to mislead or to be misled. Remember that one of the reasons for writing is *self-discovery*. The writing you will do in sociology classes—and for the rest of your life—will give you a chance to discover and confront honestly your own views on your subjects. Responsible writers keep an eye on their own biases and are honest about them with their readers.

Define Your Audience In any class that requires you to write, you may sometimes find it difficult to remember that the point of your writing is not simply to jump through the technical hoops imposed by the assignment. The point is *communication*—the transmission of your knowledge and your conclusions to readers in a way that suits you. Your task is to pass on to your readers the spark of your own enthusiasm for your topic. Readers who were indifferent to your topic before reading your paper should look at it in a new way after finishing it. This is the great challenge of writing: to enter a reader's mind and leave behind both new knowledge and new questions.

It is tempting to think that most writing problems would be solved if the writer could view the writing as if it were produced by another person. The discrepancy between the understanding of the writer and that of the audience is the single greatest impediment to accurate communication. To overcome this barrier, you must consider your audience's needs. By the time you begin drafting, most, if not all, of your ideas would be attaining coherent shape in your mind, so that virtually any words with which you try to express those ideas will reflect your thoughts accurately—to you. Your readers, however, do not already hold the conclusions that you have so painstakingly achieved. If you omit from your writing the material that is necessary to complete your readers' understanding of your argument, they may well be unable to supply that information themselves.

The potential for misunderstanding is present for any audience, whether it is made up of general readers, experts in the field, or your professor, who is reading in part to see how well you have mastered the constraints that govern the relationship between writer and reader. Make your presentation as complete as possible, bearing in mind your audience's knowledge of your topic.

2.2 THINK CREATIVELY

Discover What You Know

We have discussed various methods of selecting and narrowing the topic of a paper. As your focus on a specific topic sharpens, you will naturally begin to think about the kinds of information that will go into the paper. In the case of papers that do not require formal research, this material will come largely from your own recollections. Indeed, one of the reasons instructors assign such papers is to convince you of the incredible richness of your memory, the vastness and variety of the "database" that you have accumulated and that, moment by moment, you continue to build.

Your hoard of information is so vast that it can sometimes be difficult to find within it the material that would best suit your paper. In other words, finding out what you already know about a topic is not always easy. *Invention*, a term borrowed from classical rhetoric, refers to the task of discovering, or recovering from memory, such information. As we write, we go through an invention procedure that helps us explore our topic. Some writers seem to have little problem coming up with material; others need more help. Over the centuries, writers have devised different exercises that can help locate useful material housed in memory. We will look at a few of these briefly.

Freewriting   *Freewriting* is an activity that forces you to get something down on paper. There is no waiting around for inspiration. Instead, you set a time limit—perhaps 3–5 minutes—and write for that length of time without stopping, not even to lift the pen from the paper or your hands from the keyboard. Focus on the topic, and do not let the difficulty of finding relevant material stop you from writing. If necessary, you may begin by writing, over and over, some seemingly useless phrase, such as, "I cannot think of anything to write," or perhaps the name of your topic. Eventually, something else will occur to you. (It is surprising how long a 3-minute period of freewriting can seem to last!) At the end of the freewriting, look over what you have produced for anything you might be able to use. Much of the writing will be unusable, but there might be an insight or two that you did not know you had.

Freewriting helps you in recovering usable material from your memory for your paper and has certain other benefits. First, it takes little time, which means that you may repeat the exercise as often as you like. Second, it breaks down some of the resistance that stands between you and the act of writing. There is no initial struggle to find something to say; you just write.

For his introductory American government class, Bill Alexander had to write a paper on some aspects of local government. Bill, who felt his understanding of local government was slight, began the job of finding a topic that interested him with 2 minutes of freewriting. Thinking about local government, Bill wrote steadily for this period without lifting his pen from the paper. Here is the result of his freewriting:

Okay okay local government. Local, what does that mean? Like police? the mayor—whoever that is? judges? I got that parking ticket last year, went to court, had to pay it anyway, bummer. Maybe trace what happens to a single parking ticket—and my money. Find out the public officials who deal with it, from the traffic cop who gives it out to wherever it ends up. Point would be, what? Point point point. To find out how much the local government spends to give out and process a $35 parking ticket—how much do they really make after expenses, and where does that money go? Have to include cop's salary? judge's? Printing costs for ticket? Salary for clerk or whoever deals only with ticket. Is there somebody who lives whole life only processing traffic tickets? Are traffic tickets and parking tickets handled differently? Assuming the guy fights it. Maybe find out the difference in revenue between a contested and an uncontested ticket? Lots of phone calls to make. Who? Where to start?

Brainstorming *Brainstorming* is the process of making a list of ideas about a topic. It can be done quickly and at first without any need to order items in a coherent pattern. The point is to write down everything that occurs to you as quickly and briefly as possible, using individual words or short phrases. Once you have a good-sized list of items, you can then group them according to relationships that you see among them. Brainstorming thus allows you to uncover both ideas stored in your memory and useful associations among those ideas.

A professor in a constitutional law class asked his students to write a 700-word paper, in the form of a letter to be translated and published in a Warsaw newspaper, giving Polish readers useful advice about living in a democracy. One student, Melissa Jessup, started thinking about the assignment by brainstorming. First, she simply wrote down anything about life in society that occurred to her:

churches	welfare	social media
racism	opportunity	minorities
poverty	American Dream	injustice
the individual	job security	corporations
size of government	psychological factors	aristocracy of wealth

Thinking through her list, Melissa decided to create two new separate lists: one devoted to positive aspects of life in today's society; the other, to negative aspects. At this point, she decided to discard some items that were redundant or did not seem to have much potential.

Positive	Negative
diversity	racism
wealth	poverty
reform	injustice
opportunity	aristocracy of wealth
social media	isolation

At this point, Melissa decided that her topic would be about the ways in which money tends to accumulate in increasingly smaller portions of the population. Which items on her lists would be relevant to her paper?

Asking Questions It is always possible to ask most or all of the following questions about any topic: *Who? What? When? Where? Why? How?* They force you to approach the topic as a journalist does, setting it within different perspectives that can then be compared.

A professor asked her class on ethnicities to write a paper describing effects of cultural traditions economic vitality. One student developed the following questions as he began to think about a thesis:

Who are some groups with distinctive cultural traditions?
What specific traditions affect their prosperity?
What benefits do the traditions provide?
What costs do the traditions entail?
When during the life cycle are the traditions most important?
Where do the traditions come from?
How are they carried out?
Who benefits the most and the least from these traditions?

Can you think of other questions that would make for useful inquiry?

Maintaining Flexibility As you engage in invention strategies, you are also performing other writing tasks. You are still narrowing your topic, for example, as well as making decisions that will affect your choice of tone or audience. You are moving forward on all fronts with each decision you make affecting the others. This means that you must be flexible enough to allow for slight adjustments in understanding your paper's development and your goal. Never be so determined to prove a particular theory that you fail to notice when your own understanding of it changes. Stay objective.

Read&Write 2.2   Freewriting

Sociologists are, at heart, problem solvers. The problems of society intrigue them intensely. An often effective agent for solving societal problems is social movements. This is not to say, by any means, that all problems should be solved by social movements. Most often they require courageous, charismatic leadership.

Today in America several social movements have a variety of strength and prominence. From the Tea Party to the Main Street versus Wall Street coalitions, to the anti-immigration vigilantes, their influence waxes and wanes over time.

Social movements, therefore, present some fascinating opportunities. In this case, you have an opportunity to do some freewriting on a topic of your choice. First, find a newspaper, online or in print. Then select an article that provides information about a social movement. Following the sample in this chapter, do some freewriting. The objective of your freewriting is to establish an initial approach to find a solution to understanding the social effects of the movement you have selected.

2.3   ORGANIZE YOUR WRITING

The structure of any particular type of sociology paper is governed by a formal pattern. When rigid external controls are placed on their writing, some writers feel that their creativity is hampered by a kind of "paint-by-numbers" approach to structure. It is vital to the success of your paper that you don't allow yourself to be overwhelmed by the pattern rules for any type of paper. Remember that such controls exist not to limit your creativity but to make the paper immediately and easily useful to its intended audience. It is as necessary to write clearly and confidently in a position paper or a policy analysis paper as in a term paper for English literature, a résumé, a short story, or a job application letter.

A paper that contains all the necessary facts but presents them in an ineffective order will confuse rather than inform or persuade. Although there are various methods of grouping ideas, none is potentially more effective than outlining. Unfortunately, no organizing process is more often misunderstood.

The Importance of Outlining

Outline for Yourself   Outlining can do two jobs. First, it can force you, the writer, to gain a better understanding of your ideas by arranging them according to their interrelationships. There is one primary rule of outlining: ideas of equal weight are placed on the same level within the outline. This rule requires you to determine the relative importance of your ideas. You must decide which ideas are of the same type or order, and into which subtopic each idea best fits.

In the planning stage, if you carefully arrange your ideas in a coherent outline, your grasp of your topic will be greatly enhanced. You will have linked your ideas logically together and given a basic structure to the body of the paper. This sort of subordinating and coordinating activity is difficult, however, and as a result, inexperienced writers sometimes begin to write their first draft without an effective outline, hoping for the best. This hope is usually unfulfilled, especially in complex papers involving research.

EXERCISE Organizing Thoughts

Rodrigo, a student in a second-year class in government management, researched the impact of a worker-retraining program in his state and came up with the following facts and theories. Number them in logical order:

___ A growing number of workers in the state do not possess the basic skills and education demanded by employers.

___ The number of dislocated workers in the state increased from 21,000 in 2001 to 32,000 in 2011.

___ A public policy to retrain uneducated workers would allow them to move into new and expanding sectors of the state economy.

___ Investment in high technology would allow the state's employers to remain competitive in the production of goods and services in both domestic and foreign markets.

___ The state's economy is becoming more global and more competitive.

Outline for Your Reader   The second job of an outline is to serve as a reader's blueprint to the paper, summarizing its points and their interrelationships. By consulting your outline, a busy policymaker can quickly get a sense of your paper's goal and the argument you have used to promote it. The clarity and coherence of the outline help in determining the amount of attention your audience will pay to your ideas.

As sociology students, you will be given a great deal of help with the arrangement of your material into an outline to accompany your paper. The formats presented in Chapter 3 of this manual show the strict structure of these formal outlines. But, although you must pay close attention to these requirements, do not forget how powerful a tool an outline can be in the early planning stages of your paper.

The Formal Outline Pattern   Following this pattern accurately during the planning stage of your paper, you can place your ideas logically:

Thesis sentence (precedes the formal outline)

I. First main idea

   A. First subordinate idea

      1. Reason, example, or illustration

         a. Supporting detail

         b. Supporting detail

         c. Supporting detail

2. Reason, example, or illustration
    a. Supporting detail
    b. Supporting detail
    c. Supporting detail

B. Second subordinate idea

II. Second main idea

Notice that each level of the paper must have more than one entry; for every A there must be at least a B (and, if required, a C, a D, and so on), and for every 1 there must be a 2. This arrangement forces you to *compare ideas*, looking carefully at each one to determine its place among the others. The insistence on assigning relative values to your ideas is what makes an outline an effective organizing tool.

Read&Write 2.3 Write a Paper Outline

This is a relatively simple exercise, but it does require some thought. Start by perusing today's newspaper (local or national). When you come to an article that "gets under your skin," stop. Suppose the article is one like this, from the *New York Times*:

> HEMPSTEAD, N.Y.—A man accused of firing the bullet that fatally struck a 12-year-old girl as she sat in her Long Island home in October was retaliating after his younger brother's hoverboard was stolen, the police said on Monday.
>
> The man, Jakwan Keller, 20, wearing a bulletproof vest, declined to comment as detectives led him out of Nassau County Police Headquarters. He later pleaded not guilty to murder, weapons possession and other charges in connection with the death of the girl, Dejah Joyner.[3]

Think. What is it about the article that irritates you? Is it the waste of a person's life? Is it the availability of guns? Is it a lack of law enforcement?

Now, following the outline format described in this chapter section, write an outline of a paper you might write because you read this article. Your outline will not *summarize* the article, although a short summary might be included in your paper. Your paper outline might look something like this:

How to Reduce Accidental Gun Deaths

I. The history of accidental deaths is a long one.

A. Most Deaths on Nineteenth Century Wagon Trains Were Accidental Shootings.
    1. Loaded guns were always at hand.
    2. Bumpy trails led to frequent discharges.

B. Loaded guns at home are a danger to children.
    1. Children play with guns.
    2. Adults are not required to store guns securely.
    3. Adults want loaded guns easily available.

---

[3] Stray Bullet That Killed Long Island Girl Was Fired in Retaliation for Hoverboard Theft, Police Say." 2016. *New York Times*, January 11. Retrieved March 7, 2016 (http://www.nytimes.com/2016/01/12/nyregion/stray-bullet-that-killed-long-island-girl-was-fired-in-retaliation-for-theft-police-say.html?_r=0)

II. The number of accidental gun deaths is alarming.

    A. The number of accidental gun deaths has risen from 1860 to 2016.
        1. There were few early efforts to reduce the death rate.
        2. Gun deaths were accepted as a way of life.

    B. The prevalence of guns is increasing in the twenty-first century.
        1. Gun sales rise with each new mass shooting.
        2. The NRA presses for open carry laws.
        3. Open carry on campus and in bars becomes controversial.

III. The number of options for reducing gun deaths is growing.

    A. There are criminal penalties for negligent parents.
        1. Some parents have received long prison sentences.
        2. Capital punishment is an alternative under discussion.

    B. The outlawing of semi-automatic weapons is a controversial possibility.
        1. Critics complain about financial costs.
        2. Political costs may prevent meaningful legislation.

    C. Advocates see public education on gun safety as essential.
        1. Courses in elementary and secondary schools are becoming feasible.
        2. Enrollments in online seminars for adults are on the incline.

2.4   DRAFT, REVISE, EDIT, AND PROOFREAD

Write the Rough Draft

After planning comes the writing of the first draft. Using your thesis and outline as direction markers, you must now weave your amalgam of ideas, data, and persuasion strategies into logically ordered sentences and paragraphs. Although adequate prewriting may facilitate drafting, it still will not be easy. Writers establish their own individual methods of encouraging themselves to forge ahead with the draft, but here are some tips:

1. Remember that this is a rough draft, not the final paper. At this stage, it is not necessary that every word be the best possible choice. Do not put that sort of pressure on yourself. You must not allow anything to slow you down now. Writing is not like sculpting in stone, where every chip is permanent; you can always go back to your draft and add, delete, reword, and rearrange. *No matter how much effort you have put into planning, you cannot be sure how much of this first draft you will eventually keep.* It may take several drafts to get one that you find satisfactory.

2. Give yourself sufficient time to write. Do not delay the first draft by telling yourself there is still more research to do. You cannot uncover all the material there is to know on a particular subject, so do not fool yourself into trying. Remember

that writing is a process of discovery. You may have to begin writing before you can see exactly what sort of research you need to do. Remember that there are other tasks waiting for you after the first draft is finished, so allow for them as you determine your writing schedule.

More importantly, give yourself time to write, because the more time that passes after you have written a draft, the better your ability to view it with objectivity. It is very difficult to evaluate your writing accurately soon after you complete it. You need to cool down, to recover from the effort of putting all those words together. The "colder" you get on your writing, the better you are able to read it as if it were written by someone else and thus acknowledge the changes needed to strengthen the paper.

3. Stay sharp. Keep in mind the plan you created as you narrowed your topic, composed a thesis sentence, and outlined the material. But, if you begin to feel a strong need to change the plan a bit, do not be afraid to do so. Be ready for surprises dealt you by your own growing understanding of your topic. Your goal is to record your best thinking on the subject as accurately as possible.

Paragraph Development There is no absolute requirement for the structure of any paragraph in your paper except that all its sentences must be clearly related to each other and each must carry the job of saying what you want to say about your thesis *one step farther*. In other words, simply restating what is already said elsewhere in the paper is a waste of your time and the reader's. It isn't unusual for a paragraph to have, somewhere in it, a *topic* sentence that serves as the key to the paragraph's organization and announces the paragraph's connection to the paper's thesis. But not all paragraphs need topic sentences.

What all paragraphs in the paper *do* need is an organizational strategy. Here are four typical organizational models, any one of which, if you keep it in mind, can help you build a coherent paragraph:

- *Chronological organization*: The sentences of the paragraph describe a series of events, steps, or observations as they occur over time: this happens, then that, and then that.
- *Spatial organization*: The sentences of the paragraph record details of its subject in some logical order: top to bottom, up to down, outside to inside.
- *General-to-specific organization*: The paragraph starts with a statement of its main idea and then goes into detail as it discusses that idea.
- *Specific-to-general organization*: The paragraph begins with smaller, nuts-and-bolts details, arranging them in a larger pattern that, by the end of the paragraph, leads to the conclusion that is the paragraph's main idea.

These aren't the only organizational strategies available to you, and, of course, different paragraphs in a paper can use different strategies; however, a paragraph that employs more than one organizational plan is risking incoherence. It is important that each sentence in the paragraph must bear a logical relationship to the one before it and the one after it. It is this notion of *interconnectedness* that can prevent you from getting off track and stuffing extraneous material in your paragraphs.

Like all other aspects of the writing process, paragraph development is a challenge. But remember, one of the helpful facts about paragraphs is that they are relatively small, especially compared to the overall scope of your paper. Each paragraph can basically do only one job—handle or help to handle a single idea, which is itself only a part of the overall development of the larger thesis idea. That paragraphs are small and aimed at a single task means that it is relatively easy to revise them. By focusing clearly on the single job a paragraph does and filtering out all the paper's other claims for your attention, you should gain enough clarity of vision during the revision process to understand what you need to do to make that paragraph work better.

Authority   To be convincing, your writing has to be authoritative; that is, you have to sound as if you have complete confidence in your ability to convey your ideas in words. Sentences that sound stilted, or that suffer from weak phrasing or the use of clichés, are not going to win supporters for the positions that you express in your paper. So a major question becomes, "How can I sound confident?"

Consider these points to convey to your reader that necessary sense of authority:

Level of Formality   Tone is one of the primary methods by which you signal to the readers who you are and what your attitude is toward them and toward your topic. Your major decision is which level of language formality is most appropriate to your audience. The informal tone you would use in a letter to a friend may be out of place in a paper on "Waste in Military Spending" written for your government professor. Remember that tone is only part of the overall decision you make about presenting your information. Formality is, to some extent, a function of individual word choices and phrasing. For example, is it appropriate to use contractions such as *isn't* or *they'll*? Would the strategic use of a sentence fragment for effect be out of place? The use of informal language, the personal *I*, and the second-person *you* is traditionally forbidden—for better or worse—in certain kinds of writing. Often, part of the challenge of writing a formal paper is simply how to give your prose impact while staying within the conventions.

Jargon   One way to lose readers quickly is to overwhelm them with *jargon*— phrases that have a special, usually technical meaning within your discipline but that are unfamiliar to the average reader. The very occasional use of jargon may add an effective touch of atmosphere, but anything more than that will severely dampen a reader's enthusiasm for the paper. Often the writer uses jargon in an effort to impress the reader by sounding lofty or knowledgeable. Unfortunately, jargon usually causes confusion. In fact, the use of jargon indicates a writer's lack of connection to the audience.

Sociological writing is a haven for jargon. Perhaps writers of policy analyses and position papers believe their readers are all completely attuned to their terminology. Or some may hope to obscure damaging information or potentially unpopular ideas in confusing language. In other cases, the problem could simply be unclear thinking by the writer. Whatever the reason, the fact is that sociology papers too often sound like prose made by machines to be read by machines.

Some students may feel that, to be accepted as sociologists, their papers should conform to the practices of their published peers. *This is a mistake*. Remember that it is never better to write a cluttered or confusing sentence than a clear one, and burying your ideas in jargon defeats the effort that you went through to form them.

EXERCISE Revising Jargon

What words in the following sentence, from an article in a sociology journal, are jargon? Can you rewrite it to clarify its meaning?

> The implementation of statute-mandated regulated inputs exceeds the conceptualization of the administrative technicians.

Clichés   In the heat of composition, as you are looking for words to help you form your ideas, it is sometimes easy to plug in a *cliché*—a phrase that has attained universal recognition by overuse. (*Note:* Clichés differ from jargon in that clichés are part of the general public's everyday language, whereas jargon is specific to the language of experts in a field.) Our vocabularies are brimming with clichés:

It's *raining cats and dogs*.

That issue is as *dead as a doornail*.

It's time for the governor to *face the music*.

Angry voters *made a beeline* for the ballot box.

The problem with clichés is that they are virtually meaningless. Once a colorful means of expression, they have lost their color through overuse, and they tend to bleed energy and color from the surrounding words. When revising, replace clichés with fresh wording that more accurately conveys your point.

Descriptive Language   Language that appeals to readers' senses will always engage their interest more fully than language that is abstract. This is especially important for writing in disciplines that tend to deal in abstracts, such as sociology. A typical sociology paper, with its discussions of principles, demographics, or points of law, is usually in danger of floating off into abstraction, with each paragraph drifting further away from the felt life of the readers. Whenever appropriate, appeal to your readers' sense of sight, hearing, taste, touch, or smell.

EXERCISE Using Descriptive Language

Which of these two sentences is more effective?

1. The housing project had deteriorated badly since the last inspection.
2. The housing project had deteriorated badly since the last inspection; stench rose from the plumbing, grime coated the walls and floors, and rats scurried through the hallways.

Bias-Free and Gender-Neutral Writing   Language can be a very powerful method of either reinforcing or destroying cultural stereotypes. By treating the sexes in subtly different ways in your language, you may unknowingly be committing an act of discrimination. A common example is the use of the pronoun *he* to refer to a person whose gender has not been identified.

Some writers, faced with this dilemma, alternate the use of male and female personal pronouns; others use the plural to avoid the need to use a pronoun of either gender:

Sexist: A lawyer should always treat his client with respect.

Corrected: A lawyer should always treat his or her client with respect.

Or: Lawyers should always treat their clients with respect.

Sexist: Man is a political animal.

Corrected: People are political animals.

Remember that language is more than the mere vehicle of your thoughts. Your words shape perceptions for your readers. How well you say something will profoundly affect your readers' response to what you say. Sexist language denies to a large number of your readers the basic right to fair and equal treatment. Make sure your writing is not guilty of this form of discrimination.

Revise

After all the work you have gone through writing it, you may feel "married" to the first draft of your paper. However, revision is one of the most important steps in ensuring your paper's success. Although unpracticed writers often think of revision as little more than making sure all the *i*'s are dotted and *t*'s are crossed, it is much more than that. Revising is *reseeing* the essay, looking at it from other perspectives, trying always to align your view with the one that will be held by your audience. Research indicates that we are actually revising all the time, in every phase of the writing process, as we reread phrases, rethink the placement of an item in an outline, or test a new topic sentence for a paragraph. Subjecting your entire hard-fought draft to cold, objective scrutiny is one of the toughest activities to master, but it is absolutely necessary. You have to ensure that you have said everything that needs to be said clearly and logically. One confusing passage will deflect the reader's attention from where you want it to be. Suddenly the reader has to become a detective, trying to figure out why you wrote what you did and what you meant by it. You do not want to throw such obstacles in the path of understanding.

Here are some tips to help you with revision:

1. Give yourself adequate time for revision. As discussed above, you need time to become "cold" on your paper to analyze it objectively. After you have written your draft, spend some time away from it. Then try to reread it as if someone else had written it.

2. Read the paper carefully. This is tougher than it sounds. One good strategy is to read it aloud yourself or to have a friend read it aloud while you listen. (Note, however, that friends are usually not the best critics. They are rarely trained in revision techniques and are often unwilling to risk disappointing you by giving your paper a really thorough examination.)

3. Have a list of specific items to check. It is important to revise in an orderly fashion, in stages, first looking at large concerns, such as the overall organization, and then at smaller elements, such as paragraph or sentence structure.

4. Check for unity—the clear and logical relation of all parts of the essay to its thesis. Make sure that every paragraph relates well to the whole of the paper and is in the right place.

5. Check for coherence. Make sure there are no gaps between the various parts of the argument. Look to see that you have adequate transitions everywhere they are needed. Transitional elements indicate places where the paper's focus or attitude changes. Such elements can take the form of one word—*however, although, unfortunately, luckily*—or an entire sentence or a paragraph: *In order to fully appreciate the importance of democracy as a shaping presence in post–Cold War Polish politics, it is necessary to examine briefly the Poles' last historical attempt to implement democratic government.*

   Transitional elements rarely introduce new material. Instead, they are direction pointers, either indicating a shift to new subject matter or signaling how the writer wishes certain material to be interpreted by the reader. Because you, the writer, already know where and why your paper changes direction and how you want particular passages to be received, it can be very difficult for you to catch those places where transition is needed.

6. Avoid unnecessary repetition. Two types of repetition can annoy a reader: repetition of content and repetition of wording.

   Repetition of content occurs when you return to a subject you have already discussed. Ideally, you should deal with a topic once, memorably, and then move on to your next subject. Organizing a paper is a difficult task, however, which usually occurs through a process of enlightenment in terms of purposes and strategies, and repetition of content can happen even if you have used prewriting strategies. What is worse, it can be difficult for you to be aware of the repetition in your own writing. As you write and revise, remember that any unnecessary repetition of content in your final draft is potentially annoying to your readers, who are working to make sense of the argument they are reading and do not want to be distracted by a passage repeating material they have already encountered. You must train yourself, through practice, to look for material that you have repeated unnecessarily.

   Repetition of wording occurs when you overuse certain phrases or words. This can make your prose sound choppy and uninspired, as the following examples demonstrate:

The subcommittee's report on education reform will surprise a number of people. A number of people will want copies of the report.

The chairman said at a press conference that he is happy with the report. He will circulate it to the local news agencies in the morning. He will also make sure that the city council has copies.

I became upset when I heard how the committee had voted. I called the chairman and expressed my reservations about the committee's decision. I told him I felt that he had let the teachers and students of the state down. I also issued a press statement.

The last passage illustrates a condition known by composition teachers as the *I-syndrome*. Can you hear how such duplicated phrasing can hurt a paper? Your language should sound fresh and energetic. Make sure, before you submit your final draft, to read through your paper carefully, looking for such repetition. However, not all repetition is bad. You may want to repeat a phrase for rhetorical effect or special emphasis: "*I came. I saw. I conquered.*" Just make sure that any repetition in your paper is intentional, placed there to produce a specific effect.

Edit

Editing is sometimes confused with the more involved process of revising. But editing is done later in the writing process, after you have wrestled through your first draft—and maybe your second and third—and arrived at the final draft. Even though your draft now contains all the information you want to impart and has the information arranged to your satisfaction, there are still many factors to check, such as sentence structure, spelling, and punctuation.

It is at this point that an unpracticed writer might be less than vigilant. After all, most of the work on the paper is finished, as the "big jobs" of discovering, organizing, and drafting information have been completed. *But watch out!* Editing is as important as any other part of the writing process. Any error that you allow in the final draft will count against you in the mind of the reader. This may not seem fair, but even a minor error—a misspelling or confusing placement of a comma—will make a much greater impression on your reader than perhaps it should. Remember that everything about your paper is your responsibility, including performing even the supposedly little jobs correctly. Careless editing undermines the effectiveness of your paper. It would be a shame if all the hard work you put into prewriting, drafting, and revising were to be damaged because you carelessly allowed a comma splice!

Most of the tips given above for revising hold for editing as well. It is best to edit in stages, looking for only one or two kinds of errors each time you reread the paper. Focus especially on errors that you remember committing in the past. If, for instance, you know that you have a tendency to misplace commas, go through your paper looking at each comma carefully. If you have a weakness for writing unintentional sentence fragments, read each sentence aloud to make sure that it is indeed a complete sentence. Have you accidentally shifted verb tenses anywhere, moving from past to present tense for no reason? Do all the subjects in your sentences agree in number with their verbs? *Now is the time to find out.*

Watch out for *miscues*—problems with a sentence that the writer simply does not see. Remember that your search for errors is hampered in two ways:

1. As a writer, you hope not to find any errors in your work. This desire can cause you to miss mistakes when they do occur.
2. Because you know your material so well, it is easy, as you read, to unconsciously supply missing material—a word, a piece of punctuation—as if it were present.

How difficult is it to see that something is missing in the following sentence?

Unfortunately, legislators often have too little regard their constituents.

We can guess that the missing word is probably *for*, which should be inserted after *regard*. It is quite possible, however, that the writer of the sentence would automatically supply the missing *for* as if it were on the page. This is a miscue, which can be hard for writers to spot because they are so close to their material.

One tactic for catching mistakes in sentence structure is to read the sentences aloud, starting with the last one in the paper and then moving to the next-to-last, then to the previous sentence, and thus going backward through the paper (reading each sentence in the normal, left-to-right manner, of course) until you reach the first sentence of the introduction. This backward progression strips each sentence of its rhetorical context and helps you focus on its internal structure.

Editing is the stage in which you finally answer those minor questions that you had put off when you were wrestling with wording and organization. Any ambiguities regarding the use of abbreviations, italics, numerals, capital letters, titles (When do you capitalize the title *president*, for example?), hyphens, dashes (usually created on a typewriter or computer by striking the hyphen key twice), apostrophes, and quotation marks have to be cleared up now. You must also check to see that you have used the required formats for footnotes, endnotes, margins, page numbers, and the like.

Guessing is not allowed. Sometimes unpracticed writers who realize that they do not quite understand a particular rule of grammar, punctuation, or format do nothing to fill that knowledge gap. Instead, they rely on guesswork and their own logic—which is not always up to the task of dealing with so contrary a language as English—to get them through problems that they could solve if they referred to a writing manual. Remember that it does not matter to the reader why or how an error shows up in your writing. It only matters that you have dropped your guard. You must not allow a careless error to undo all the good work that you have done.

Proofread

Before you hand in the final version of your paper, it is vital that you check it one more time to ensure that there are no errors of any sort. This job is called *proofreading* or *proofing*. In essence, you are looking for many of the same things you had checked for during editing, but now you are doing it on the last draft, which is about to be submitted to your audience. Proofreading is as important as editing; you may have missed an error that you still have time to find, or an error may have been introduced when the draft was recopied or typed for the last time. Like every other stage of the writing process, proofreading is your responsibility.

At this point, you must check for typing mistakes: transposed or deleted letters, words, phrases, or punctuation. If you have had the paper professionally typed, you still must check it carefully. Do not rely solely on the typist's proofreading. If you are creating your paper on a computer or a word processor, it is possible for you to unintentionally insert a command that alters your document drastically by slicing out a word, line, or sentence at the touch of a key. Make sure such accidental deletions have not occurred.

Above all else, remember that your paper represents you. It is a product of your best thinking, your most energetic and imaginative response to a writing challenge. If you have maintained your enthusiasm for the project and worked through the stages of the writing process honestly and carefully, you should produce a paper you can be proud of, one that will serve its readers well.

Read&Write 2.4 Discover Your Own Style

Here is another opportunity to do some freewriting. The wisdom of the Oracle of Delphi was noted by Socrates, who affirmed the Oracle's belief that the key to wisdom itself was to "Know Yourself." Fulfilling this admonition can become a life-long occupation. As psychologists may tell you, helping others know themselves offers a potentially fulfilling career. Let's start our writing project by accepting, though with apologies for an ancient philosopher's gender bias, Aristotle's observation that "man is a political animal."[4] If you are a political animal, what does this mean about you personally? In this case, think about politics in the broadest sense, not just running for office, but as a mode of conduct in which you exert influence on other people, most specifically to get your needs and desires met. Have fun! When you are done freewriting, write one solid paper in which you describe who you are as a "political animal."

[4] Aristotle. *Politics.* 1.1253a. Retrieved March 7, 2016 (http://data.perseus.org/citations/urn:cts: greekLit:tlg0086.tlg035.perseus-eng1:1.1253a).

3

PRACTICE THE CRAFT

OF SCHOLARSHIP

3.1   THE COMPETENT WRITER

Good writing places your thoughts in your readers' minds in exactly the way you want them to be there. Good writing tells your readers just what you want them to know without telling them anything you do not want them to know. This may sound odd, but the fact is that writers have to be careful not to let unwanted messages slip into their writing. Look, for example, at the passage below, taken from a paper analyzing the impact of a worker-retraining program. Hidden within the prose is a message that jeopardizes the paper's success. Can you detect the message?

> Recent articles written on the subject of dislocated workers have had little to say about the particular problems dealt with in this paper. Because few of these articles focus on the problem at the state level.

Chances are, when you reached the end of the second "sentence," you felt that something was missing and perceived a gap in logic or coherence, so you went back through both sentences to find the place where things had gone wrong. The second sentence is actually not a sentence at all. It does have certain features of a sentence—for example, a subject (*few*) and a verb (*focus*)—but its first word (*Because*) subordinates the entire clause that follows, taking away its ability to stand on its own as a complete idea. The second "sentence," which is properly called a *subordinate clause*, merely fills in some information about the first sentence, telling us why recent articles about dislocated workers fail to deal with problems discussed in the present paper.

The sort of error represented by the second "sentence" is commonly called a *sentence fragment*, and it conveys to the reader a message that no writer wants to send: that the writer either is careless or, worse, has not mastered the language. Language errors such as fragments, misplaced commas, or shifts in verb tense send out warnings to the readers' minds. As a result, readers lose some of their concentration on the issue being discussed; they become distracted and begin to wonder about the language competency of the writer. The writing loses its effectiveness.

Note: Whatever goal you set for your paper—whether to persuade, describe, analyze, or speculate—you must also set one other goal: to display your language competence. If your paper does not meet this goal, it will not completely achieve its other aims. Language errors spread doubt like a virus; they jeopardize all the hard work you have done on your paper.

Language competence is especially important in sociology, for credibility in politics depends on such skill. Anyone who doubts this should remember the beating that Vice President Dan Quayle took in the press for misspelling the word *potato* at a 1992 spelling bee. The error caused a storm of humiliating publicity for the hapless Quayle, adding to an impression of his general incompetence.

Correctness Is Relative

Although they may seem minor, the sort of language errors we are discussing—often called *surface errors*—can be extremely damaging in certain kinds of writing. Surface errors come in various types, including misspellings, punctuation problems, grammar errors, and the inconsistent use of abbreviations, capitalization, and numerals. These errors are an affront to your readers' notion of correctness, and therein lies one of the biggest problems with surface errors. Different audiences tolerate different levels of correctness. You know that you can get away with surface errors in, say, a letter to a friend, who will probably not judge you very harshly for them, whereas those same errors in a job application letter might eliminate you from being considered for the position. Correctness depends to an extent on the context.

Another problem is that the rules governing correctness shift over a period of time. What would have been an error to your grandmother's generation—the splitting of an infinitive, for example, or the ending of a sentence with a preposition—is taken in stride by most readers today.

So how do you write correctly when the rules shift from person to person and over a period of time? Here are some tips:

Consider Your Audience   One of the great risks of writing is that even the simplest of choices regarding wording or punctuation can sometimes prejudice your audience against you in ways that may seem unfair. For example, look again at the old grammar rule forbidding the splitting of infinitives. After decades of telling students to never split an infinitive (something just done in this sentence), most composition experts now concede that a split infinitive is *not* a grammar crime. Suppose you have written a position paper trying to convince your city council of the need to hire security personnel for the library, and half of the council members—the people you wish to convince—remember their eighth-grade grammar teacher's warning about splitting infinitives. How will they respond when you tell them, in your introduction, that librarians are compelled "to always accompany" visitors to the rare book room because of the threat of vandalism? How much of their attention have you suddenly lost because of their automatic recollection of what is now a nonrule? It is possible, in other words, to write correctly and still offend your readers' notions of your language competence.

Make sure that you tailor the surface features and the degree of formality in your writing to the level of competency that your readers require. When in doubt, take a conservative approach. Your audience might be just as distracted by a contraction as by a split infinitive.

Aim for Consistency   When you are dealing with a language question for which there are different answers—such as whether to use a comma before the conjunction in a series of three ("The mayor's speech addressed taxes, housing for the poor, and the job situation.")—always use the same strategy throughout your paper. If, for example, you avoid splitting one infinitive, avoid splitting *all* infinitives.

Have Confidence in What You Know About Writing!

It is easy for unpracticed writers to allow their occasional mistakes to shake their confidence in their writing ability. The fact is, however, that most of what we know about writing is correct. We are all capable, for example, of writing grammatically sound phrases, even if we cannot list the rules by which we achieve coherence. Most writers who worry about their chronic errors make fewer mistakes than they think. Becoming distressed about errors makes writing even more difficult.

Read&Write 3.1   Correct a Sentence Fragment

See how many ways you can rewrite this two "sentence" passage to eliminate the fragment and make the passage syntactically correct.

Although married couples often both work full time, women do most of the house work. Except when the men work second or third shifts.

3.2   AVOID ERRORS IN GRAMMAR AND PUNCTUATION

As various composition theorists have pointed out, the word *grammar* has several definitions. One meaning is "the formal patterns in which words must be arranged in order to convey meaning." We learn these patterns very early in life and use them spontaneously, without even thinking. Our understanding of grammatical patterns is extremely sophisticated, despite the fact that few of us can actually cite the rules by which the patterns work. Patrick Hartwell tested grammar learning by asking native English speakers of different ages and levels of education, including high school teachers, to arrange these words in natural order:

French   the   young   girls   four

Everyone could produce the natural order for this phrase: "the four young French girls." Yet none of Hartwell's respondents said they knew the rule that governs the order of the words.[1]

---

[1] Patrick Hartwell. 1985. "Grammar, Grammars, and the Teaching of Grammar." *College English* 47(2): 105–127.

Eliminate Chronic Errors   If just thinking about our errors has a negative effect on our writing, then how do we learn to write more correctly? Perhaps the best answer is simply to write as often as possible. Give yourself lots of practice in putting your thoughts into written shape—and then in revising and proofing your work. As you write and revise, be honest with yourself—and patient. Chronic errors are like bad habits; getting rid of them takes time.

You probably know of one or two problem areas in your writing that you could have eliminated but have not. Instead, you may have "fudged" your writing at the critical points, relying on half-remembered formulas from past English classes or trying to come up with logical solutions to your writing problems. (*Warning:* The English language does not always work in a way that seems logical.) You may have simply decided that comma rules are unlearnable or that you will never understand the difference between the verbs *lay* and *lie*. And so you guess, and you come up with the wrong answer a good part of the time. What a shame, when just a little extra work would give you mastery over those few gaps in your understanding and boost your confidence as well.

Instead of continuing with this sort of guesswork and living with the holes in your knowledge, why not face the problem areas now and learn the rules that have heretofore escaped you? What follows is a discussion of those surface features of writing in which errors most commonly occur. You will probably be familiar with most, if not all, of the rules discussed, but there may well be a few you have not yet mastered. Now is the time to do so.

Apostrophes

An apostrophe is used to show possession. When you wish to say that something belongs to someone or something, you add either an apostrophe and an *s* or an apostrophe alone to the word that represents the owner.

- When the owner is singular (a single person or thing), the apostrophe precedes an added *s:*

    According to CEO Anderson's secretary, the senior staff meeting has been canceled.

    The union's lawyers challenged the government's policy in court.

    Somebody's briefcase was left in the auditorium.

- The same rule applies if the word showing possession is a plural that does not end in *s:*

    The women's club sponsored several benefit concerts during their annual charity drive.

    Father Garrity has proven himself a tireless worker for improved children's services.

- When the word expressing ownership is a plural ending in *s*, the apostrophe follows the *s:*

    The new initiation ceremony was discussed at the club secretaries' conference.

There are two ways to form the possessive for two or more nouns:

1. To show joint possession (both nouns owning the same thing or things), the last noun in the series is possessive:

   The president and first lady's invitations were sent out yesterday.

2. To indicate that each noun owns an item or items individually, each noun must show possession:

   Superintendent Scott's and Principal MacKay's speeches took different approaches to the same problem.

The importance of the apostrophe is obvious when you consider the difference in the meaning between the following two sentences:

Be sure to pick up the volunteer's bags on your way to the airport.

Be sure to pick up the volunteer's bags on your way to the airport.

In the first sentence, you have only one volunteer to worry about, whereas in the second, you have at least two!

Capitalization

Here is a brief summary of some hard-to-remember capitalization rules:

1. You may, if you choose, capitalize the first letter of the first word in a sentence that follows a colon. However, make sure you use one pattern consistently throughout your paper:

   Our instructions are explicit: Do not allow anyone into the conference without an identification badge.

   Our instructions are explicit: do not allow anyone into the conference without an identification badge.

2. Capitalize *proper nouns* (names of specific people, places, or things) and *proper adjectives* (adjectives made from proper nouns). A common noun following a proper adjective is usually not capitalized, nor is a common adjective preceding a proper adjective (such as *a*, *an*, or *the*):

Proper Nouns	Proper Adjectives
Poland	Polish officials
Iraq	the Iraqi ambassador
Shakespeare	a Shakespearean tragedy

Proper nouns include:

- *Names of monuments and buildings:* the Washington Monument, the Empire State Building, the Library of Congress
- *Historical events, eras, and certain terms concerning calendar dates:* the Civil War, the Dark Ages, Monday, December, Columbus Day

- *Parts of the country:* North, Southwest, Eastern Seaboard, the West Coast, New England.

> **Note:** When words like *north*, *south*, *east*, *west*, and *northwest* are used to designate direction rather than geographical region, they are not capitalized: "We drove east to Boston and then made a tour of the East Coast."

- *Words referring to race, religion, and nationality:* Islam, Muslim, Caucasian, White (or white), Asian, Negro, Black (or black), Slavic, Arab, Jewish, Hebrew, Buddhism, Buddhists, Southern Baptists, the Bible, the Koran, American
- *Names of languages:* English, Chinese, Latin, Sanskrit
- *Titles of corporations, institutions, universities, and organizations:* Dow Chemical, General Motors, the National Endowment for the Humanities, University of Tennessee, Colby College, Kiwanis Club, American Association of Retired Persons, Oklahoma State Senate

> **Note:** Some words once considered proper nouns or adjectives have, over time, become common and are no longer capitalized, such as *french fries, pasteurized milk, arabic numerals, and italics.*

3. Titles of individuals may be capitalized if they precede a proper name; otherwise, titles are usually not capitalized:

The committee honored Senator Jones.

The committee honored the senator from Kansas.

We phoned Doctor Jessup, who arrived shortly afterward.

We phoned the doctor, who arrived shortly afterward.

A story on Queen Elizabeth's health appeared in yesterday's paper.

A story on the queen's health appeared in yesterday's paper.

Pope John Paul's visit to Colorado was a public relations success.

The pope's visit to Colorado was a public relations success.

When Not to Capitalize　In general, you do not capitalize nouns when your reference is nonspecific. For example, you would not capitalize *the senator*, but you would capitalize *Senator Smith*. The second reference is as much a title as it is a term of identification, whereas the first reference is a mere identifier. Likewise, there is a difference in degree of specificity between *the state treasury* and *the Texas State Treasury*.

> **Note:** The meaning of a term may change somewhat depending on its capitalization. What, for example, might be the difference between a *Democrat* and a *democrat*? When capitalized, the word refers to a member of a specific political party; when not capitalized, it refers to someone who believes in the democratic form of government.

Capitalization depends to some extent on the context of your writing. For example, if you are writing a policy analysis for a specific corporation, you may capitalize words and phrases that refer to that corporation—such as *Board of Directors, Chairman of the Board*, and *the Institute*—that would not be capitalized in a paper written for a more general audience. Likewise, in some contexts, it is not unusual to see the titles of certain powerful officials capitalized even when not accompanying a proper noun:

The President took few members of his staff to Camp David with him.

Colons

We all know certain uses for the colon. A colon can, for example, separate the parts of a statement of time (*4:25 A.M.*), separate chapter and verse in a biblical quotation (*John 3:16*), and close the salutation of a business letter (*Dear Director Keaton:*). But the colon has other, less well-known uses that can add extra flexibility to sentence structure.

The colon can introduce into a sentence certain kinds of material, such as a list, a quotation, or a restatement or description of material mentioned earlier:

List

The committee's research proposal promised to do three things: (1) establish the extent of the problem, (2) examine several possible solutions, and (3) estimate the cost of each solution.

Quotation

In his speech, the mayor challenged us with these words: "How will your council's work make a difference in the life of our city?"

Restatement or Description

Ahead of us, according to the senator's chief of staff, lay the biggest job of all: convincing our constituents of the plan's benefits.

Commas

The comma is perhaps the most troublesome of all marks of punctuation, no doubt because its use is governed by so many variables, such as sentence length, rhetorical emphasis, and changing notions of style. The most common problems are outlined below.

The Comma Splice   A *comma splice* is the joining of two complete sentences with only a comma:

An impeachment is merely an indictment of a government official, actual removal usually requires a vote by a legislative body.

An unemployed worker who has been effectively retrained is no longer an economic problem for the community, he has become an asset.

It might be possible for the city to assess fees on the sale of real estate, however, such a move would be criticized by the community of real estate developers.

In each of these passages, two complete sentences (also called *independent clauses*) have been spliced together by a comma, which is an inadequate break between the two sentences.

One foolproof way to check your paper for comma splices is to read the structures on both sides of each comma carefully. If you find a complete sentence on each side, and if the sentence following the comma does not begin with a coordinating conjunction (*and, but, for, nor, or, so, yet*), then you have found a comma splice.

Simply reading the draft to try to "hear" the comma splices may not work because the rhetorical features of your prose—its "movement"—may make it hard to detect this kind of error in sentence completeness. There are five commonly used ways to correct comma splices:

1. Place a period between the two independent clauses:

INCORRECT   A political candidate receives many benefits from his or her affiliation with a political party, there are liabilities as well.

CORRECT   A political candidate receives many benefits from his or her affiliation with a political party. There are liabilities as well.

2. Place a comma and a coordinating conjunction (*and, but, for, or, nor, so, yet*) between the independent clauses:

INCORRECT   The councilman's speech described the major differences of opinion over the economic situation, it also suggested a possible course of action.

CORRECT   The councilman's speech described the major differences of opinion over the economic situation, and it also suggested a possible course of action.

3. Place a semicolon between the independent clauses:

INCORRECT   Some people feel that the federal government should play a large role in establishing a housing policy for the homeless, many others disagree.

CORRECT   Some people feel that the federal government should play a large role in establishing a housing policy for the homeless; many others disagree.

4. Rewrite the two clauses as one independent clause:

INCORRECT   Television ads played a big part in product promotion, however they were not the deciding factor in the gaining the greatest market share.

CORRECT   Television ads played a large but not a decisive role in gaining the greatest market share.

5. Change one of the independent clauses into a dependent clause by beginning it with a subordinating word (*although, after, as, because, before, if, though, unless, when, which, where*), which prevents the clause from being able to stand on its own as a complete sentence.

INCORRECT   The sports gear sale was held last Tuesday, there was a poor consumer turnout.

CORRECT   When the sports gear sale was held last Tuesday, there was a poor consumer turnout.

Commas in a Compound Sentence   A *compound sentence* is composed of two or more independent clauses—two complete sentences. When these two clauses are joined by a coordinating conjunction, the conjunction should be preceded by a comma to signal the reader that another independent clause follows. (This is method number 2 for fixing a comma splice, described above.) When the comma is missing, the reader is not expecting to find the second half of a compound sentence and may be distracted from the text.

As the following examples indicate, the missing comma is especially a problem in longer sentences or in sentences in which other coordinating conjunctions appear. Notice how the comma sorts out the two main parts of the compound sentence, eliminating confusion:

INCORRECT   The archbishop promised to visit the hospital and investigate the problem and then he called the press conference to a close.

CORRECT   The archbishop promised to visit the hospital and investigate the problem, and then he called the press conference to a close.

INCORRECT   The water board can neither make policy nor enforce it nor can its members serve on auxiliary water committees.

CORRECT   The water board can neither make policy nor enforce it, nor can its members serve on auxiliary water committees.

An exception to this rule arises in shorter sentences, where the comma may not be necessary to make the meaning clear:

The executive director phoned and we thanked him for his support.

However, it is never wrong to place a comma after the conjunction between independent clauses. If you are the least bit unsure of your audience's notion of "proper" grammar, it is a good idea to take the conservative approach and use the comma:

The executive director phoned, and we thanked him for his support.

Commas with Restrictive and Nonrestrictive Elements   A *nonrestrictive element* is a part of a sentence—a word, phrase, or clause—that adds information about another element in the sentence without restricting or limiting its meaning. Although this information may be useful, the nonrestrictive element is not needed for the sentence to make sense. To signal its inessential nature, the nonrestrictive element is set off from the rest of the sentence with commas.

The failure to use commas to indicate the nonrestrictive nature of a sentence element can cause confusion. See, for example, how the presence or absence of commas affects our understanding of the following sentence:

The gardener was talking with the volunteer coordinator, who won the outstanding service award last year.

The gardener was talking with the volunteer coordinator who won the outstanding service award last year.

Can you see that the comma changes the meaning of the sentence? In the first version of the sentence, the comma makes the information that follows it incidental: *The gardener was talking with the volunteer coordinator, who happens to have won the service award last year.* In the second version of the sentence, the information following the title *volunteer coordinator* is vital to the sense of the sentence; it tells us specifically *which* volunteer coordinator—presumably there are more than one—the gardener was addressing. Here, the lack of a comma has transformed the material following the word *policeman* into a *restrictive element*, which means that it is necessary to our understanding of the sentence.

Be sure that you make a clear distinction in your paper between nonrestrictive and restrictive elements by setting off the nonrestrictive elements with commas.

Commas in a Series A series is any two or more items of a similar nature that appear consecutively in a sentence. These items may be individual words, phrases, or clauses. In a series of three or more items, the items are separated by commas:

The butler, the baker, and the chauffeur all attended the ceremony.

Because of the new zoning regulations, all trailer parks must be moved out of the neighborhood, all small businesses must apply for recertification and tax status, and the two local churches must repave their parking lots.

The final comma in the series, the one before *and*, is sometimes left out, especially in newspaper writing. This practice, however, can make for confusion, especially in longer, complicated sentences like the second example above. Here is the way this sentence would read without the final, or serial, comma:

Because of the new zoning regulations, all trailer parks must be moved out of the neighborhood, all small businesses must apply for recertification and tax status and the two local churches must repave their parking lots.

Notice that, without a comma, the division between the second and third items in the series is not clear. This is the sort of ambiguous structure that can cause a reader to backtrack and lose concentration. You can avoid such confusion by always using that final comma. Remember, however, that if you decide to include it, do so consistently; make sure it appears in every series in your paper.

Misplaced Modifiers

A *modifier* is a word or group of words used to describe, or modify, another word in the sentence. A *misplaced modifier*, sometimes called a dangling modifier, appears at either the beginning or the end of a sentence and seems to be describing some word other than the one the writer obviously intended. The modifier therefore "dangles," disconnected from its correct meaning. It is often hard for the writer to spot a dangling modifier, but readers can—and will—find them, and the result can be disastrous for the sentence, as the following examples demonstrate:

INCORRECT	Flying low over Beverly Hills, the Oral Robert's mansion was seen.
CORRECT	Flying low over Beverly Hills, we saw Oral Robert's Mansion.
INCORRECT	Worried at the cost of the menu, the desert was eliminated by the committee.
CORRECT	Worried at the cost of the menu, the committee eliminated the desert.
INCORRECT	To lobby for prison reform, a lot of effort went into the television ads.
CORRECT	The lobby group put a lot of effort into the television ads advocating prison reform.
INCORRECT	Stunned, the television broadcast the defeated senator's concession speech.
CORRECT	The television broadcast the stunned senator's concession speech.

Note that, in the first two incorrect sentences above, the confusion is largely due to the use of *passive-voice* verbs: "the White House *was seen*," "sections of the bill *were trimmed*." Often, although not always, a dangling modifier results because the actor in the sentence—*we* in the first sentence, *the committee* in the second—is either distanced from the modifier or obliterated by the passive-voice verb. It is a good idea to avoid using the passive voice unless you have a specific reason for doing so.

One way to check for dangling modifiers is to examine all modifiers at the beginning or end of your sentences. Look especially for to be phrases or for words ending in -*ing* or -*ed* at the start of the modifier. Then see if the modified word is close enough to the phrase to be properly connected.

Parallelism

Series of two or more words, phrases, or clauses within a sentence should have the same grammatical structure, a situation called *parallelism*. Parallel structures can add power and balance to your writing by creating a strong rhetorical rhythm. Here is a famous example of parallelism from the Preamble to the U.S. Constitution (the capitalization follows that of the original eighteenth-century document; parallel structures have been italicized):

> We the People of the United States, in Order to *form a more perfect Union, Establish justice, insure Domestic Tranquility, provide for the common defense, promote the general Welfare*, and *secure the Blessings of Liberty to ourselves and our Posterity*, do *ordain* and *establish* this Constitution for the United States of America.

There are actually two series in this sentence: the first, composed of six phrases, each of which completes the infinitive phrase beginning with the word to [*to form*, (*to*) *Establish*, (*to*) *insure*, (*to*) *provide*, (*to*) *promote*, and (*to*) *secure*]; the second, consisting of two verbs (*ordain* and *establish*). These parallel series appeal to our love of balance and pattern, and give an authoritative tone to the sentence. The writer, we feel, has thought long and carefully about the matter at hand and has taken firm control of it.

Because we find a special satisfaction in balanced structures, we are more likely to remember ideas phrased in parallelisms than in less highly ordered language.

For this reason, as well as for the sense of authority and control that they suggest, parallel structures are common in political utterances:

> *We hold these truths to be self-evident, that all men are created equal, that they are endowed by their Creator with certain unalienable rights, that among these are life, liberty, and the pursuit of happiness.*
>
> —The Declaration of Independence, 1776

> *Ask not what your country can do for you, ask what you can do for your country.*
>
> —John F. Kennedy, Inaugural Address, 1961

Faulty Parallelism   If the parallelism of a passage is not carefully maintained, the writing can seem sloppy and out of balance. Scan your writing to ensure that all series and lists have parallel structures. The following examples show how to correct faulty parallelism:

INCORRECT   The mayor promises not only *to reform* the police department but also *the giving of raises* to all city employees. (Connective structures such as *not only . . . but also* and *both . . . and* introduce elements that should be parallel.)

CORRECT   The mayor promises not only *to reform* the police department but also *to give* raises to all city employees.

INCORRECT   The cost *of doing nothing* is greater than the cost *to renovate* the apartment block.

CORRECT   The cost *of doing nothing* is greater than the cost *of renovating* the apartment block.

INCORRECT   Here are the items on the committee's agenda: (1) *to discuss* the new property tax; (2) *to revise* the wording of the city charter; (3) *a vote* on the city manager's request for an assistant.

CORRECT   Here are the items on the committee's agenda: (1) *to discuss* the new property tax; (2) *to revise* the wording of the city charter; (3) *to vote* on the city manager's request for an assistant.

Fused (Run-on) Sentences

A *fused sentence* is one in which two or more independent clauses (passages that can stand as complete sentences) have been run together without the aid of any suitable connecting word, phrase, or punctuation. There are several ways to correct a fused sentence:

INCORRECT   The council members were exhausted they had debated for two hours.

CORRECT   The council members were exhausted. They had debated for two hours. (The clauses have been separated into two sentences.)

CORRECT   The council members were exhausted; they had debated for two hours. (The clauses have been separated by a semicolon.)

CORRECT   The council members were exhausted, having debated for two hours. (The second clause has been rephrased as a dependent clause.)

INCORRECT   Our policy analysis impressed the committee it also convinced them to reconsider their action.

CORRECT   Our policy analysis impressed the committee and also convinced them to reconsider their action. (The second clause has been rephrased as part of the first clause.)

CORRECT   Our policy analysis impressed the committee, and it also convinced them to reconsider their action. (The clauses have been separated by a comma and a coordinating word.)

Although a fused sentence is easily noticeable to the reader, it can be maddeningly difficult for the writer to catch. Unpracticed writers tend to read through the fused spots, sometimes supplying the break that is usually heard when sentences are spoken. To check for fused sentences, read the independent clauses in your paper carefully, ensuring that there are adequate breaks among all of them.

Pronouns

Its* Versus *It's   Do not make the mistake of trying to form the possessive of *it* in the same way that you form the possessive of most nouns. The pronoun *it* shows possession by simply adding an *s*.

The Boy Scout leader selected a campsite on its merits.

The word *it's* is a contraction of *it is*:

It's the most expensive program ever launched by the school board.

What makes the *its/it's* rule so confusing is that most nouns form the singular possessive by adding an apostrophe and an *s*:

The jury's verdict startled the crowd.

When proofreading, any time you come to the word *it's* substitute the phrase *it is* while you read. If the phrase makes sense, you have used the correct form. If you have used the word *it's*:

The newspaper article was misleading in it's analysis of the election.

then read it as *it is*:

The newspaper article was misleading in it is analysis of the election.

If the phrase makes no sense, substitute *its* for *it's*:

The newspaper article was misleading in its analysis of the election.

Vague Pronoun References   Pronouns are words that take the place of nouns or other pronouns that have already been mentioned in your writing. The most common pronouns include *he, she, it, they, them, those, which,* and *who.* You must make sure there is no confusion about the word to which each pronoun refers:

The priest said that he would support our bill if the archbishop would also back it.

The word that the pronoun replaces is called its *antecedent.* To check the accuracy of your pronoun references, ask yourself, "To what does the pronoun refer?" Then answer the question carefully, ensuring that there is not more than one possible antecedent. Consider the following example:

Several special interest groups decided to defeat the new health care bill. This became the turning point of the government's reform campaign.

To what does the word *this* refer? The immediate answer seems to be the word *bill* at the end of the previous sentence. It is more likely that the writer was referring to the attempt of the special interest groups to defeat the bill, but there is no word in the first sentence that refers specifically to this action. The pronoun reference is thus unclear. One way to clarify the reference is to change the beginning of the second sentence:

Several special interest groups decided to defeat the new health care bill. Their attack on the bill became the turning point of the government's reform campaign.

Here is another example:

When John F. Kennedy appointed his brother Robert to the position of U.S. attorney general, he had little idea how widespread the corruption in the Teamsters Union was.

To whom does the word *he* refer? It is unclear whether the writer is referring to John or Robert Kennedy. One way to clarify the reference is simply to repeat the antecedent instead of using a pronoun:

When John F. Kennedy appointed his brother Robert to the position of U.S. attorney general, Robert had little idea how widespread the corruption in the Teamsters Union was.

Pronoun Agreement   A pronoun must agree with its antecedent in both gender and number, as the following examples demonstrate:

Bank manager Smith said that he appreciated our club's support in the fund raising campaign.

One reporter asked the reporter what she would do if the editor offered her a promotion.

Having listened to our proposal, the coach decided to put it into effect within the week.

Engineers working on the housing project said they were pleased with the renovation so far.

Certain words, however, can be troublesome antecedents because they may look like plural pronouns but are actually singular:

anyone	each	either	everybody	everyone
nobody	no one	somebody	someone	

A pronoun referring to one of these words in a sentence must be singular too:

INCORRECT   Each of the women in the support group brought their children.

CORRECT   Each of the women in the support group brought her children.

INCORRECT   Has everybody received their ballot?

CORRECT   Has everybody received his or her ballot? (The two gender-specific pronouns are used to avoid sexist language.)

CORRECT   Have all the delegates received their ballots? (The singular antecedent has been changed to a plural one.)

A Shift in Person

It is important to avoid shifting unnecessarily among first person (*I, we*), second person (*you*), and third person (*she, he, it, one, they*). Such shifts can cause confusion:

INCORRECT Most people (third person) who run for office find that if you (second person) tell the truth during your campaign, you will gain the voters' respect.

CORRECT   Most people who run for office find that if they tell the truth during their campaigns, they will gain the voters' respect.

INCORRECT One (first person) cannot tell whether they (third person) are suited for public office until they decide to run.

CORRECT   One cannot tell whether one is suited for public office until one decides to run.

Quotation Marks

It can be difficult to remember when to use quotation marks and where they go in relation to other punctuation. When faced with these questions, unpracticed writers often try to rely on logic rather than on a rule book, but the rules do not always seem to rely on logic. The only way to make sure of your use of quotation marks is to memorize the rules. Luckily, there are not many.

The Use of Quotation Marks   Use quotation marks to enclose direct quotations that are no longer than 100 words or eight typed lines:

In a stinging rebuke to those members of the committee who voted against the measure, Mayor Jenkins, in a press conference hastily called today, said, "In all my years in public office, never have I had to put up with so much shortsightedness, ingratitude, and cowardice. It makes me wonder how our coalition can survive much longer, or even if it should."

Longer quotations, called *block quotations*, are placed in a double-spaced indented block, without quotation marks:

Lincoln clearly explained his motive for continuing the Civil War in his August 22, 1862, response to Horace Greeley's open letter:

> I would save the Union. I would save it the shortest way under the Constitution. The sooner the National authority can be restored, the nearer the Union will be the Union as it was. If there be those who would not save the Union unless they could at the same time save Slavery, I do not agree with them. If there be those who would not save the Union unless they could at the same time destroy Slavery, I do not agree with them.[2]

---

[2] Abraham Lincoln. N.d. "Letter to Horace Greeley" (August 22, 1862). Abraham Lincoln Online. Retrieved March 25, 2016 (http://www.abrahamlincolnonline.org/lincoln/speeches/greeley.htm).

Use single quotation marks to set off quotations within quotations:

"I intend," said the senator, "to use in my speech a line from Frost's poem, 'The Road Not Taken.'"

Note: When the quote occurs at the end of the sentence, both the single and double quotation marks are placed outside the period.

Use quotation marks to set off titles of the following:
Short poems (those not printed as a separate volume)
Short stories
Articles or essays
Songs
Episodes of television or radio shows

Use quotation marks to set off words or phrases used in special ways:

- To convey irony:

  The "liberal" administration has done nothing but cater to big business.

- To indicate a technical term:

  To "filibuster" is to delay legislation, usually through prolonged speechmaking. The last notable filibuster occurred just last week in the Senate. (Once the term is defined, it is not placed in quotation marks again.)

Quotation Marks in Relation to Other Punctuation Place commas and periods *inside* closing quotation marks:

"My fellow Americans," said the president, "there are tough times ahead of us."

Place colons and semicolons *outside* closing quotation marks:

In his speech on voting, the governor warned against "an encroaching indolence"; he was referring to the middle class.

There are several victims of the government's campaign to "Turn Back the Clock": the homeless, the elderly, the mentally impaired.

Use the context to determine whether to place question marks, exclamation points, and dashes inside or outside closing quotation marks. If the punctuation is part of the quotation, place it inside the quotation mark:

"When will Congress make up its mind?" asked the ambassador.

The demonstrators shouted, "Free the hostages!" and "No more slavery!"

If the punctuation is not part of the quotation, place it outside the quotation mark:

Which president said, "We have nothing to fear but fear itself"?

Note that although the quote is a complete sentence, you do not place a period after it. There can only be one piece of "terminal" punctuation (punctuation that ends a sentence).

Semicolons

The semicolon is a little-used punctuation mark that you should learn to incorporate into your writing strategy because of its many potential applications. For example, a semicolon can be used to correct a comma splice:

INCORRECT   The union representatives left the meeting in good spirits, their demands were met.

CORRECT   The union representatives left the meeting in good spirits; their demands were met.

INCORRECT   Several guests at the fundraiser had lost their invitations, however, we were able to seat them anyway.

CORRECT   Several guests at the fundraiser had lost their invitations; however, we were able to seat them anyway.

It is important to remember that conjunctive adverbs such as *however, therefore,* and *thus* are not coordinating words (such as *and, but, or, for, so, yet*) and cannot be used with a comma to link independent clauses. If the second independent clause begins with *however*, it must be preceded by either a period or a semicolon. As you can see from the second example above, connecting two independent clauses with a semicolon instead of a period preserves the suggestions that there is a strong relationship between the clauses.

Semicolons can also separate items in a series when the series items themselves contain commas:

The newspaper account of the rally stressed the march, which drew the biggest crowd; the mayor's speech, which drew tremendous applause; and the party in the park, which lasted for hours.

Avoid misusing semicolons. For example, use a comma, not a semicolon, to separate an independent clause from a dependent clause:

INCORRECT   Students from the college volunteered to answer phones during the pledge drive; which was set up to generate money for the new arts center.

CORRECT   Students from the college volunteered to answer phones during the pledge drive, which was set up to generate money for the new arts center.

Do not overuse semicolons. Although they are useful, too many semicolons in your writing can distract your readers' attention. Avoid monotony by using semicolons sparingly.

Sentence Fragments

A *fragment* is an incomplete part of a sentence that is punctuated and capitalized as if it were an entire sentence. It is an especially disruptive error because it obscures the connections that the words of a sentence must make to complete the reader's understanding.

Students sometimes write fragments because they are concerned that a sentence needs to be shortened. Remember that cutting the length of a sentence merely by adding a period somewhere often creates a fragment. When checking a writing for fragments, it is essential that you read each sentence carefully to determine whether it has (1) a complete subject and a verb; and (2) a subordinating word before the subject and verb, which makes the construction a subordinate clause rather than a complete sentence.

Some fragments lack a verb:

INCORRECT   The chairperson of our committee, receiving a letter from the surveyor. (Watch out for words that look like verbs but are being used in another way.)

CORRECT   The chairperson of our committee received a letter from the surveyor.

Some fragments lack a subject:

INCORRECT   Our study shows that there is broad support for improvement in the health-care system. And in the unemployment system.

CORRECT   Our study shows that there is broad support for improvement in the health care system and in the unemployment system.

Some fragments are subordinate clauses:

INCORRECT   After the latest edition of the newspaper came out. [This clause has the two major components of a complete sentence: a subject (*edition*) and a verb (*came*). Indeed, if the first word (*After*) were deleted, the clause would be a complete sentence. But that first word is a *subordinating word*, which prevents the following clause from standing on its own as a complete sentence. Watch out for this kind of construction. It is called a *subordinate clause*, and it is not a sentence.]

CORRECT   After the latest edition of the newspaper came out, the editor's secretary was overwhelmed with phone calls. (A common method of correcting a subordinate clause that has been punctuated as a complete sentence is to connect it to the complete sentence to which it is closest in meaning.)

INCORRECT   Several representatives asked for copies of the vice president's position paper. Which called for reform of the Environmental Protection Agency.

CORRECT   Several representatives asked for copies of the vice president's position paper, which called for reform of the Environmental Protection Agency.

Spelling

All of us have problems spelling certain words that we have not yet committed to memory. But most writers are not as bad at spelling as they believe they are. Usually, an individual finds only a handful of words troubling. It is important to be as sensitive as possible to your own particular spelling problems—and to keep a dictionary handy. There is no excuse for failing to check spelling.

What follows are a list of commonly confused words and a list of commonly misspelled words. Read through the lists, looking for those words that tend to give you trouble. If you have any questions, consult your dictionary.

Commonly Confused Words

accept/except	envelop/envelope	quiet/quite
advice/advise	every day/everyday	rain/reign/rein
affect/effect	fair/fare	raise/raze
aisle/isle	formally/formerly	reality/realty
allusion/illusion	forth/fourth	respectfully/respectively
an/and	hear/here	reverend/reverent
angel/angle	heard/herd	right/rite/write
ascent/assent	hole/whole	road/rode
bare/bear	human/humane	scene/seen
brake/break	its/it's	sense/since
breath/breathe	know/no	stationary/stationery
buy/by	later/latter	straight/strait
capital/capitol	lay/lie	taught/taut
choose/chose	lead/led	than/then
cite/sight/site	lessen/lesson	their/there/they're
complement/compliment	loose/lose	threw/through
conscience/conscious	may be/maybe	too/to/two
corps/corpse	miner/minor	track/tract
council/counsel	moral/morale	waist/waste
dairy/diary	of/off	waive/wave
descent/dissent	passed/past	weak/week
desert/dessert	patience/patients	weather/whether
device/devise	peace/piece	were/where
die/dye	personal/personnel	which/witch
dominant/dominate	plain/plane	whose/who's
elicit/illicit	precede/proceed	your/you're
eminent/immanent/	presence/presents	
imminent	principal/principle	

Commonly Misspelled Words

acceptable	accompany	against
accessible	accustomed	annihilate
accommodate	acquire	apparent

arguing	humorous	practical
argument	hurried	preparation
authentic	hurriedly	probably
before	hypocrite	process
begin	ideally	professor
beginning	immediately	prominent
believe	immense	pronunciation
benefited	incredible	psychology
bulletin	innocuous	publicly
business	intercede	pursue
cannot	interrupt	pursuing
category	irrelevant	questionnaire
committee	irresistible	realize
condemn	irritate	receipt
courteous	knowledge	received
definitely	license	recession
dependent	likelihood	recommend
desperate	maintenance	referring
develop	manageable	religious
different	meanness	remembrance
disappear	mischievous	reminisce
disappoint	missile	repetition
easily	necessary	representative
efficient	nevertheless	rhythm
environment	no one	ridiculous
equipped	noticeable	roommate
exceed	noticing	satellite
exercise	nuisance	scarcity
existence	occasion	scenery
experience	occasionally	science
fascinate	occurred	secede
finally	occurrences	secession
foresee	omission	secretary
forty	omit	senseless
fulfill	opinion	separate
gauge	opponent	sergeant
guaranteed	parallel	shining
guard	parole	significant
harass	peaceable	sincerely
hero	performance	skiing
heroes	pertain	stubbornness

studying	tendency	until
succeed	therefore	vacuum
success	tragedy	valuable
successfully	truly	various
susceptible	tyranny	vegetable
suspicious	unanimous	visible
technical	unconscious	without
temporary	undoubtedly	women

Read&Write 3.2 Proofread for the President

It's January 1941, and you're on the staff of the thirty-second President of the United States. Franklin Roosevelt is about to make one of the most important speeches of his presidency, and it's your job to proofread the text before it can be printed for the world to read. There are 15 errors embedded in the copy of the speech that appears below this paragraph. As you locate the errors, circle them with a pencil. When you have finished, check the error key on the following page. Below the error key you'll find a copy of this selection from Roosevelt's speech as it was originally published without the embedded errors.

A Selection from "Franklin D. Roosevelts' 'Four Freedoms Speech' Annual Message to Congress on the State of the Union," January 6, 1941.

In the future days, which we seek to make secure, we look forward to a world founded upon four essential human freedoms.

The first is freedom of speach and expression—everywhere in the world.

The second is freedom of every person to worship God in their own way—everywhere in the world.

The third is freedom from want—which translated into world terms, means economic understandings which will secure to every nation a healthy peacetime life for it's inhabitants everywhere in the world.

The fourth is freedom from fear—which, translated into world terms, means a world-wide reduction of armaments to such a point and in such a thorough fashion that no nation will be in a position to commit an act of physical aggression against any neighbor—anywhere in the world.

That is no vision of a distant milennium, it is a definite basis for a kind of world attainable in our own time and generation. That kind of world is the very antithesis of the so-called new order of tyranny which the dictator's seek to create with the crash of a bomb.

To that new order we oppose the greater conception—the moral order, a good society is able to face schemes of world domination and foreign revolutions alike without fear.

Since the beginning of our American history; we have been engaged in change—in a perpetual peaceful revolution—a revolution which goes on steady, quietly adjusting itself to changing conditions—without the concentration camp or the quick-lime in the ditch. The world order which we seek is the cooperation of free countries. Working together in a friendly, civilized society.

This nation has placed it's destiny in the hands and heads and hearts of its millions of free men and women; and its faith in freedom under the guidance of God. Freedom means the supremacy of human rights everywhere, our support goes to those who struggle to gain those rights or keep them. Our strength is our unity of purpose. To that high concept there can be no end save victory.

Key to "Find the Errors"

The letters, words, and punctuation in **bold font** and underlined below indicate locations of grammar, spelling, and other errors. You can also check the original, error-free copy to find the correct forms of grammar and usage.

A Selection from "Franklin D. Roosevelt**s'** 'Four Freedoms Speech' Annual Message to Congress on the State of the Union**"**, January 6, 1941.

In the future days, which we seek to make secure, we look forward to a world founded upon four essential human freedoms.

The first is freedom of spe**a**ch and expression—everywhere in the world.

The second is freedom of every person to worship God in **their** own way—everywhere in the world. **[NOTE: Nowadays, it is becoming acceptable, in certain types of writing, to allow the plural "their" to stand in place of "his," which is considered sexist. Another acceptable alternative is "his or her." Think about what pronoun to use, when you come to such a circumstance.]**

The third is freedom from want—whic**h** translated into world terms, means economic understandings which will secure to every nation a healthy peacetime life for **it's** inhabitants everywhere in the world.

The fourth is freedom from fear—which, translated into world terms, means a world-wide reduction of armaments to such a point and in such a thorough fashion that no nation will be in a position to commit an act of physical aggression against any neighbor—anywhere in the world.

That is no vision of a distant mi**l**ennium**, it** is a definite basis for a kind of world attainable in our own time and generation. That kind of world is the very antithesis of the so-called new order of tyranny which the dictator**'s** seek to create with the crash of a bomb.

To that new order we oppose the greater conception—the moral order**, a** good society is able to face schemes of world domination and foreign revolutions alike without fear.

Since the beginning of our American history**;** we have been engaged in change—in a perpetual peaceful revolution—a revolution which goes on stead**y** quietly adjusting itself to changing conditions—without the concentration camp or the quick-lime in the ditch. The world order which we seek is the cooperation of free countries**. W**orking together in a friendly, civilized society.

This nation has placed **it's** destiny in the hands and heads and hearts of its millions of free men and women; and its faith in freedom under the guidance of God.

Freedom means the supremacy of human rights everywhere, our support goes to those who struggle to gain those rights or keep them. Our strength is our unity of purpose. To that high concept there can be no end save victory.

Original Four Freedoms Speech

A Selection from "Franklin D. Roosevelt's 'Four Freedoms Speech' Annual Message to Congress on the State of the Union," January 6, 1941.

In the future days, which we seek to make secure, we look forward to a world founded upon four essential human freedoms.

The first is freedom of speech and expression—everywhere in the world.

The second is freedom of every person to worship God in his own way—everywhere in the world.

The third is freedom from want—which, translated into world terms, means economic understandings which will secure to every nation a healthy peacetime life for its inhabitants everywhere in the world.

The fourth is freedom from fear—which, translated into world terms, means a world-wide reduction of armaments to such a point and in such a thorough fashion that no nation will be in a position to commit an act of physical aggression against any neighbor—anywhere in the world.

That is no vision of a distant millennium. It is a definite basis for a kind of world attainable in our own time and generation. That kind of world is the very antithesis of the so-called new order of tyranny which the dictators seek to create with the crash of a bomb.

To that new order we oppose the greater conception—the moral order. A good society is able to face schemes of world domination and foreign revolutions alike without fear.

Since the beginning of our American history, we have been engaged in change—in a perpetual peaceful revolution—a revolution which goes on steadily, quietly adjusting itself to changing conditions—without the concentration camp or the quick-lime in the ditch. The world order which we seek is the cooperation of free countries, working together in a friendly, civilized society.

This nation has placed its destiny in the hands and heads and hearts of its millions of free men and women; and its faith in freedom under the guidance of God. Freedom means the supremacy of human rights everywhere. Our support goes to those who struggle to gain those rights or keep them. Our strength is our unity of purpose. To that high concept there can be no end save victory.[3]

[3] Franklin D. Roosevelt. 1941. "'Four Freedoms Speech': Annual Message to Congress on the State of the Union." Franklin D. Roosevelt Presidential Library and Museum. January 6. Retrieved March 8, 2016 (http://www.fdrlibrary.marist.edu/pdfs/fftext.pd).

3.3   FORMAT YOUR PAPER PROFESSIONALLY

Your format makes your paper's first impression. Justly or not, accurately or not, it announces your professional competence—or the lack of it. A well-executed format implies that your paper is worth reading. More importantly, however, a proper format brings information to your readers in a familiar form that has the effect of setting their minds at ease. Your paper's format should therefore impress your readers with your academic competence as a sociologist by following accepted professional standards. Like the style and clarity of your writing, your format communicates messages that are often more readily and profoundly received than the content of the document itself.

The formats described in this chapter are in conformance with generally accepted standards in the discipline of sociology, including instructions for the following elements:

General page formats	Table of contents
Title page	Reference page
Abstract	List of tables and figures
Executive summary	Text
Outline page	Appendices

Except for special instructions from your instructor, follow the directions in this manual exactly.

General Page Formats

Sociology assignments should be printed on 8-by-11-inch premium white bond paper, 20 pound or heavier. Do not use any other size or color except to comply with special instructions from your instructor, and do not use off-white or poor-quality (draft) paper. Sociology that is worth the time to write and read is worth good paper.

Always submit to your instructor an original typed or computer-printed manuscript. Do not submit a photocopy! Always make a second paper copy and back up your electronic copy for your own files in case the original is lost.

Margins, except in theses and dissertations, should be one inch on all sides of the paper. Unless otherwise instructed, all papers should be *double-spaced* in a 12-point word-processing font or typewriter pica type. Typewriter elite type may be used if another font is not available. Select a font that is plain and easy to read, such as Helvetica, Courier, Garamond, or Times Roman. Do not use script, stylized, or elaborate fonts.

Page numbers should appear in the upper right-hand corner of each page, starting immediately after the title page. No page number should appear on the title page or on the first page of the text. Page numbers should appear one inch from the right side and one-half inch from the top of the page. They should proceed consecutively beginning with the title page (although the first number is not actually printed on the title page). You may use lowercase roman numerals (i, ii, iii, iv, v, vi, vii, viii, ix, x, and so on) for the pages, such as the title page, table of contents, and table of figures, that precede the first page of text, but if you use them, the numbers must be placed at the center of the bottom of the page.

Ask your instructor about bindings. In the absence of further directions, do not bind your paper or enclose it within a plastic cover sheet. Place one staple in the upper left-hand corner, or use a paper clip at the top of the paper. Note that a paper to be submitted to a journal for publication should not be clipped, stapled, or bound in any form.

Title Page

The following information will be centered on the title page:

Title of the paper

Name of writer

Course name, section number, and instructor

College or university

Date

Marital Satisfaction among College Students

by

Nicole Garcia

The Family

SOC 3403

Dr. LaShonda Brown

University of Kansas

January 1, 2017

As the sample title page above shows, the title should clearly describe the problem addressed in the paper. If the paper discusses juvenile recidivism in Albemarle County jails, for example, the title "Recidivism in the Albemarle County Criminal Justice System" is professional, clear, and helpful to the reader. "Albemarle County," "Juvenile Justice," or "County Jails" are all too vague to be effective. Also, the title should not be "cute." A cute title may attract attention for a play on Broadway, but it will detract from the credibility of a paper in sociology. "Inadequate Solid Waste Disposal Facilities in Denver" is professional. "Down in the Dumps" is not.

In addition, title pages for position papers and policy analysis papers must include the name, title, and organization of the public official who has the authority and responsibility to implement the recommendation of your paper. The person to whom you address the paper should have the responsibility and the authority to make the necessary decision in your paper. The "address" should include the person's name, title, and organization, as shown in the example of a title page for a position paper that follows. To identify the appropriate official, first carefully define the problem and the best solution. Then ascertain the person, or persons, who have the authority to solve the problem. If you recommend installation of a traffic signal at a particular intersection, for example, find out who makes the decisions regarding such actions in your community. It may be the public safety director, a transportation planning commission, or a town council.

Oak City Police Department Personnel Policy Revisions

submitted to

Farley Z. Simmons

Director of Personnel

Police Department

Oak City, Arkansas

by

Luke Tyler Linscheid

Political Sociology

SOC 3603

Dr. Hickory Stonecipher

Randolph Scott College

January 21, 2016

Abstract

An abstract is a brief summary of a paper written primarily to allow potential readers to see if the paper contains information of sufficient interest for them to read. People conducting research want specific kinds of information, and they often read dozens of abstracts looking for papers that contain relevant data. Abstracts have the designation "Abstract" centered at the top of the page. Next is the title, also centered, followed by a paragraph that precisely states the paper's topic, research and analysis methods, and results and conclusions. The abstract should be written in one paragraph of no more than 150 words. Remember, an abstract is not an introduction; instead, it is a summary, as demonstrated in the sample below.

Bertrand Russell's View of Mysticism

This paper reviews Bertrand Russell's writings on religion, mysticism, and science, and defines his perspective of the contribution of mysticism to scientific knowledge. Russell drew a sharp distinction between what he considered to be (1) the essence of religion, and (2) dogma or assertions attached to religion by theologians and religious leaders. Although some of his writings, including *Why I Am Not a Christian*, appear hostile to all aspects of religion, Russell actually asserts that religion, freed from doctrinal encumbrances, not only fulfills certain psychological needs but evokes many of the most beneficial human impulses. He believes that religious mysticism generates an intellectual disinterestedness that may be useful to science, but that it is not a source of a special type of knowledge beyond investigation by science.

Executive Summary

An executive summary, like an abstract, summarizes the content of a paper but does so in more detail. A sample executive summary is given on the next page. Although abstracts are read by people doing research, executive summaries are more likely to be read by people who need some or all of the information in the paper in order to make a decision. Many people, however, will read the executive summary to fix clearly in their minds the organization and results of a paper before reading the paper itself.

Executive Summary

Municipal parks in Springfield are deteriorating because of inadequate maintenance, and one park in particular, Oak Ridge Community Park, needs immediate attention. The problem is that parking, picnic, and restroom facilities at Oak Ridge Community Park have deteriorated because of normal wear, adverse weather, and vandalism, and are inadequate to meet public demand. The park was established as a public recreation "Class B" facility in 1967. Only one major renovation has occurred: in the summer of 1987 general building repair was done, and new swing sets were installed. The Park Department estimates that 10,000 square feet of new parking space, 14 items of playground equipment, 17 new picnic tables, and repairs on current facilities would cost about $43,700.

Three possible solutions have been given extensive consideration in this paper. One option is to do nothing. Area residents will use the area less as deterioration continues, but no immediate outlay of public funds will be necessary. The first alternative solution is to make all repairs immediately. Area residents will enjoy immediate and increased use of facilities. Taxpayers have turned down the last three tax increase requests. Revenue bonds may be acceptable to a total of $20,000, according to the City Manager, but no more than $5,000 per year is available from general city revenues.

A second alternative is to make repairs, according to a priority list, over a five-year period, using a combination of general city revenues and a $20,000 first-year bond issue that will require City Council and voter approval. Residents will enjoy the most needed improvements immediately.

The recommendation of this report is that the second alternative be adopted by the City Council. The City Council should, during its May 15 meeting, (1) adopt a resolution of intent to commit $5,000 per year for five years from the general revenue fund dedicated to this purpose, and (2) approve for submission to public vote in the November 2007 election a $20,000 bond issue.

Outline Page

An outline page is a specific type of executive summary. Most often found in position papers and policy analysis papers, an outline page provides more information about the organization of the paper than does an executive summary. The outline shows clearly the sections in the paper and the information in each. An outline page is an asset because it allows busy decision-makers to understand the entire content of a paper without reading it all or to refer quickly to a specific part for more information. Position papers and policy analysis papers are written for people in positions of authority who normally need to make a variety of decisions in a short period. Outline pages reduce the amount of time these people need to understand a policy problem, the alternative solutions, and the author's preferred solution.

Outline pages sequentially list the complete topic sentences of the major paragraphs of a paper, in outline form. In a position paper, for example, you will be stating a problem, defining possible solutions, and then recommending the best solution. These three steps will be the major headings in your outline. (See Chapter 1 for instructions on writing an outline.) Wait until you have completed the paper before writing the outline page. Take the topic sentences from the leading (most important) paragraph in each section of your paper and place them in the appropriate places in your outline. A sample outline page is given on page 74.

Table of Contents

A table of contents does not provide as much information as an outline, but it does include the titles of the major divisions and subdivisions of a paper. Tables of contents are not normally required in student papers or papers presented at professional meetings but may be included. They are normally required, however, in books, theses, and dissertations. The table of contents should consist of the chapter or main section titles, and the headings used in the text, with one additional level of titles, along with their page numbers, as the sample on page 75 demonstrates.

Text

Ask your instructor for the number of pages required for the paper you are writing. The text should follow the directions explained in Chapter 1 of this manual and should conform to the format shown on page 73.

Sample Passage of Text   The problem is that parking, picnic, and restroom facilities at Oak Ridge Community Park have deteriorated because of normal wear, adverse weather, and vandalism, and are of inadequate quantity to meet public demand. The paved parking lot has crumbled and eroded. As many as 200 cars park on the lawn during major holidays. Only one of the five swing sets is in safe operating condition. Each set accommodates four children, but during weekends and holidays many children wait turns for the available sets. Spray paint vandalism has marred the rest room facilities, which are inadequate to meet major holiday demands.

The Department of Parks and Recreation established the park as a public recreation Class B facility in 1993. In the summer of 2015, the department conducted general building repair and installed new steel swing sets. Only minimal annual maintenance has occurred since that time.

The department estimates that 10,000 square feet of new parking lot space, 14 items of playground equipment, 17 new picnic tables, and repairs on current facilities would cost about $43,700 (Department of Parks and Recreation 2005). Parking lot improvements include a new surface of coarse gravel on the old paved lot and expansion of the new paved lot by 10,000 square feet. The State Engineering Office estimates the cost of parking lot improvements to be $16,200.

Chapter Headings

Your paper should include no more than three levels of headings:

1. *Primary*, which should be all in caps and left-justified (i.e., beginning at the left margin)
2. *Secondary*, which is left-justified, in italics, and uses headline-style capitalization.
3. *Tertiary*, which is indented at the beginning of the paragraph, in italics, uses sentence-style capitalization, and ends with a period, followed immediately by the paragraph.

The following illustration shows the proper use of chapter headings:

REVIEW OF LITERATURE   *(Primary Heading)*

Marital Satisfaction and the Number of Children   (Secondary Heading)

   Families with more than two children. Although many people believe that large families lead to increased marital satisfaction, the results of . . .   (Tertiary Heading)

Reference Page

The format for references is discussed in the source citation information in Section 3.4. See the Sample Reference page on pages 99–100.

Tables, Illustrations, Figures, and Appendices

If your paper includes tables, illustrations, or figures, include a page after the Table of Contents listing each of them, under the name for it used in the paper's text. List the items in the order in which they appear in the paper, along with their page numbers. You may list tables, illustrations, and figures together under the title "Figures" (and call them all "Figures" in the text), or if you have more than a half page of entries, you may have separate lists for tables, illustrations, and figures (and title them accordingly in the text). An example of the format for such lists is given below.

Outline of Contents

I. The problem is that parking, picnic, and restroom facilities at Oak Ridge Community Park have deteriorated because of normal wear, adverse weather, and vandalism, and are inadequate to meet public demand.

   A. Only one major renovation has occurred since 1967, when the park was opened.

   B. The Park Department estimates that 10,000 square feet of new parking space, 14 items of playground equipment, 17 new picnic tables, and repairs on current facilities would cost about $43,700.

II. The municipal government has given extensive consideration to three possible solutions.

   A. One option is to do nothing. Area residents will use the area less as deterioration continues, but no immediate outlay of public funds will be necessary.

   B. The first alternative solution is to make all repairs immediately. Area residents will enjoy immediate and increased use of facilities. $43,700 in funds will be needed. Sources include: (1) Community Development Block Grant funds, (2) increased property taxes, (3) revenue bonds, and (4) general city revenues.

   C. A second alternative is to make repairs according to a priority list over a five-year period, using a combination of general city revenues and a $20,000 first-year bond issue. Residents will enjoy the most needed improvements immediately. The bond issue will require City Council and voter approval.

III. The recommendation of this report is that alternative C be adopted by the City Council. The benefit/cost analysis demonstrates that residents will be satisfied if basic improvements are made immediately. The City Council should, during its May 15 meeting, (1) adopt a resolution of intent to commit $5,000 per year for five years from the general revenue fund, dedicated to this purpose; and (2) approve for submission to public vote in the November 2017 election a $20,000 bond issue.

Contents

Figures

Tables

Tables are used in the text to show relationships among data, to help the reader come to a conclusion or understand a certain point. Tables that show simple results or "raw" data should be placed in an appendix. They should not reiterate the content of the text. They should say something new and stand on their own. In other words, the reader should be able to understand the table without reading the text. The columns and rows in the table must be labeled clearly. Each word in the title

TABLE 3.1

Projections of the Total Population of Selected States, 2015–2035 (in thousands)

State	2020	2025	2030	2035
Alabama	4,451	4,631	4,956	5,224
Illinois	12,051	12,266	12,808	13,440
Maine	1,259	1,285	1,362	1,423
New Mexico	1,860	2,016	2,300	2,612
Oklahoma	3,373	3,491	3,789	4,057
Tennessee	5,657	5,966	6,365	6,665
Virginia	6,997	7,324	7,921	8,466

Source: U.S. Census Bureau.

(except articles, prepositions, and conjunctions) should be capitalized. The source of the information should be shown immediately below the table, not in a footnote or endnote (see Table 3.1).

Illustrations and Figures

Illustrations are not normally inserted in the text of a sociology paper, even in an appendix, unless they are necessary to explain the content. If illustrations are necessary, do not paste or tape photocopies of photographs or similar materials to the text or the appendix. Instead, photocopy each one on a separate sheet of paper and center it, along with its typed title, within the normal margins of the paper. The format of illustration titles should be the same as that for tables and figures.

Figures in the form of charts and graphs may be very helpful in presenting certain types of information, as the example shows on page 143.

Appendices

Appendices are reference materials provided for the convenience of the reader at the back of the paper, after the text. They provide information that supplements important facts in the text and may include maps, charts, tables, and selected documents. Do not place materials that are merely interesting or decorative in your appendix. Use only items that will answer questions raised by the text or are necessary to explain the text. Follow the guidelines for formats of tables, illustrations, and figures when adding material in an appendix. At the top center of the page, label your first appendix as "Appendix A," your second appendix as "Appendix B," and so on. Do not append an entire government report, journal article, or other publication, but only the portions of such documents that are necessary to support your paper. The source of the information should always be evident on the appended pages.

Read&Write 3.3 Explain the Data in This Table

Your assignment in this chapter is to

1) Locate, using the sources of information described above, a currently posted chart or table of statistics compiled by a government agency on a topic of your choice.
2) Write a "Data Interpretation Essay" in which you *interpret* what this table tells you.
3) Find an independent source of information that corroborates your interpretation of the data.

The following sample data and essay will help guide your efforts in completing this exercise.

SAMPLE DATA AND ESSAY

Data Interpretation Essay:
Civilian Casualties in Japan in World War II
Luke Linscheid
Sociology 101
Dr. Harry Longabaugh
Sundance University
February 28, 2017

Having enjoyed the opportunity to participate in a study group tour to Japan in the summer of 2016, I decided to explore population growth in Japan cities from 1900 to the present. I found some interesting trends, especially in the period from 1940 to 1947. From a table that covered a wider time period I selected the data provided for my chosen time period. Table 3.2, therefore, presents an abridged set of data derived from *Statistics Japan*, the Statistics Bureau, Ministry of Internal Affairs and Communications, nation of Japan, through this web portal: http://www.stat.go.jp/english/info/guide/2014guide.htm.

TABLE 3.2

Population of Selected Cities of Japan, 1940–1947

City	Population 1940	Population 1947	Change, 1940–1947
Sendai-shi	223,630	293,816	70,186
Yamaguchi-shi	34,579	97,975	63,396
Akita-shi	61,791	116,300	54,509
Niigata-shi	150,903	204,477	53,574
Sapporo-shi	206,103	259,602	53,499
Kumamoto-shi	194,139	245,841	51,702
Saitama-shi	59,671	106,176	46,505
Kanazawa-shi	186,297	231,441	45,144
Kochi-shi	106,644	147,120	40,476

Fukushima-shi	48,287	86,763	38,476
Matsuyama-shi	117,534	147,967	30,433
Chiba-shi	92,061	122,006	29,945
Yamagata-shi	69,184	98,632	29,448
Morioka-shi	79,478	107,096	27,618
Miyazaki-shi	66,497	92,144	25,647
Nara-shi	57,273	82,399	25,126
Fukuoka-shi	306,763	328,548	21,785
Nagano-shi	76,861	94,993	18,132
Saga-shi	50,406	64,978	14,572
Otsu-shi	67,532	81,426	13,894
Toyama-shi	127,859	137,818	9,959
Oita-shi	76,985	86,570	9,585
Utsunomiya-shi	87,868	97,075	9,207
Tottori-shi	49,261	57,218	7,957
Matsue-shi	55,506	62,136	6,630
Maebashi-shi	86,997	90,432	3,435
Kofu-shi	102,419	104,993	2,574
Tsu-shi	68,625	68,662	37
Mito-shi	66,293	61,416	−4,877
Gifu-shi	172,340	166,995	−5,345
Shizuoka-shi	212,198	205,737	−6,461
Aomori-shi	99,065	90,828	−8,237
Takamatsu-shi	111,207	101,403	−9,804
Tokushima-shi	119,581	103,320	−16,261
Fukui-shi	94,595	77,320	−17,275
Kagoshima-shi	190,257	170,416	−19,841
Okayama-shi	163,552	140,631	−22,921
Wakayama-shi	195,203	171,800	−23,403
Kawasaki-shi	300,777	252,923	−47,854
Nagasaki-shi	252,630	198,642	−53,988
Kyoto-shi	1,089,726	999,660	−90,066
Hiroshima-shi	343,968	224,100	−119,868
Yokohama-shi	968,091	814,379	−153,712
Kobe-shi	967,234	607,079	−360,155
Nagoya-shi	1,328,084	853,085	−474,999
Osaka-shi	3,252,340	1,559,310	−1,693,030
Ku-area	6,778,804	4,177,548	−2,601,256
Total change			**−4,925,902**

Source: The data in the table is a partial compilation of data from the document *Population of Cities (1920–2005) Excel: 37KB.*[4]

[4] "Population of Cities (1920–2005)," in "Historical Statistics of Japan: Chapter 2 Populations and Households." *Statistics Japan*. Retrieved March 8, 2016 (http://www.stat.go.jp/english/data/chouki/02.htm).

Even without confirmation from other historical or statistical resources, an examination of this chart detailing the population changes in select Japanese cities over a brief but very significant span of time in the middle of the twentieth century leads to one overwhelming conclusion: war is hell—especially a war that features the widespread aerial bombardment of cities. Two salient features of the chart back this interpretation, the specific time period for which the statistics have been taken and the sharp contrast between the group of Japanese cities that lost population during these dates and the group that gained population.

The Second World War began in 1939 and ended in 1945, a time that coincides closely with the time represented by the chart's statistics, 1940–1947. It is common knowledge that, during the beginning of the war as it was fought in the Pacific the Japanese, expanding out from their island, enjoyed many victories and added much territory to their empire, and just as well known that, by the end of the war, their empire had shrunk back, almost exclusively, to the contours of the main island. In those last days of the war the Allies dropped hundreds of tons of bombs on Japanese cities either to prepare the island for an Allied invasion or to compel unconditional surrender from the Japanese without the need of an invasion.

The cities in the chart describe a dramatic pattern of population shift, with slightly less than half of them (twenty-two) losing thousands of inhabitants over the time period covered by the chart, and a slightly larger number (twenty-seven) experiencing an intensive population increase. The likeliest reason for this shift is the devastation of Allied bombing, which suggests that the time in which much of the shift actually took place occupies only a fraction of the chart's time frame, say, 1944–1945. How harrowing is it to observe that the population increases in those cities that grew in size are not nearly as large as the decreases in population of those cities that lost inhabitants. Sendai-shi, the city that had the highest growth in population, added an amazing total of 70,186 inhabitants, but Ku-area, the city with the biggest decrease, lost a staggering 2,601,256 people. The total change in population density, as reported in the chart, reveals a loss, over these war years, of almost five million people. Now, since statistical sources estimate that Japan's military causalities in World War II amount to between two and two and a half million, perhaps as many as three million Japanese died in America's conventional weapon bombing campaign.

Why these specific cities? It is likely to assume that those losing population were industrial centers, prime targets for the Allied strategists working to destroy Japan's ability to wage war. People from the devastated cities must have struggled to reach the safety of cities not directly concerned with the war effort and, therefore, not targeted by the bombers. But two cities famously don't fit the profile: Hiroshima, which according to the chart lost 119,868 of its citizens, and Nagasaki, which lost 53,988. These cities, neither of which contributed significantly to the Japanese war effort, were chosen by the Allies for a special bombardment, namely, the first two—and, so far, the only two—deployments of the atom bomb on civilian populations.

In essence, this population chart serves to underscore the effectiveness of the bombing campaign that ended World War II. But hidden in its numbers is the incalculable cost, in human terms, of that campaign. In order to determine if *our interpretation* of the data in our chart is correct we need to find an independent source of information that corroborates our conclusion. One source is Director Errol Morris' Academy Award winning documentary *The Fog of War* in which former Secretary of Defense Robert McNamara recounts his first-hand participation, as a military intelligence officer in World War II, in planning and executing the conventional fire-bombing campaigns that resulted in the approximately three million civilian casualties indicated as highly likely by the data in our chart.

3.4 CITE YOUR SOURCES PROPERLY IN ASA STYLE

One of your most important jobs as a research writer is to document your use of source material carefully and clearly. Failure to do so causes confusion in your reader, damages the effectiveness of your paper, and perhaps makes you vulnerable to a charge of plagiarism. Proper documentation is more than just good form; it is a powerful indicator of your own commitment to scholarship and the sense of authority that you bring to your writing. Good documentation demonstrates your expertise as a researcher and increases the reader's trust in you and your work; it gives credibility to what you are writing.

Unfortunately, as anybody who has ever written a research paper knows, getting the documentation right can be a frustrating, confusing job, especially for the novice writer. Accurately positioning each element of a single reference citation can require what seems an inordinate amount of time spent thumbing through the style manual. Even before you begin to work on specific citations, there are important questions of style and format to answer.

What to Document

Direct quotes must always be credited, as must certain kinds of paraphrased material. Information that is basic—important dates, and facts, or opinions universally acknowledged—need not be cited. Information that is not widely known, whether fact or opinion, should be documented.

What if you are unsure whether or not a certain fact is widely known? You are, after all, very probably a newcomer to the field in which you are conducting your research. If in doubt, supply the documentation. It is better to overdocument than to fail to do justice to a source.

The Choice of Style   Although the question of which documentation style to use may be decided for you in some classes by your instructor, others may allow you to choose. There are several styles available, each designed to meet the needs of writers in particular fields. The citation and reference systems approved by the Modern Language Association (MLA) and the American Psychological Association (APA) are often used in the humanities and social sciences.

The American Sociological Association (ASA) has its own system that is widely used by sociology students and professionals. The ASA has adopted a modification of the author-date style elaborated in Section 15 of the sixteenth edition of the *Chicago Manual of Style* (CMS), perhaps the most universally approved of all documentation authorities. One of the advantages of using the ASA style, which is outlined in the fifth edition of the *ASA Style Guide* (2014), is that it is designed to guide the professional sociologist in preparing a manuscript for submission to a journal. The ASA style is required for all papers submitted to the *American Sociological Review*, the official journal of the ASA and the most influential sociology journal in publication. It is also required for all the leading journals in sociology and many of the less prestigious ones.

Citing Sources

In the author-date citation style, a parenthetical reference or citation is a note placed within the text, near where the source material occurs. In order not to distract the reader from the argument, the citation is as brief as possible, containing just enough information to refer the reader to the full reference listing that appears in the bibliography or reference section following the text. Usually, the minimum information necessary is the author's last name—meaning the name by which the source is alphabetized in the references at the end of the paper—and the year of the publication of the source. As indicated by the following models, this information can be given in a number of ways. Models for listing bibliographical entries that correspond to parenthetical citations are given in the next section of this chapter.

Text Citations   Citations within the text should include the author's last name and the year of publication.

Page numbers should be included only when quoting directly from a source or referring to specific passages. Subsequent citations of the same source should be identified the same way as the first. The following examples identify the *ASA Style Guide's* (2014) citation system for a variety of possibilities.

When the author's name is in the text, it should be followed by the publication year in parentheses:

Freedman (2004) postulates that when individuals . . .

When the author's name is not in the text, the last name and publication date should be enclosed within parentheses:

. . . encourage more aggressive play (Perrez 1999).

The page number should be included when the material referred to is quoted directly, or when you wish to refer the reader to a specific page of the source text. However, some instructors prefer page numbers for all citations in order to check for plagiarism. Ask your instructor what system you should follow. When the page number is included, it should follow the publication year and be preceded by a colon, with no space between the colon and the page number:

Thomas (1999:741) builds on this scenario . . .

In both the in-text citations and the references, the *ASA Style Guide* (2014) follows the format recommended by the *Chicago Manual of Style* (2010) for recording a range of page numbers:

For any range of numbers in which the first number is below 100, use all digits:

D'Ambrosio (2016:14–19) denies this possibility.

. . . endorses the project enthusiastically (Jenkins 2007:78–79).

For any range in which the first number is 100 or a multiple of 100, use all digits:

. . . according to Squires (2008:400–409).

In which case the vote will fail (Piplin 2014:1200–1201).

For any range in which the first number is 101 through 109, 201 through 209, 301 through 309, and so on, use the changed part only for the second number:

. . . counters any lateral move, according to Givan (1998:103–4).

. . . a cogent argument for the opposite opinion (Fells 2004:1108–9).

For any range in which the first number is 110 through 199, 210 through 299, 310 through 399, and so on, use two or more digits as needed:

Alexandro (2007:221–23) supports the proposition . . .

. . . in which case, according to Stevens (1999), the Congress will act (1299–302).

In a range of page numbers in which the second number contains four digits, three of which are changed, use all four digits:

. . . refused to acknowledge the request (Austin 2008:1298–1305).

Rankin (2015:3489–3510) claims attorney–client privilege . . .

When the publication has two authors, cite both last names:

. . . establish a sense of self (Holmes and Watson 1872:114–16).

If no date of publication can be determined, perhaps because of the age of the document or the fact that it has not yet been published, use the abbreviation *n.d.* for "no date," unless the document is to be published, in which case, use the word "forthcoming."

. . . gave the Roundheads no secure license (Hallows n.d.).

Bartholi (forthcoming) places the blame squarely on Congress.

When a publication has three authors, cite all three last names in the first citation, with *et al.* (in roman type) used for subsequent citations in the text. Thus a first citation would read:

. . . found the requirements very restrictive (Mollar, Querley, and McLarry 1926).

Thereafter, the following form is sufficient:

. . . proved to be quite difficult (Mollar et al. 1926).

For more than three authors, use *et al.* (in roman type) in all citations.

When citing two authors with the same last name, use a first initial to differentiate between them.

. . . the new child custody laws (K. Grady 2016).

. . . stimulate community development (B. Grady 1993).

When citing two works by the same author, in the same note, place a comma between the publication dates of the works.

George (1996, 2004) argues for . . .

If the two works were published in the same year, differentiate between them by adding lowercase letters to the publication dates. Be sure to add the letters to the references in the bibliography, too.

. . . the city government (Estrada 2002a, 2002b).

Direct quotes of fewer than 50 words should be placed in the text, with quotation marks at the beginning and end. The citation should include the page number in one of the following formats:

The majority of these ads promote the notion that "If you are slim, you will also be beautiful and sexually desirable" (Rockett and McMinn 1999:278).

Smith and Hill (1997) found that "women are far more likely to obsess about weight" (p. 127).

Direct quotes of 50 words or more should be indented as a block, with no tab set for the first line. Such longer quotes should not be contained within quotation marks:

Especially pernicious is the fact that, according to what research has been done, the situation is universal and does not correct itself with age, education, or any type of socialization therapy. According to Brown (2005):

There are few girls and women of any age or culture raised in white America, who do not have some manifestation of the concerns discussed here, i.e., distortion of body image, a sense of "out-of-control" in relationship to food, addiction to dieting, binging, or self-starvation. (P. 61)

Note that in the block quote the author, date, and/or page number follows the period at the end, and that the *P* for *page* is capitalized when the page number appears alone without the author and date, as in this example.

Sometimes information is obtained from a source that is cited in a secondary source. Although it is always best to locate and cite the original source, sometimes this is not possible. When citing a source that is itself cited in a secondary source, refer in your parenthetical citation to the original source, and not to the later source in which the original is quoted. For example, if you wish to cite a passage from a 1999 article by John Smith that you found cited in a 2003 article by Arleen Michaels, your citation should look like this:

. . . the promise of a subsequent generation (Smith 1999).

See "Article Cited in a Secondary Source" on page 91 for information on how to list this citation in your references.

Section 14.80 of the *Chicago Manual of Style* (2010) indicates that if the authorship of an anonymous work is known, the name is given in brackets:

([Morey, Cynthia] 1977)

According to Section 14.79 of the *Chicago Manual of Style* (2010), if the name of the author of an anonymous work cannot be ascertained, the reference begins with the title of the work. The first of the following models refers to a magazine article, the second to a book. Note that in the case of the book title, the initial article "The" is moved to the end of the title.

("The Case for Prosecuting Deadbeat Dads" 1996:36–38)

(*Worst Way to Learn: The Government's War on Education, The* 2003)

Cite chapters, tables, appendices, and the like as follows:

. . . (Johnson 1995, chap. 6).

. . . (Blake 2009, table 4:34).

. . . (Shelby 1976, appendix C:177).

When citing a work reprinted from an earlier publication, give the earliest date of publication in brackets, followed immediately by the date of the version you have used:

. . . Baldwin ([1897] 2002) interpreted this . . .

When citing more than one source, separate the citations by a semicolon and order them in a manner of your choice. You may arrange them in alphabetical order, date order, or order of importance to your argument, but whatever order you choose, use it consistently throughout your paper:

. . . are related (Harmatz 1999:48; Marble et al. 1996:909; Powers and Erickson 2001:48; Rackley et al. 1988:10; Thompson and Thompson 2000:1067).

Give the date for dissertation and unpublished papers. When the date is not available, use "n.d." (no date) in place of the date. Use the word "forthcoming" when materials cited are unpublished but scheduled for publication.

Studies by Barkley (forthcoming) and Jorden (n.d.) lend support . . .

According to Section 15.49 of the *Chicago Manual of Style* (2010), when citing manuscript collections in author-date citation style place the date of the document under discussion in the body of the text rather than within the parentheses, since most collections include materials from different dates:

Johnson wrote to Scott on March 12 (Nora Manuscripts) to explain the publishing disaster.

According to Section 14.304 of *The Chicago Manual of Style* (2010), cite any of the unpublished documents of the United States Government housed in the National Archives (NA)—including films, photographs, and sound recordings as well as written materials—by the record group number (RG).

(NA, RG 43)

Classic Texts   When citing classic texts, such as the Bible, standard translations of ancient Greek texts, or numbers of the Federalist Papers, you may use the systems by which they are subdivided. Since any edition of a classic text employs the standard subdivisions, this reference method has the advantage of allowing your reader to find the source passage in any published edition of the text. It is not necessary to include a citation for a classic text in the reference section.

You may cite a biblical passage by referring to the particular book, chapter, and verse, all in roman type, with the translation given after the verse number:

"But the path of the just is as the shining light, that shineth more and more unto the perfect day" (Proverbs 4:18 King James Version).

The Federalist Papers are numbered:

Madison addresses the problem of factions in a republic (Federalist 10).

Newspapers According to the *Chicago Manual of Style* (2010: Section 15.47), references to material in daily newspapers should be handled within the syntax of your sentence:

In an August 10, 1999, editorial, the *New York Times* painted the new regime in glowing colors.

An article entitled "Abuse in Metropolis," written by Harry Black and published in the *Daily News* on December 24, 2001, took exception to the mayor's remarks.

According to the *Chicago Manual of Style* (2010), references to newspaper items are not usually included in the reference list or bibliography. If you wish to include newspaper references, however, there is a model of a bibliographical entry in the next section of this chapter.

Public Documents When citing a public (government) document or one with institutional authorship, include in your text citation only a minimum of information from the beginning of the reference list citation, followed, if applicable, by the page number. While the information in the text citation is minimal, it must be sufficient to make the connection clearly with the full citation in the reference list.

. . . only in areas of large population growth (U.S. Bureau of the Census 2009:223).

Documents for which author's names are provided are cited just as non-public documents:

. . . making a positive impact on local economies (McSweeney and Marshall 2009:5).

The following models are based largely on information from the *ASA Style Guide* (2014) and from the *Chicago Manual of Style* (2010). Corresponding reference list entries appear in the next section.

Congressional Journals Parenthetical text references to both the *Senate Journal* and the *House Journal* start with the journal title, the session year, and, if applicable, the page:

(Senate Journal 2009:24)

Congressional Debates Congressional debates are printed in the daily issues of the *Congressional Record*, which are bound biweekly and then collected and bound at the end of the session. Whenever possible, you should consult the bound yearly collection instead of the biweekly compilations. The "H" preceding the page number stands for House of Representatives.

(U.S. Congress 2001:H10403)

Congressional Reports and Documents References to congressional reports and documents, which are numbered sequentially in one- or two-year periods, include the name of the body generating the material, the year, and, if applicable, the page:

(U.S. Congress 2004: 17)

Any reference that begins with *U.S. Congress, U.S. Senate,* or *U.S. House* may omit the *U.S.* if it is clear from the context that you are referring to the United States. Whichever form you use, be sure to use it consistently, in both the notes and the bibliography.

State and Local Government Documents References for state and local government publications are modeled on those for corresponding national government documents:

(Oklahoma Legislature 2008)

(Marder 1977:37)

Laws You must structure a citation to a law according to the place where you found the law published. Initially published separately in pamphlets, as slip laws, statutes are eventually collected and incorporated, first into a set of volumes called *U.S. Statutes at Large* and later into the *U.S. Code*, a multivolume set that is revised every six years. You should use the latest edition.

Statutes at Large

(*Statutes at Large* 2006:2083)

U.S. Code

(*Declaratory Judgment Act, U.S. Code* 28, sec. 1562)

State Law

(*Ohio Revised Code Annotated*)

United States Constitution References to the United States Constitution include the number of the article or amendment, the section number, and the clause, if necessary:

(U.S. Constitution, art. 3, sec. 3)

Executive Department Document A reference to a report, bulletin, circular, or any other type of material issued by the Executive Department starts with the name of the agency issuing the document, although you may use the name of the author, if known:

(Department of Labor 2004:334)

Legal References Court decisions at any level of government are rarely given their own citations in the author-date system but are instead identified in the running text. If you wish to use a formal reference, however, this manual recommends that, for the in-text citation, you place within the parentheses only the title of the case, in italics, followed by the year.

(*AT&T Corporation v. Iowa Utilities Board* 1999)

The next section of this manual provides models of citations for court decisions suitable to the list of references.

Publications of Government Commissions According to the fifteenth edition of the *Chicago Manual of Style* (2003: Section 17.320), references to bulletins, circulars, reports, and study papers that are issued by various government commissions should include the name of the commission, the date of the document, and the page:

(Securities and Exchange Commission 1984:57)

Because government documents are often credited to a corporate author with a lengthy name, you may devise an acronym or a shortened form of the name and indicate in your first reference to the source that this name will be used in later citations:

(*Bulletin of Labor Statistics* 1997: 154; hereafter BLS)

Interviews According to the Chicago Manual of Style (2010: Sections 14.219), citations to unpublished interviews should be handled by references within the text or in notes.

In a March 1997 interview with O. J. Simpson, Barbara Walters asked questions that seemed to upset and disorient the former superstar.

For published or broadcast interviews, no parenthetical reference is necessary, but there should be a complete citation under the interviewer's name in the bibliography.

An unpublished interview conducted by the writer of the paper should also be cited in the syntax of the sentence:

In an interview with the author on April 23, 2003, Dr. Kennedy expressed her disappointment with the new court ruling.

If you are citing material from an interview that you conducted, identify yourself as "the author" and give the date of the interview. Cite the interview by placing the date in parentheses following the name of the person interviewed:

Marsha Cummings (2009), Director of the Children's Hospital in Oklahoma City, was interviewed by the author on November 14, 2009.

References

In the author-date referencing system, parenthetical citations in the text point the reader to the fuller source descriptions at the end of the paper known as the references or bibliography. This reference list, which always directly follows the text under the heading References, is arranged alphabetically according to the first element in each citation. Some instructors prefer papers to be structured in article format, with everything presented as tightly compressed and succinct as possible. If your instructor favors this system, your reference section should immediately follow (after a double space) the last line of your discussion section. Other instructors prefer the references to be listed on a separate page. Ask your instructor which system you should follow.

As with most alphabetically arranged bibliographies, there is a kind of reverse-indentation system, or "hanging indent": After the first line of a citation, all subsequent lines are indented five spaces. The entire references section is double-spaced.

The ASA uses standard, or "headline style," capitalization for titles in the reference list. In this style, all first and last words in a title, and all other words except articles (*a, an, the*), coordinating words (*and, but, or, for, nor*), and prepositions (*among, by, for, of, to, toward*, etc.) are capitalized.

Remember that every source cited in the text, with those exceptions noted in the examples below, must have a corresponding entry in the references section. Do not include references to any work not cited in the text of your paper.

Many of the following formats are based on those given in the *ASA Style Guide* (2014). Formats for bibliographical situations not covered by the ASA guide are taken from the *Chicago Manual of Style* (2010).

Books

One Author   The author's name appears first, inverted, then the date of publication, followed by the title of the book, the place of publication, and the name of the publishing house. Use first names for all authors or initials if no first name is provided. Add a space after each initial, as in the example below. When giving the place of publication, if the city of publication is well known (New York, Dallas, Los Angeles), it is not necessary to identify the name of the state in which the city is located. Likewise, do not repeat the identification of the state if its name is embedded in the publisher's name (University Press of Virginia). If the location of the city of publication is not clear, use a postal abbreviations to denote the state (OK, MA, etc.).

Periods divide most of the elements in the citation, although a colon separates the place of publication from the name of the publisher. Custom dictates that the main title and subtitle be separated by a colon, even though a colon may not appear in the title as printed on the title page of the book.

Northrup, A. K. 2002. *Living High off the Hog: Recent Pork Barrel Legislation in the Senate*. Cleveland: Johnstown.

If no date of publication can be determined, perhaps because of the age of the document or the fact that it has not yet been published, use the abbreviation *N.d.* for "no date." If the document is to be published, end the reference with the word "forthcoming."

Hallows, Gerard. N.d. *On the Latest Indignities Suffered by the Crown*. London: Southwall.

Bartholi, Kenneth. N.d. *Ineptitudes of Scale: Business Practices in the New Century*. New York: Balfour. Forthcoming.

Two Authors   Only the name of the first author is reversed, since it is the one by which the citation is alphabetized. Note that there is no comma between the first name of the first author and the *and* following:

Spence, Michelle and Kristen Ruell. 1996. *Hiring and the Law*. Boston: Tildale.

Three or More Authors   The use of *et al.* is not acceptable in the references section; list the names of all authors of a source. Place commas between all names. Note also that the ASA does not advocate abbreviating the word University in the name of a press, as indicated in the model below.

Moore, J. B., Allen Rice, and Natasha Traylor. 2002. *Down on the Farm: Culture and Folkways*. Norman: University of Oklahoma Press.

Anonymous Source   Section 15.33 of the *Chicago Manual of Style* (2010) states that if you can ascertain the name of the author when that name is not given in the work itself, place the author's name in brackets:

[Morey, Cynthia]. 1977. *How We Mate: American Dating Customs, 1950–2000*. New York: Putney.

Do not use *anonymous* to designate an author whose name you cannot determine; instead, according to Section 15.32 of the *Chicago Manual of Style* (2010), begin your reference entry with the title of the book, followed by the date. You may, if you wish, move initial articles (*a, an, the*) to the end of the title:

Worst Way to Learn: The Government's War on Education, The. 1997. San Luis Obispo, CA: Blakeside.

Editor, Compiler, or Translator as Author   When no author is listed on the title page, begin the citation with the name of the editor, compiler, or translator:

Trakas, Dylan, comp. 1998. *Making the Road-Ways Safe: Essays on Highway Preservation and Funding*. El Paso: Del Norte Press.

Editor, Compiler, or Translator with Author

Pound, Ezra. 1953. *Literary Essays*. Edited by T. S. Eliot. New York: New Directions.

Stomper, Jean. 2000. *Grapes and Rain*. Translated by John Picard. New York: Baldock.

Untranslated Book   If your source is in a foreign language, it is not necessary, according to Section 14.107 of the *Chicago Manual of Style* (2010), to translate the title into English. Use the capitalization format of the original language.

Picon-Salas, Mariano. 1950. *De la Conquesta a la Independencia*. Mexico, DF: Fondo de Cultura Económica.

If you wish to provide a translation of the title, do so in brackets following the title. Set the translation in roman type, and capitalize only the first word of the title and subtitle, proper nouns, and proper adjectives:

Wharton, Edith. 1916. *Voyages au front* [Visits to the Front]. Paris, France: Plon.

Two or More Works by the Same Author In citations for different works by the same author, always give the author's full name. List the works in the order of the year of publication, starting with the earliest year:

Russell, Henry. 1978. *Famous Last Words: Notable Supreme Court Cases of the Last Five Years*. New Orleans: Liberty Publications.

Russell, Henry. 1988. *Great Court Battles*. Denver: Axel and Myers.

Chapter in a Multiauthor Collection

Gray, Alexa North. 1998. "Foreign Policy and the Foreign Press." pp. 188–204 in *Current Media Issues*, edited by Barbara Bonnard and Luke F. Guinness. New York: Boulanger.

The parenthetical text reference may include the page reference:

(Gray 1998:195–97)

You must repeat the name if the author and the editor are the same person:

Farmer, Susan A. 1995. "Tax Shelters in the New Dispensation: How to Save Your Income." Pp. 58–73 in *Making Ends Meet: Strategies for the Nineties*, edited by Susan A. Farmer. Nashville: Burkette and Hyde.

Author of a Foreword or Introduction According to Section 14.91 of the *Chicago Manual of Style* (2010), there is no need to cite the author of a foreword or introduction in your bibliography, unless you have used material from that author's contribution to the volume. In that case, list the bibliography entry under the name of the author of the foreword or introduction. Place the name of the author of the work itself after the title of the work:

Farris, Carla. 2000. Foreword to *Marital Stress among the Professoriat: A Case Study*, by Basil Givan. New York: Galapagos.

The parenthetical text reference cites the name of the author of the foreword or introduction, not the author of the book:

(Farris 2000)

Subsequent Editions If you are using an edition of a book other than the first, you must cite the number of the edition or the status, such as *Rev. ed.* for *Revised edition*, if there is no edition number:

Hales, Sarah. 2002. *The Coming Water Wars*. 3rd ed. Pittsburgh: Blue Skies.

Multivolume Work If you are citing a multivolume work in its entirety, use the following format:

Graybosch, Charles. 1988–89. *The Rise of the Unions*. 3 vols. New York: Starkfield.

If you are citing only one of the volumes in a multivolume work, use the following format:

Graybosch, Charles. 1988. *The Beginnings*. Vol. 1, *The Rise of the Unions*.
New York: Starkfield.

Reprints

Adams, Sterling R. [1964] 2001. *How to Win an Election: Promotional Campaign Strategies*. New York: Starkfield.

Classic Texts   According to the *Chicago Manual of Style* (2010: Sections 15.256), references to classic texts such as sacred books and Greek verse and drama are usually confined to the text and not given as citations in the bibliography.

Periodicals

Journal Articles   Journals are periodicals, usually published either monthly or quarterly, that specialize in serious scholarly articles in a particular field.

Hunzecker, Joan. 2010. "Teaching the Toadies: Cronyism in Municipal Politics." *Review of Local Politics* 4(2):250–62.

Johnson, J. D., N. E. Noel and J. Sutter-Hernandez. 2000. "Alcohol and Male Acceptance of Sexual Aggression: The Role of Perceptual Ambiguity." *Journal of Applied Social Psychology* 30(July):1186–1200.

Note that the name of the journal, which is italicized, is followed without punctuation by the volume number, which is itself followed by the issue number—or, if there is no issue number, the month—in parentheses, a colon, and the page numbers. The recommendation that the issue number or month be included in the citation marks a change from previous editions of the *ASA Style Guide*, which did not recommend it. There should be no space between the journal and issue numbers or the colon and the page numbers, which are inclusive. Do not use *p.* or *pp.* to introduce the page numbers.

Article Published in More Than One Journal Issue

Crossitch, Vernelle. 1997. "Evaluating Evidence: Calibrating Ephemeral Phenomena," parts 1–4. *Epiphanic Review* 15(4):22–29; 16(1):46–58; 17(1):48–60.

Articles Published in Foreign-Language Journals

Sczaflarski, Richard. 2001 "The Trumpeter in the Tower: Solidarity and Legend" (in Polish). *World Political Review* 32(3):79–95.

Article Cited in a Secondary Source   When referencing a source that has itself been cited in a secondary source, first list the complete citation of the source you cited, followed by the words *cited in*, and a listing of the source from which you obtained your citation.

Johnson, William A. and Richard P. Rettig. 2006. "Drug Assessment of Juveniles in Detention." *Social Forces* 28(3):56–69, cited in John Duncan and Mary Ann Hopkins. 2009. "Youth and Drug Involvement: Families at Risk." *British Journal of Addiction* 95:45.

Gonzalez, Tim, Lucy Hammond, Fred Luntz and Virginia Land. 2007. "Free Love and Nickel Beer: On Throwaway Relationships." *The Journal of Sociology and Religion* 12(2):14–29, cited in Emanuel Hiddocke, Cheryl Manson and Ruth Mendez. 2010. *The Death of the American Family.* Upper Saddle River, NJ: Prentice Hall, p. 107.

Magazine Articles   Magazines, which are usually published weekly, bimonthly, or monthly, appeal to the popular audience and generally have a wider circulation than journals. *Newsweek* and *Scientific American* are examples of magazines.

Monthly Magazine

Stapleton, Bonnie and Ellis Peters. 1981. "How It Was: On the Trail with Og Mandino." *Lifetime Magazine*, April, pp. 23–24, 57–59.

Weekly or Bimonthly Magazine

Bruck, Connie. 1997. "The World of Business: A Mogul's Farewell." *The New Yorker*, October 18, pp. 12–15.

Newspaper Articles

Everett, Susan. 2002. "Beyond the Alamo: How Texans View the Past." *The Carrollton Tribune*, February 16, pp. D1, D4.

Sources Stored in Archives   According to the *ASA Style Guide* (2014), if you refer to a number of archival sources, you should group them in a separate part of the references section and name it *Archival Sources*. A sample entry follows:

Clayton Fox Correspondence, Box 12. July–December 1903. File: Literary Figures 2. Letter to Edith Wharton, dated September 11.

According to the *Chicago Manual of Style* (2010: Section 14.304), materials housed in the National Archives or in one of its branches are cited according to their record group (RG) number. The citation may also include title, subsection, and file number:

National Archives. RG 43. Records of the National Committee on Poverty and Aging. File 78A-M22.

Public Documents   Section 4.4.1 of the *ASA Style Guide* (2014) notes that non-legal works generally identify legal documents—for example, constitutions, executive orders, or amicus briefs—in the running text and not in the list of references. The ASA guide goes on, however, to say that it is possible to include public documents among the references and gives several examples. The following reference models are based on those found in the ASA guide and in the third edition of the *Chicago Manual of Style* (2003).

Congressional Journals References to either the *Senate Journal* or the *House Journal* begin with the journal's title and include the years of the session, the number of the Congress and session, and the month and day of the entry:

U.S. Senate Journal. 1997. 105th Cong., 1st sess., 10 December.

While Section 2.5 of the *ASA Style Guide* (2014) recommends that ordinal numbers *second* and *third* usually be expressed as *nd* (52nd) and *rd* (103rd), respectively, it makes an exception for legal citations, in which either ordinal may be expressed as *d* (52d, 103d).

Congressional Debates Congressional debates are printed in the daily issues of the *Congressional Record*, which are bound biweekly and then collected and bound at the end of the session. Whenever possible, you should consult the bound yearly collection instead of the biweekly compilations. The "H" preceding the page number stands for House of Representatives.

U.S. Congress. House of Representatives. 2001. *District of Columbia Police Coordination Amendment Act of 2001*. H.R. 2199, 107th Congress, 1st Session, 2001. *Congressional Record* 147 (December 19, 2001): H10403.

Congressional Reports and Documents

U.S. Congress. Senate. Select Committee on Intelligence. 2004. *Report on the U.S. Intelligence Community's Prewar Intelligence Assessments on Iraq.* Committee Report. 108th Congress, 2nd Session.

State and Local Government Documents References for state and local government publications are modeled on those for corresponding national government documents:

Oklahoma Legislature. Joint Committee on Public Recreation. 1995. *Final Report to the Legislature, Regular Session, on Youth Activities.* Oklahoma City.

Sidney M. Marder.1977. *Review and Synopsis of Public Participation regarding Sulfur Dioxide and Particulate Emissions.* Illinois Institute for Environmental Quality. IIEQ Document no. 77/21. Chicago.

Remember to start the reference with the author's name, when available, as in the second model above.

Laws According to Section 14.294 of the *Chicago Manual of Style* (2010), laws may be cited to the *Statutes at Large* or the *U.S. Code* or both.

Statutes at Large

National Defense Authorization Act for Fiscal Year 2007. Public Law 109–364, 120 U.S. Statutes at Large 2083 (2006).

The number "120" designates the volume and "2083" the page number.

U.S. Code

Declaratory Judgment Act, 28 U.S.C., Section 2201 (1952).

The number "28" designates volume number.

State Law

Ohio Revised Code Annotated, Section 3566 (West 2000).

United States Constitution

U.S. Constitution, Article 2, Section 2.

Executive Department Document

U.S. Department of Labor. Employment Standards Administration. 1984. *Resource Book: Training for Federal Employee Compensations Specialists.* Washington, D.C.: U.S. Government Printing Office.

Legal References   Note that in all cases or court decisions, case names, including the abbreviation *v.,* are italicized.

Supreme Court   Since 1875 all Supreme Court decisions have been published in the *United States Supreme Court Reports,* which is designated by the abbreviation U.S. The number preceding the abbreviation is the volume number, and the number following is the opening page of the decision:

AT&T Corporation v. Iowa Utilities Board, 525 U.S. 366 (1999).

Before 1875, Supreme Court decisions were published under the names of official court reporters. The reference below is to William Cranch, *Reports of Cases Argued and Adjudged in the Supreme Court of the United States, 1801–1815,* 9 vols. (Washington, D.C., 1804–17). The number preceding the clerk's name is the volume number; the last number is the page:

*Marbury v. Madison.*1803.1 Cranch 137.

Lower Federal Courts   Decisions of the lower federal courts are usually cited to the *Federal Reporter,* abbreviated as F., or the *Federal Supplement* (F. Supp.). The material in the parentheses in the model reference is the name of the court, abbreviated, and the year of the decision:

Eaton v. IBM Corp., 925 F. Supp. 487 (S. D. Tex. 1996).

State Courts   In the model reference below, "Cal." Is the abbreviated name of the official court reporter, "27" is the volume number, "2d" identifies the series number, and 746 is the opening page of the decision.

Williams v. Davis, 27 Cal. 2d 746 (1946).

Note that the titles of court cases, including the "v," are italicized.

Publications of Government Commissions

U.S. Securities and Exchange Commission. 1984. *Annual Report of the Securities and Exchange Commission for the Fiscal Year*. Washington, D.C.: U.S. Government Printing Office.

Note: See the section on formatting citations for electronic sources, below, for information on citing public documents found in Internet sources.

Interviews   According to Section 14.221 of the *Chicago Manual of Style* (2010), published interviews are cited like a periodical article or a book chapter.

Untitled Interview in a Book

Jorgenson, Mary. 1998. Interview by Alan McAskill. pp. 62–86 in *Hospice Pioneers*, edited by Alan McAskill. Richmond, VA: Dynasty Press.

Titled Interview in a Periodical

Simon, John. 1997. "Picking the Patrons Apart: An Interview with John Simon," by Selena Fox. *Media Week*, March 14, pp. 40–54.

Interview on Television

Snopes, Edward. 2002. Interview by Klint Gordon. *Oklahoma Politicians*. WKY Television, June 4.

Unpublished Interview

Kennedy, Melissa. 1997. Interview by author. Tape recording. Portland, ME, April 23.

Unpublished Sources

Personal Communications   According to Section 14.222 of the *Chicago Manual of Style* (2010), references to personal communications may be handled completely in the text of the paper:

In a letter to the author, dated July 16, 1997, Mr. Bentley admitted the organizational plan was flawed.

If, however, you wish to include a reference to an unpublished communication in the list of references, you may do so using one of the following models:

Bentley, Jacob. 1997. Letter to author, July 16.

Duberstein, Cindy. 2008. Telephone conversation with the author, June 5.

Timrod, Helen. 1997. E-mail to author, April 25.

Theses and Dissertations

Longley, Klint. 1999. "Populism and the Free Soil Movement." Ph.D. dissertation, Department of Sociology, Lamont University, Cleveland.

Paper Presented at a Meeting

Zelazny, Kim and Ed Gilmore. 2005. "Art for Art's Sake: Funding the NEA in the Twenty-First Century." Presented at the annual meeting of the Conference of Metropolitan Arts Boards, June 15, San Francisco.

Unpublished Manuscripts

Borges, Rita V. 1993. "Mexican–American Border Conflicts, 1915–1970." Department of History, University of Texas at El Paso, El Paso. Unpublished manuscript.

Working and Discussion Papers

Blaine, Emory and Ralph Cohn. 2009. "Analysis of Social Structure in Closed Urban Environments." Discussion Paper No. 312, Institute for Sociological Research, Deadwood College, Deadwood, SD.

Electronic Sources

Online Sources   The need for a reliable online citation system continues to grow, but attempts to establish one are hampered by a number of factors. For one thing, there is no foolproof method of clearly reporting even such basic information as the site's author(s), title, or date of establishment. Occasionally authors identify themselves clearly; sometimes they place a link to their home page at the bottom of the site. But it is not always easy to determine exactly who authored a particular site. Likewise, it can be difficult to determine whether a site has its own title or instead exists as a subsection of a larger document with its own title. Perhaps the biggest problem facing online researchers is the instability of Internet sites. Although some sites may remain in place for weeks, months, or years, others either move to another site—not always leaving a clear path for you to find it—or disappear.

As in other issues concerning the formatting of research material, the *ASA Style Guide* (2014) has adopted methods established in the *Chicago Manual of Style* (2010) as a direction for its own system for handling electronic sources.

Text Citations for Electronic Sources   Format parenthetical text citations for most types of electronic sources just as you do for text citations for printed materials. See exceptions below for websites and e-mail messages.

References for Electronic Sources

Books, Sections of Books, and Reports   To cite a book, a chapter or section of a book, or a separately published report that you have accessed online, list the reference citation in the same format that you use for a print edition, including, if available, the place of publication, the name of the publisher, and the date of publication. Follow this information with the date on which you last retrieved the material and, in parentheses, the URL (Uniform Resource Locator, the address for the document on the World Wide Web). According to Section 14.12 of the *Chicago Manual of Style* (2010), it is possible to break a URL at the end of a line after a single (/) or a double slash (//), before a tilde(~), period, comma, hyphen, underline, question mark, number sign, or percent symbol (%). You may break a URL at the end of a line either before or after an equals sign (=) or an ampersand (&). Never add a hyphen to a URL to indicate a line break. Do not place a hyphen after the period. Remember one thing that is absolutely required to find a site on the Internet is the site address, so make sure you copy it accurately.

Squires, Nora and Avery Cook. 2009. *Negotiating Stress in the Home: A Primer.* New York: Cally Press. Retrieved March 13, 2009 (http://www.jc. familiesagainstgloomdoom&despair.org/html book09/s&c).

You may, if you wish, list other formats in which the book appears:

Snyder, Howard N. and Melissa Sickmund. 2006. *Juvenile Offenders and Victims: 2006 National Report.* Pittsburgh, PA: National Center for Juvenile Justice. (Also available at http://ojjdp.ncjrs.gov/ojstatbb/nr2006/downloads/NR2006.pdf).

Online Periodicals

Journal Article Available in Print and Online   Begin with the information required for a reference to the print edition, and end with the date accessed and the online location, in parentheses.

Bucknell, Vespasia. 2008. "Servitude as a Way of Life: Religious Denominations in Middle America." *Skeptic's Journal* 4(2):22–37. Retrieved September 25, 2009 (http://www. religio.org/protest/skepjrnl/my03.html).

Journal Article Available Only in Online Form   Include as much as possible the information required for a citation for an article available in print, followed by the date you last retrieved the article and, in parentheses, the URL.

Linklater, Philip and Lucy Beall. 2007. "My Papa's Waltz: Alcoholism and Culture." *High Art Quarterly* 12(2). Retrieved April 1, 2009. (http://www.linkbeall/lennox.org/litcult.html).

For journal articles you have accessed through an online database such as JSTOR or SocINDEX, list the database just before the retrieval date.

Asbridge, Mark and Swarna Weerasinghe. 2009. "Homicide in Chicago from 1890 to 1930: Prohibition and Its Impact on Alcohol- and Non-Alcohol-Related Homicides." *Addiction* 104(3):355-64. (Retrieved from ScoINDEX on March 13, 2009.)

Online Newspaper Article

Squires, Amanda. 2000. "Hard Times for Social Workers, Says Mayor." *El Paso Sun Times*, July 14, pp. A2, A8. Retrieved November 12, 2000 (http://www.elpasosun.com/2000-12/12.html).

Newsletter

Lampert, James. 2008. "Slouching toward Armageddon." *Desert Technologies*, July. Retrieved January 22, 2009 (http://www.phoenixites.org/destech/Jul09/dt3 .html).

Websites Any website from which you have used material that is important to the work you are doing in your manuscript should receive a text citation and a full citation in the reference list.

Document retrieved from an institution with a known location:

Text: (SPM 2008)

Reference:

Society for the Prevention of Malnutrition. 2008. "Score Card for the Decade." Juneau, AL: Society for the Prevention of Malnutrition. Retrieved June 6, 2009 (http://www.spmal.org/rs/westhem/stat).

Document retrieved from a corporate website with an unknown location:

Text: (Okydata 2009)

Reference:

Okydata Corp. 2009. "Sports that Stigmatize: The Impact of Noodling on the State's Cultural Profile." Retrieved September 12, 2009 (http://www .okydata.com/sportrec/channelcat.html).

Public Documents A great number of public texts, including congressional debates, bills, and laws; federal, state, and local reports and documents; and court cases can now be found on the Internet. Over the last few years there has been a flowering of government-centered websites, such as THOMAS, a website established by the Library of Congress, under the direction of Congress, to make all manner of federal legislative information available to the general public.

Citations for public documents found on the Internet use the citation format for a print document as far as it is practicable, ending with the date of retrieval and URL. For documents found on databases and websites such as LexisNexis and THOMAS, list the name of the database or website before the retrieval date.

U.S. Congress. House of Representatives. 2009. *Omnibus Appropriations Act of 2009*. H.R. 1105, 111th Congress, 1st Session, 2009. (Retrieved from THOMAS on March 13, 2009.)

Blog Entries Give full citations for any significant Web log references included in your manuscript.

Text: (Hochenauer 2009)

Reference:

Hochenauer, Kurt. "No New Tax Cuts." *Okie Funk: Notes From The Outback*, March 13, 2009. Retrieved March 14, 2009. (http://www.okiefunk.com/).

E-Mail Document   A reference to an email message should be handled within the text of the manuscript and referenced in a footnote or endnote. Do not cite the e-mail address, and be sure to obtain permission from the owner of the e-mail before using it.

Text: Bennett assured the author in an e-mail message that the negotiations would continue.[4]

Footnote: [4]Albert Bennett, e-mail message to author, March 22, 2009.

CD-ROM. References to materials housed on CD-ROM are cited in much the same way as printed sources. You may omit the place of publication and date, unless relevant.

Complete National Geographic: 110 Years of National Geographic Magazine. 2000. CD-ROM. Mindscape.

DVD-ROM and Videocassettes   Citations for video recordings resemble those for printed materials. Section 14.279 of the *Chicago Manual of Style* (2010) notes that scenes from a video work, which are accessible individually on DVDs, should be treated as book chapters and cited by title or number. Material incidental to the primary work on the DVD or videocassette—for example, critical commentaries—should be cited by author and title.

"Crop Duster Attack." 1959; 2000. *North by Northwest.* DVD. Directed by Alfred Hitchcock. Burbank, CA: Warner Home Video.

The first date listed above is the date the film was first shown; the second is the date the DVD was published.

Cleese, John, Terry Gilliam, Eric Idle, Terry Jones, and Michael Palin. 2001. "Commentaries." Disc 2. *Monty Python and the Holy Grail*, special ed. DVD. Directed by Terry Gilliam and Terry Jones. Culver City, CA: Columbia Tristar Home Entertainment.

The date in the above citation refers to the Commentaries being cited, material original to the 2001 DVD edition of the movie. The original date of the film is omitted as irrelevant.

A sample reference page follows.

Sample Reference Page

Asbridge, Mark and Swarna Weerasinghe. 2017. "Homicide in Chicago from 1890 to 1930: Prohibition and Its Impact on Alcohol- and Non-Alcohol-Related Homicides." *Addiction* 104(3):355–64. (Retrieved from ScoINDEX on March 13, 2016.)

Johnson, J. D., N. E. Noel, and J. Sutter-Hernandez. 2000. "Alcohol and Male Acceptance of Sexual Aggression: The Role of Perceptual Ambiguity." *Journal of Applied Social Psychology* 30(6):1186–1200. *(Continued on Next Page)*

(Continued from Previous Page)

Johnson, William A. and Richard P. Rettig. 2006. "Drug Assessment of Juveniles in Detention." Social Forces 28(3):56–69, cited in John Duncan and Mary Ann Hopkins. 2015. "Youth and Drug Involvement: Families at Risk." *British Journal of Addiction* 95:45.

Moore, J. B., Allen Rice and Natasha Traylor. 1998. *Down on the Farm: Culture and Folkways.* Norman: University of Oklahoma Press.

Sczaflarski, Richard. 2001 "The Trumpeter in the Tower: Solidarity and Legend" (in Polish). *World Political Review* 32(3):79–95.

Squires, Amanda. 2000. "Hard Times for Social Workers, Says Mayor." *El Paso Sun Times*, July 14, p. 2. Retrieved November 12, 2000 (http://www.elpasosun.com/2000–12/12.html).

Stapleton, Bonnie and Ellis Peters. 1981. "How It Was: On the Trail with Og Mandino." *Lifetime Magazine*, April, pp. 23–24, 57–59.

Stomper, Jean. 2000. *Grapes and Rain.* Translated by John Picard. New York: Baldock.

Read & Write 3.4 Create a Scholarly Bibliography

Using the directions in this and previous sections, create a 12-item scholarly biography that includes at least one *actually published* entry from each of the following information types:

- A Federalist paper
- Congressional debate
- A publication of a government commission
- A recent (within the last three years) book
- A recent article from a sociology journal
- A recent article from a popular political commentary magazine
- A blog post
- A social media comment (e.g., Twitter, Instagram)

3.5 AVOID PLAGIARISM

You want to use your source material as effectively as possible. This will sometimes mean that you should quote from a source directly, whereas at other times you will want to express such information in your own words. At all times, you should work to integrate the source material skillfully into the flow of your written argument.

When to Quote

You should quote directly from a source when the original language is distinctive enough to enhance your argument, or when rewording the passage would lessen its impact. In the interest of fairness, you should also quote a passage to which you will take exception. Rarely, however, should you quote a source at great length (longer than two or three paragraphs). Nor should your paper, or any substantial section of it, be merely a string of quoted passages. The more language you take from the writings of others, the more the quotations will disrupt the rhetorical flow of your own words. Too much quoting creates a choppy patchwork of varying styles and borrowed purposes in which your sense of your own control over your material is lost.

Quotations in Relation to Your Writing

When you do use a quotation, make sure that you insert it skillfully. According to *CMS* 16 (13.9–10), quotations of fewer than 100 words (approximately eight typed lines) should generally be integrated into the text and set off with quotation marks:

"In the last analysis," Alice Thornton argued in 2006, "we cannot afford not to embark on a radical program of fiscal reform" (p. 12).

A quotation of 100 words or longer (eight typed lines or longer) should be formatted as a *block quotation*; it should begin on a new line, be indented from the left margin, and not be enclosed in quotation marks.

Blake's outlook for the solution to the city's problem of abandoned buildings is anything but optimistic:

> If the trend in demolitions due to abandonment continues, the cost of doing nothing may be too high. The three-year period from 2004 to 2007 shows an annual increase in demolitions of roughly twenty percent. Such an upward trend for a sustained period of time would eventually place a disastrous hardship on the city's resources. And yet the city council seems bent on following the tactic of inaction. (2016:8)

Acknowledge Quotations Carefully

Failing to signal the presence of a quotation skillfully can lead to confusion or choppiness:

The U.S. Secretary of Labor believes that worker retraining programs have failed because of a lack of trust within the American business culture. "The American business community does not visualize the need to invest in its workers" (Winn 2016:11).

The first sentence in the above passage seems to suggest that the quote that follows comes from the Secretary of Labor. Note how this revision clarifies the attribution:

According to reporter Fred Winn, the U.S. Secretary of Labor believes that worker retraining programs have failed because of a lack of trust within the American business culture. Summarizing the secretary's view, Winn writes, "The American business community does not visualize the need to invest in its workers" (2016:11).

The origin of each quote must be indicated within your text at the point where the quote occurs as well as in the list of works cited, which follows the text.

Quote Accurately

If your transcription of a quotation introduces careless variants of any kind, you are misrepresenting your source. Proofread your quotations very carefully, paying close attention to such surface features as spelling, capitalization, italics, and the use of numerals.

Occasionally, in order to make a quotation fit smoothly into a passage, to clarify a reference, or to delete unnecessary material, you may need to change the original wording slightly. You must, however, signal any such change to your reader. Some alterations may be noted by brackets:

"Several times in the course of his speech, the attorney general said that his stand [on gun control] remains unchanged" (McAffrey 2016:2).

Ellipses indicate that words have been left out of a quote:

"The last time voters refused to endorse one of the senator's policies . . . was back in 1982" (Laws 2005:143).

When you integrate quoted material with your own prose, it is unnecessary to begin the quote with ellipses:

Benton raised eyebrows with his claim that "nobody in the mayor's office knows how to tie a shoe, let alone balance a budget" (Williams 2006:12).

Paraphrasing

Your writing has its own rhetorical attributes, its own rhythms, and structural coherence. Inserting several quotations into one section of your paper can disrupt the patterns of your prose and diminish its effectiveness. Paraphrasing, or recasting source material in your own words, is one way to avoid the choppiness that can result from a series of quotations.

Remember that a paraphrase is to be written in your language; it is not a near-copy of the source writer's language. Merely changing a few words of the original does justice to no one's prose and frequently produces stilted passages. This sort of borrowing is actually a form of plagiarism. To integrate another's material into your own writing fully, use your own language.

Paraphrasing may actually increase your comprehension of source material, because in recasting a passage you will have to think very carefully about its meaning—more carefully, perhaps, than if you had merely copied it word for word.

Avoiding Plagiarism When Paraphrasing

Paraphrases require the same sort of documentation as direct quotes. The words of a paraphrase may be yours, but the idea belongs to someone else. Failure to give that person credit, in the form of references within the text and in the bibliography, may make you vulnerable to a charge of plagiarism.

Plagiarism is the use of someone else's words or ideas without proper credit. Although some plagiarism is deliberate, produced by writers who understand that they are guilty of a kind of academic thievery, much of it is unconscious, committed by writers who are not aware of the varieties of plagiarism or who are careless in recording their borrowings from sources. Plagiarism includes:

- Quoting directly without acknowledging the source
- Paraphrasing without acknowledging the source
- Constructing a paraphrase that closely resembles the original in language and syntax

One way to guard against plagiarism is to keep careful notes of when you have directly quoted source material and when you have paraphrased—making sure that the wording of the paraphrases is yours. Be sure that all direct quotes in your final draft are properly set off from your own prose, either with quotation marks or in indented blocks.

What kind of paraphrased material must be acknowledged? Basic material that you find in several sources need not be documented by a reference. For example, it is unnecessary to cite a source for the information that Franklin Delano Roosevelt was elected to a fourth term as President of the United States shortly before his death, because this is a commonly known fact. However, Professor Smith's opinion, published in a recent article, that Roosevelt's winning of a fourth term hastened his death is not a fact, but a theory based on Smith's research and defended by her. If you wish to use Smith's opinion in a paraphrase, you need to credit her, as you do for all judgments and claims from another source. Any information that is not widely known, either factual or open to dispute, should be documented. This includes statistics, graphs, tables, and charts taken from sources other than your own primary research.

Read&Write 3.5 Properly Summarize an Article from *Rolling Stone* or *The Economist*

Select an article from a recent copy of *The Economist* or *Rolling Stone*, and summarize it properly in your own words, without plagiarizing, in approximately 500 words. Attach the original article to your summary.

4

BECOME FAMILIAR WITH GOVERNMENT AND PRIVATE INFORMATION SOURCES

4.1 WELCOME TO THE AMERICAN SOCIOLOGICAL ASSOCIATION (ASA)

The American Sociological Association (ASA) is an excellent first stop for many different sorts of sociology research and writing projects. It is the front door to a large community of sociologists and others interested in studying life in society. At the "About ASA" link on its home page, you can find the following information:

The American Sociological Association is:

- a non-profit membership association based in Washington, DC
- dedicated to advancing sociology as a scientific discipline and profession serving the public good
- 100 years old in 2005 (founded in 1905)
- an association of over 13,000+ members
- home to 52 special interest sections with more than 21,000 members
- host of an annual meeting with more than 6,000 participants
- publisher of 9 professional journals and magazines

Members include:

- college and university faculty
- researchers
- students
- practitioners
- About 20 percent of the members work in government, business, or nonprofit organizations.[1]

---

[1] "About ASA." N.d. American Sociological Association. Retrieved March 25, 2016. (http://www.asanet.org/about/about_asa.cfm).

In the *To the Student* introduction to this manual, you will find the names of the 52 current ASA sections, which study a wide variety of aspects of society and human behavior.

If you seek out the list of sections on ASA's site (http://www.asanet.org/sections/list.cfm), at the top of the list appears a link to the Aging and the Life Course section. Clicking on this link will give you the following description of what this section contains:

> Sociology of Aging and the Life Course provides an analytical framework for understanding the interplay between human lives and changing social structures. Its mission is to examine the interdependence between (a) aging over the life course as a social process and (b) societies and groups as stratified by age, with succession of cohorts as the link connecting the two. This special field of age draws on sociology as a whole and contributes to it through reformulation of traditional emphases on process and change, on the multiple interdependent levels of the system, and on the multidimensionality of sociological concerns as they touch on related aspects of other disciplines. The field is concerned with both basic sociological research on age and its implications for public policy and professional practice.[2]

Suppose you are interested in researching some aspect of the aging process in American society. If you continue to follow ASA links, you can find some highly beneficial links. For example, you will find information about scholars actively engaged in investigating the aging process.

The Meetings tab shows you what else was in store at the annual meeting. In fact, 4,600 scholars and other researchers participated in 600 sessions, presenting 3,000 research papers. *This is a gold mine of current sociological research.* You may surmise that attending the meeting would have given you a rich experience, but *you don't need to attend such meetings to tap the rich resources they provide!*

Apart from information on the national meeting, you will find many other sources of information about the vibrant, dynamic world of sociology.

Read & Write 4.1 Write an Email to an ASA Section Chair

Your task here is simple. You begin by identifying a topic of your interest in sociology. If you need an idea of where to start, browse the names of the ASA sections. Once you identify a topic, clearly explain in several sentences exactly what you are interested in researching. Next, in ASA's website, locate the section that covers your topic, and then go to that section's website to find the Chair of that section. Then, compose an email to that person. Ask her or him to provide you with: (1) names of scholars in the United States (and abroad) who are knowledgeable in this subject and (2) the names of journals, research institutes, university departments, and other resources of information on your topic. Be sure to thank the chair for any information he or she may be able to provide. You may then present both the email you wrote to the section Chair and the Chair's response to your course professor.

For example, let's suppose you are interested in aging. After examining some articles on aging in your library's online card catalog, you decide that you want to know more about

---

[2] "Section on Aging and the Life Course." N.d. American Sociological Association. Retrieved March 25, 2016 (http://www.asanet.org/sections/aging.cfm).

the extent to which family cohesion changes as people age. On ASA's Aging section website, you find the following list of section officers:

Section Officers 2015–2016

Chair: Jeylan T Mortimer, University of Minnesota

Chair-Elect: Jessica A. Kelley-Moore, Case Western Reserve University

Past Chair: Deborah Carr, Rutgers University

Secretary/Treasurer: J. Jill Suitor, Purdue University 2016

Next, you could locate Professor Mortimer's email address on the University of Minnesota website and write her an email as described above.

Who is the section Chair for your chosen topic?

4.2 HOW TO LOCATE SOCIOLOGY DISSERTATIONS AND THESES

Dissertations and theses are papers written to fulfill requirements for masters and doctoral degrees. To be accepted by universities that issue graduate degrees, dissertations and theses normally must exhibit both (1) a demonstrated ability to meet widely recognized standards of scholarship, and (2) an original contribution to knowledge. In the United States, the word dissertation normally refers to papers written to achieve the Doctor of Philosophy and other doctoral degrees, whereas the term thesis is most often attached to a paper written for a master's degree. In Europe and elsewhere, however, this distinction is less common. Dissertations are often published after graduation as monographs, articles, or books. While quantitative dissertations—papers dealing largely with statistics and statistical analyses—are often less than 50 pages in length, qualitative dissertations, which tend to use descriptive language to argue specific viewpoints, may run to several hundred pages.

A good place to start your search for dissertations is the search engine for the Online Catalog of the Global Resources Network's Center for Research Libraries (CRL) (http://catalog.crl.edu/search~S4). Using the information link, on the homepage of CRL, you can find the following statements:

> The Center for Research Libraries (CRL) is an international consortium of university, college, and independent research libraries. Founded in 1949, CRL supports original research and inspired teaching in the humanities, sciences, and social sciences by preserving and making available to scholars a wealth of rare and uncommon primary source materials from all world regions.
>
> CRL's deep and diverse collections are built by specialists and experts at the major U.S. and Canadian research universities, who work together to identify and preserve unique and uncommon documentation and evidence, and to ensure its long-term integrity and accessibility to researchers in the CRL community.
>
> CRL is based in Chicago, Illinois, and is governed by a Board of Directors drawn from the library, research and higher education communities.[3]

---

[3] "About CRL." N.d. Center for Research Libraries: Global Resources Network. Retrieved March 28, 2016 (http://www.crl.edu/about).

The dissertation's link on your college library's web page will also provide databases with varied strengths depending upon the library's research capabilities.

Read&Write 4.2 Collect Six Dissertations on a Topic of Interest

Using the dissertation location services described above, (1) locate six dissertations of importance to a research topic of your choice, and (2) write a summary of each one that describes the value of the dissertation to the topic at hand.

4.3 HOW TO LOCATE STUDIES BY THINK TANKS

Private research institutes, popularly known as think tanks, provide a wealth of information on virtually any topic you can imagine. Google search provides lists of think tanks, but an excellent place to start is the Harvard Kennedy School's Think Tank Search (http://guides.library.harvard.edu/hks/think_tank_search). In this search engine, you can search for specific topics (e.g., family) or specific institutes (e.g., the Hoover Institution).

Read&Write 4.3 Collect Six Think Tank Studies on a Subject of Interest

Your task here is similar to the one you completed for finding dissertations. Using the Harvard Kennedy School's search engine, (1) locate six studies of importance to a research topic of your choice, and (2) write a summary of each one that describes the value of the study to the topic at hand.

4.4 WELCOME TO THE LIBRARY OF CONGRESS

Expect to be amazed once again at the phenomenal collections of the Library of Congress (www.loc.gov). Here, you can access millions of documents of every conceivable source.

The manuscripts section alone declares: "The Library of Congress holds approximately sixty million manuscript items in eleven thousand separate collections, including some of the greatest manuscript treasures of American history and culture."[4]

---

[4] "Collections with Manuscripts." N.d. Library of Congress. Retrieved March 7, 2016 (https://www.loc.gov/manuscripts/ collections/).

Though massive today, the library's collections had a more modest beginning, as the website's history link (http://www.loc.gov/about/history-of-the-library/) describes:

> The Library of Congress was established by an act of Congress in 1800 when President John Adams signed a bill providing for the transfer of the seat of government from Philadelphia to the new capital city of Washington. The legislation described a reference library for Congress only, containing "such books as may be necessary for the use of Congress - and for putting up a suitable apartment for containing them therein..."
>
> Established with $5,000 appropriated by the legislation, the original library was housed in the new Capitol until August 1814, when invading British troops set fire to the Capitol Building, burning and pillaging the contents of the small library.
>
> Within a month, retired President Thomas Jefferson offered his personal library as a replacement. Jefferson had spent 50 years accumulating books, "putting by everything which related to America, and indeed whatever was rare and valuable in every science"; his library was considered to be one of the finest in the United States. In offering his collection to Congress, Jefferson anticipated controversy over the nature of his collection, which included books in foreign languages and volumes of philosophy, science, literature, and other topics not normally viewed as part of a legislative library. He wrote, "I do not know that it contains any branch of science which Congress would wish to exclude from their collection; there is, in fact, no subject to which a Member of Congress may not have occasion to refer."
>
> In January 1815, Congress accepted Jefferson's offer, appropriating $23,950 for his 6,487 books, and the foundation was laid for a great national library. The Jeffersonian concept of universality, the belief that all subjects are important to the library of the American legislature, is the philosophy and rationale behind the comprehensive collecting policies of today's Library of Congress.[5]

Read&Write 4.4 Summarize a Webcast Presented by the American Folklife Center

Your task in this exercise is to peruse the American Folklife Center's collections, select a webcast, and write a brief paper describing and evaluating the content and importance of the information it contains.[6]

4.5 FINDING GOVERNMENT STATISTICS

Your first stop for government statistics is USA.gov: Data and Statistics about the United States (https://www.usa.gov/statistics). Through the search engine on this page, you can find information on any topic, but you will also find the following list of sources for statistics available from federal, state, and local government

---

[5] "History of the Library." N.d. Library of Congress. Retrieved March 7, 2016 (https://www.loc.gov/about/history-of-the-library/).

[6] "AFC Concerts, Lectures, and Symposia with Webcasts, Photographs, and Essays." N.d. The American Folklife Center. Retrieved March 28, 2016 (https://www.loc.gov/folklife/events/pasteventsmenu.html).

agencies, and you may find what you want faster if you select a specific agency to search:

Federal Government Data and Statistics

There are principal statistical agency programs that collect, analyze, and disseminate statistical data and information. These programs include:

Bureau of Economic Analysis (BEA) collects information on economic indicators, national and international trade, accounts, and industry.

Bureau of Justice Statistics (BJS) collects and publishes information on crime, criminal offenders, victims of crime, and the operation of justice systems at all levels of government.

Bureau of Labor Statistics (BLS) measures labor market activity, working conditions, and price changes in the economy.

Bureau of Transportation Statistics (BTS) collects and disseminates transportation statistics.

Census Bureau is the main source of data about our nation's people and economy.

DAP Public Dashboard provides a window into how people are interacting with the government online. The data comes from a unified Google Analytics account for U.S. federal government agencies known as the Digital Analytics Program (DAP), sponsored by the General Services Administration (GSA).

Data.gov is the home of the U.S. Government's open data. Find Federal, state and local data, tools, and resources to conduct research, build apps, design data visualizations, and more.

Economic Research Service (ERS) informs and enhances public and private decision making on economic and policy issues related to agriculture, food, the environment, and rural development.

Energy Information Administration (EIA) collects, analyzes, and disseminates independent and impartial energy information.

National Agricultural Statistical Service (NASS) provides information on agriculture in the U.S.

National Center for Education Statistics (NCES) collects and analyzes data related to education.

National Center for Health Statistics (NCHS) provides statistical information that guides actions and policies to improve the health of the American people.

National Center for Science and Engineering Statistics (NCSES) is the nation's leading provider of statistical data on the U.S. science and engineering enterprise.

Office of Personnel Management (OPM) provides data and analysis from its Enterprise Human Resources Integration-Statistical Data mart (EHRI-SDM) and other data sources like FedScope, which is statistical information about the Federal civilian workforce.

Social Security Administration Office of Research Evaluation and Statistics (ORES) collects, analyzes, and disseminates information on Social Security.

Statistics of Income (SOI) publishes an annual publication of statistics related to the operations of the internal revenue laws.

You may also search a federal government agency's website to see what types of statistical information they provide. Find the U. S. government department or agency you want to search.[7]

State/Local Government Data and Statistics

State and local government agencies also compile and maintain statistical information. Contact a state or local government for more information.

Read&Write 4.5 Collect and Explain the Meaning of Statistics on a Subject of Interest

Using the information above, *and the directions in Section 3.3 of this manual*, (1) locate three sets of statistics that would be of importance to a research topic of your choice, and (2) write a summary of each set that describes the value of the statistics to the topic at hand.

4.6 HOW TO FIND STUDIES BY GOVERNMENT AGENCIES

As you begin work on any research topic, remember that no strategy is more important than simply keeping your own imagination in play. Bits and pieces of memories that predate your assignment, and may seem to have no direct link to a specific research topic, may, in fact, provide valuable clues to your hunt for useful information. Here is a case in point:

The fall of 2015 saw some major storms along the nation's east coast. Because her uncle and aunt's house was devastated by one of these storms, Robin, a student looking for a research topic for her sociology class, decided to research the possible impact future storms such as these might have on the country. She began her research by looking for government studies about future flooding risks along the North Atlantic shore. Here is one of the studies she found:

U.S. Army Corps of Engineers releases report on coastal storm and flood risk in the North Atlantic region of the United States

Posted 1/28/2015
Release no. 15-001

---

[7] "Data and Statistics about the United States." N.d. USA.gov. Retrieved March 28, 2016 (https://www.usa.gov/statistics).

Contact

Justin Ward
347-370-4550
justin.m.ward@usace.army.mil

or

Lin Miller
347-370-4772
lin.c.miller@usace.army.mil

BROOKLYN, NY—The U.S. Army Corps of Engineers today released to the public a report detailing the results of a two-year study to address coastal storm and flood risk to vulnerable populations, property, ecosystems, and infrastructure in the North Atlantic region of the United States affected by Hurricane Sandy in October, 2012. Congress authorized this report in January 2013 in the Disaster Relief Appropriations Act of 2013 (Public Law 113-2).

The report, known as the North Atlantic Coast Comprehensive Study (NACCS), brought together experts from Federal, state, and local government agencies, as well as non-governmental organizations and academia, to assess the flood risks facing coastal communities and ecosystems and collaboratively develop a coastal storm risk management framework to address increasing risks, which are driven in part by increased frequency and intensity of storm events and rising sea levels due to a changing climate.

The NACCS provides tools and information, including a nine-step Coastal Storm Risk Management Framework that can be used by communities, states, tribes, and the Federal government to help identify coastal risk and develop strategies for reducing those risks.

In addition, the study offers a number of conclusions, including several findings, outcomes, and opportunities, that can help guide future coastal flood risk reduction efforts at all levels of government. These include: the importance of land use planning, wise use of floodplains, and strategic retreat as cost-effective risk management tactics; the value in considering the full array of risk reduction measures (e.g., nonstructural, structural, natural and nature-based, and programmatic) in project planning and combining measures, where appropriate; the need for greater institutional alignment and financing; better use of prestorm planning and post-storm monitoring tools; and better education on flood risk and the availability of flood risk management solutions.

"The North Atlantic Coast Comprehensive Study is an unprecedented effort by the U.S. Army Corps of Engineers in collaboration with our partners to develop a coastal plan that considers future sea levels and climate change," said Jo-Ellen Darcy, the Assistant Secretary of the Army for Civil Works. "The report provides a framework for communities that will arm them for the reality of future extreme weather."

The report also identifies nine high-risk areas along the Northeast coast that warrant additional analysis. These are (in no particular order): Rhode Island Coastline; Connecticut Coastline; New York-New Jersey Harbor and Tributaries; Nassau County Back Bays, New York; New Jersey Back Bays; Delaware Inland Bays and Delaware Bay Coast; City of Baltimore, Maryland; Washington, DC; and City of Norfolk, Virginia.

"Hurricane Sandy brought to light the reality that coastal storms are intensifying and that sea-level change and climate change will only heighten the vulnerability of coastal communities," said Brig. Gen. Kent D. Savre, commanding general of the U.S. Army Corps of Engineers North Atlantic Division. "Coastal storm risk management is a shared responsibility, and we believe there should be shared tools used by all decision makers to assess risk and identify solutions. This report provides those tools."

The report and all associated documents and tools are now available at the following web page: http://www.nad.usace.army.mil/compstudy[8]

How did Robin uncover this study? She started with USA.gov—always a smart step for researching significant goings-on in the nation. One of the links at the very top of the USA.gov home page reads "Government Agencies and Elected Officials" (https://www.usa.gov/agencies). From this link, Robin accessed another link: "A-Z Index of U.S. Government Departments and Agencies" (https://www.usa.gov/federal-agencies/a).

During the fall of 2015, the time when her uncle and aunt's house was destroyed by a storm, Robin had seen a news broadcast featuring a spokesperson from the Army Corps of Engineers talking about flood conditions, so she selected a link to that agency. This brought her to the Corps' website, where she typed "flooding" into the search engine (http://search.usa.gov/search?affiliate=u.s.armycorpsofengineersheadquart&query=flooding), and the above study appeared.

Read & Write 4.6   Report the Results of Studies on a Selected Topic

Using the information above, (1) locate two studies of importance to a research topic of your choice and (2) write a summary of each one that describes the value of the study to the topic at hand.

---

[8] "U.S. Army Corps of Engineers Releases Report on Coastal Storm and Flood Risk in the North Atlantic Region of the United States." 2015. US Army Corps of Engineers, January 28. Retrieved March 28, 2016. (http://www.usace.army.mil/Media/NewsReleases/NewsRelease ArticleView/tabid/231/Article/562301/us-army-corps-of-engineers-releases-report-on-coastal-storm-and-flood-risk-in-t.aspx).

5

INTRODUCTION TO SKILLED OBSERVATIONS

5.1   SOCIAL LIFE

The idea of *social life* is very broad and certainly encompasses a lot of our existence. It can be seen as the time we spend enjoying activities with our friends or as the opportunities to do things that we enjoy such as going bowling, out to dinner, or on a date; being with family during the holidays; or having coffee with friends at Starbucks. College students are often as much or more concerned about their social life as they are about achieving good grades in their courses. They may join a fraternity or sorority to enhance their social life.

How might a sociologist go about observing social life? How might he or she ascertain the social life of college students? Of course, one way is to go where students are participating in fun activities, for example a dance sponsored by a university or a leisure activity at a local bar. The sociologist can observe from a distance, which may lend to greater objectivity, or he or she can participate in the observed activity. Sociologists refer to the latter method as *participant observation*.

Another way to measure the social life of college students is, simply, to ask them. You can create an *open-ended questionnaire* (one without fixed responses) that allows respondents to talk about their experiences. For example, you might ask the person you are interviewing a basic question—"What is your favorite thing to do on Saturday night?"—and then record his response. The open-ended structure allows the respondent to continue talking, and may lead to information that is not necessarily related to the original question. But this is okay, because that's the nature of the open-ended questionnaire; in this case, its function is to get the respondent to talk about his social life, and the question is just a tool for that purpose.

Read&Write 5.1   Interview Fellow Students

Now it's time for you to try your hand at the open-ended questionnaire method of sociological research. Construct a list of five or six open-ended questions like the example above.

They should be designed to allow students to tell you about their social life. Then, select a small sample of your classmates (nine or ten), and administer the questionnaire to them. You should record their responses so that you can listen to them later as you look for trends that seem to be occurring in most, if not all, of their responses. Finally, write an essay that compiles and analyzes the students' responses.

5.2 RACE AND ETHNICITY

It doesn't require much effort to observe the impact of race and ethnicity on our everyday lives. Many of the headlines we see in the media reflect the racial and/or ethnic strife in the United States and the world: WHITE MALE COPS SHOOT YOUNG BLACK MALE, BLACK MALE SHOOTS TWO WHITE COPS WHILE THEY SET IN THEIR POLICE CAR, MIDDLE-EASTERN COUPLE GOES ON KILLING RAMPAGE IN A GOVERNMENT BUILDING, and on and on. Today, when Americans are asked what they fear the most, the answer most often given is terrorism, which in its broadest sense includes home-grown racial and ethnic violence.

When fear becomes the greatest motivating factor in their lives, people begin to think about sacrificing basic freedoms to feel safe. This usually puts the Bill of Rights in harm's way. A very real question is, how many of the freedoms guaranteed by the Constitution are we as a people willing to relinquish to attain greater security?

Read&Write 5.2 Conduct a Focus Group

One way that a researcher might approach this dilemma in a sociology class is through *focus groups*. If your teacher decides that he or she would like you to apply this research method to this or some other issue related to race and ethnicity, now might be a good time to go to Chapter 6 (Section 6.1) of this manual and read about how sociologists do different kinds of qualitative research. Toward the end of this section, you'll find a brief discussion about focus groups.

In a class assignment, focus groups often work best when the class size ranges between 12 and 25 students. This allows the group size to be three to five students. One neat thing about this approach is that each group can be given the same topic/issue, or they can each be given a different issue. In fact, each group could be given more than one topic/issue. A focus group exercise can be very flexible in both structure and the pursuit of outcomes. That's why, if the groups are all pursuing the same question, the outcomes can vary greatly, a fact that can bring up other questions concerning how such variation might occur.

Here's a suggestion: Knowing that your teacher might wish to go another direction, let's divide the class into three to five groups with three to five students in each group. Here is the question we will pose to each of the groups:

Given the racial and ethnic tensions that are present in the United States today, what action would you propose to reduce these tensions and work toward greater harmony between majority and minority groups?

The task of each group is to address this question and formulate a proposal (one-and-a-half to two pages in length) that will be shared with the other groups in the class. Someone from each group will read his or her group's proposal to the class and generate a class discussion. Then, the next group does the same, until each group's proposal has been read and discussed by all the students in the class.

BECOMING A SOCIOLOGIST BY LEARNING SCHOLARSHIP SKILLS

6

READ AND WRITE
PROFESSIONALLY AND
CRITICALLY

6.1   READ QUALITATIVE SCHOLARLY
ARTICLES IN SOCIOLOGY

What Is *Qualitative* Scholarship?

In our era of dizzying digital development, it may be unwise to assume that arithmetical measurement has its limits. Today your iPhone can take an excellent photo of a prospective date, but it can't tell you how interested he or she is in you. Does your photo subject's enigmatic smile mean you are all right for an off-night, or is it a signal that he or she is playing hard to get? Someday your iPhone will tell you these things and more because people are now conducting qualitative studies to discover insights about what questions have to be asked to develop new iPhone capabilities.

Consider another example. Today we can easily measure the height, volume, circumference, temperature, density, and aridity of Oregon's Mount Hood. But how do we measure its beauty? Perhaps Google Earth can model anticipated environmental effects if Mount Hood were to suddenly evaporate. But what unanticipated effects might the mountain's disappearance precipitate? Might there be a crop failure in the Congo or a sudden loss of volume in the Mississippi River? *Qualitative research* is what we do when the knowledge we want is not easy to quantify. Whereas good quantitative research brings us precise answers, good qualitative research helps us discover new interesting questions we have not thought to ask.

Qualitative research methods use techniques that are semistructured and more in-depth than quantitative methods. Sociologists who utilize a qualitative approach are not interested in calibrating precisely their subject's thoughts or actions according to some absolute scale. They structure their research so that subjects can describe their thoughts, feelings, and experiences in their own words, or so that they can behave naturally in the social setting being studied. Some of the methods used by qualitative researchers include observation, participant observation, open-ended surveys, unstructured interviews, and life histories.

If the research you're conducting is not intended to limit its subjects' behavior or the conditions under which they respond, then the qualitative approach offers a real advantage over quantitative methodology. This is especially true in situations in which social status puts constraints on subjects' freedom to respond. We know that when someone has power over us, we feel less free to respond naturally. But when asked the same questions by a social researcher with no ability or desire to configure our responses, we usually feel comfortable telling it as we see it. This is one reason why a well-designed and administered qualitative study can elicit the in-depth responses that are more likely to give us the full range of meanings we desire in describing a given social setting.

While qualitative research is advantageous in some situations, it also has some disadvantages. The ability to generalize the findings to other populations is limited because: (1) the data are not quantified; (2) the samples tend to be nonprobability, that is, not susceptible to statistical analysis; and (3) the conclusions are very specific to the group(s) being studied. If you are interviewing employees of a department store about their job satisfaction and asking them to give in-depth responses to open-ended questions, the findings are limited to the setting that you are assessing. This sort of limitation often occurs with qualitative research. Therefore, qualitative methods are usually applied when we want to better understand some particular aspect of a given social setting. We also apply this type of research when our goal is to allow theoretical arguments to emerge and expand.

There are several forms of qualitative research. Two of the most widely utilized are *field research* and *in-depth interviews*. The goal of field research is to directly observe behavior in some predetermined site or setting. One type of field research that is widely used by sociologists is *ethnography*. This method is often employed when the researchers want to describe a particular group, organization, institution, setting, and so on. Maybe the researcher enters some group, like the Fraternal Order of Police in Muskogee, Oklahoma, or some setting, like Los Angeles International Airport, to observe and record peoples' behavior. Perhaps the researcher is only interested in describing the behavior in these environments. Or, as is often the case with *ethnomethodology*, the researchers may have some predetermined idea or notion—theory or perspective—that they wish to explore with the new data that emerges from their observations. So ethnographies are also used as "theory builders"; they expand the research or even change the direction of the theoretical perspective that the researchers entered the research project with. The researchers may begin with one set of assumptions but discover that these are not supported by the data. This requires the researchers to rethink the notions or ideas that they began with, and in most cases, to formulate new ones. Hence, with ethnomethodology the data is always reshaping the theoretical perspective.

Because the major goal of ethnographies is to know about the culture and patterns of the behavior and thinking of some group or organization, one important early step is to find a qualified informant, someone in the know who can assist in discovering important patterns about the group in question. Anthropologists who study other cultures have long relied on informants. They are valuable tools. In her study on *Coming of Age in Samoa* (first published in 1928), Margaret Mead relied heavily on older members of the society she was studying who knew about the values, norms, and status variations of their social environment.[1] Another famous sociologist/anthropologist, William Lloyd Warner, in his book on *Social Class in America* (first published in 1949), describes how he used this tool to study the social stratification of communities in the United States. Warner felt that the class structure of any community would be revealed though interviews with his informants. He also believed that not all communities had the same number of social classes and that the number and description of each social class could be determined through extensive interviews with these informants. He was the first to give us the academic definitions and descriptions for the labels we still use today in social stratification: lower class, middle class, upper-middle class, and upper class. But he allowed his theory to emerge and be guided by his use of ethnomethodology.[2]

Another form of ethnomethodology is to actually become a part of the group you are studying. In sociology, we refer to this type of research method as *participant observation*. In some cases, the people in the group may know that they are being observed, which, of course, can influence their responses. In other cases, the researcher may be "under cover" and the data collection process is not known to the subjects being observed. For example, perhaps the researcher is also a member of Overeaters Anonymous and wants to do research on the process and outcomes of this organization. As a member of the particular group, the researcher can inform the group of his or her intent to also observe and record the process and seek their approval to do so. Or the researcher can proceed without their knowledge and probably encounter less bias in the responses of the group.

Do you see any ethical concerns here? As a sociologist doing participant observation research, which method would you employ? Why? There's also the reality that being a member of the group you are studying can cause you to develop a bias that could affect the process and the outcomes you are observing. It's very difficult to move back and forth between being a participant in the group and also observing the group as a researcher.

The second widely used qualitative research method is *in-depth interviews*. This form of sociological research uses a preset list of open-ended questions. Unlike the more structured questionnaire used in quantitative research, this research methodology allows respondents to expand in their own words and elaborate more fully when the researcher asks them to do so. Subjects often feel more comfortable with this process than with questionnaires that limit their responses. Maybe there is a question that asks the subject what it was like growing up in Oklahoma City. As he responds to this question, the researcher becomes aware that during the subject's teenage years he experienced the arrival of the Thunder NBA team. Now the researcher may want the subject to elaborate on how this affected the community, the state, and him personally. The in-depth interview allows the researcher flexibility and the opportunity to enrich the data being collected.

---

[1] Margaret Mead. 1928. *Coming of Age in Samoa: A Psychological Study of Primitive Youth for Western Civilization.* New York: William Morrow.

[2] William Lloyd Warner. 1947. *Social Class in America: A Manual of Procedure for the Measurement of Social Status.* Chicago: Science Research Associates.

This interviewing technique can be a part of the observational research design, or it can be the complete design itself. For example, when Howard Becker (1953) studied the process of "Becoming a Marijuana User," he interviewed 50 users and asked them to elaborate on their personal experiences with marijuana and how they felt about the whole drug experience.[3] Without the open-ended questions and the in-depth interviewing process, he might not have discovered how individuals actually learn how to experience the drug; he found out that the norms within the user culture dictate the process of experiencing the high.

Of course, there's always the possibility that the subjects are lying or that they don't completely understand the situation. Therefore, those conducting this type of research should be aware of how deception or bias can influence the responses.

Several other types of qualitative research methods are used less extensively than the two described above, but they are very effective for what they are attempting to accomplish. They include examining archival data like newspapers, magazines, or public records, analyzing biographies, or conducting group interviews. Using *focus groups*, which involves loosely structured interviews with small groups, allows the researcher to obtain a wide range of responses to the same questions. For example, maybe the Sociology Department at the University of Oklahoma is interested in how their majors feel about being required to take a course in sociological statistics and research, as well as how they feel about other relevant issues concerning the curriculum. The focus group that they use to assess these issues could be the members of the local Sociology Club. After one of the club's monthly meetings, the department researchers could ask if some of the students would be willing to answer some questions about the departmental curriculum. When part of a focus group being questioned, one student's response can stimulate others to get involved in the discussion, which generates multiple perspectives on the question. While there is usually a set of questions designed to get at the issues in question, the focus group model is flexible enough to allow input outside the original design.

Two other popular methods for examining archival data are *content analysis* and *narrative analysis*. While content analysis looks for social trends in things like newspaper articles and other forms of media (television programming, films, books, or blogs), diaries, and certain public records, narrative analysis is usually concerned with how someone's personal life story reflects meaningful information about larger social events. Both of these research methods offer effective ways of examining targeted aspects of the social environment. As with most qualitative research, and especially with narrative analysis, it's important to be cautious about the bias and error that can be present. And remember that while qualitative research methods do not possess the rigor, reliability, and ability to generalize past their own results that are found in many quantitative studies, they are significantly more flexible and richly descriptive than their quantitative counterparts. Qualitative methods are far more likely to allow the researcher to see the world from the perspective of those being studied.

---

[3] Howard Becker. 1953. "Becoming a Marijuana User." *AJS: American Journal of Sociology* 59(3):235–42.

How Should We *Read* Qualitative Scholarship?

When you read anything, especially scholarship, you will get more out of it if you ask yourself some questions as you begin. What am I reading? Why am I reading it? What, exactly, do I expect to get out of it?

First of all, when you read an academic article, you are reading scholarship. Scholars are people on a quest for knowledge. They want to know *what* exists (detecting, identifying, and categorizing phenomena), *how* it came to be or how it does what it does, and *why* something acts or reacts in a certain way. To qualify as scholarship accepted by the academic community, the article must make an *original contribution to knowledge*. When scholars achieve this goal, they participate in an ongoing discussion, becoming members of a community of people contributing to the ever-expanding universal storehouse of knowledge. Scholarship is rarely easy reading. Since its audience is scholars, it assumes basic and sometimes advanced knowledge of languages and practices employed in a particular discipline.

So, what is the best approach to reading scholarship? First consider some general principles:

- Read slowly, carefully, deeply, and repeatedly.
- Read everything one section at a time.
- Reread everything one section at a time.
- Refuse to not understand anything you encounter:

  –Understand the article.
  –Understand the article's implications.
  –Imagine applications of the article's insights and discoveries.

- Question everything. Scholars are by no means infallible.
- Take lots of notes.
- Be sure to include important points, questions you can't answer, and interesting insights you have or the article provides.
- Create outlines as you go along that include the structure of the argument (logic) and the process by which information in the article unfolds.
- Before reading check out the author. Find his or her web page, and identify his or her specialty and credentials.
- You will find that the article includes:

  –An abstract, a brief summary of what the article purports to have accomplished
  –An introduction that includes reasons for conducting the research
  –A research question that reveals what the article intends to discover
  –Methods used to produce knowledge
  –Findings, or, in other words, the outcomes of applying the methods
  –A discussion of the importance and implications of the findings
  –A conclusion that explains the significance of the findings
  –References, that is, a list of the sources of information used in the study.

Scholarship always has an agenda, something the scholar is trying to prove. Precisely identify the agenda. Then identify the sequence of points in the argument employed to support the agenda. Is the pattern of points logical? Is it biased?

Read&Write 6.1　Evaluate a Recent Qualitative Article from a Sociology Journal

Among the journals sponsored by the American Sociological Association (ASA) (asanet.org) is *Sociological Methodology* (*SM*) (http://smx.sagepub.com). Enter "qualitative" in the *SM* web page search engine. Select an article that employs qualitative methods. Read it slowly, attempting to understand what it is all about. Then re-read the article, taking notes as described above.

Using your notes, write an essay that includes a description in your own words of:

- What the author(s) attempted to do
- Why they wanted to do it
- How they went about doing it
- What they claimed to have discovered
- What they inferred about the benefits and importance of knowing what they discovered

6.2　READ AND WRITE CASE STUDIES

One of the most common forms of qualitative research is the case study, although in some instances this approach can also be quantitative. We will take the remainder of this chapter to describe and outline this approach to qualitative research, followed by an example of a qualitative case study.

Definition and Purpose

A *case study* is an in-depth investigation of a social unit such as a person, gang, business, political party, or church undertaken to identify the factors that influence the manner in which the unit functions. Some examples of case studies are:

- An evaluation of the industrial efficiency of a Western Electric plant
- A study of ritual and magic in the culture of the Trobriand Islanders
- A study of the social service agency behavior of forest rangers
- A description of the role of secretary in the corporation

Case studies have long been used in law schools, where students learn how the law develops by reading actual court case decisions. Business schools began to develop social service agency case studies to help students understand actual management situations. Courses in social organization, public administration, and social institutions adopt the case study method as a primary teaching tool less often than business or law schools, but case studies have become a common feature of many courses in these areas.

Psychologists have used the case histories of mental patients for many years to support or refute a particular theory. Sociologists use the case study approach to describe and draw conclusions about a wide variety of subjects, such as labor unions, police departments, medical schools, gangs, public and private bureaucracies, religious groups, cities, and social class.[4] The success of this type of research depends heavily on the open-mindedness, sensitivity, insights, and integrative abilities of the investigator.

Case studies fulfill many educational objectives in the social sciences. As a student in a sociology course, you may write a case study to improve your ability to do the following:

- Carefully and objectively analyze information
- Solve problems effectively
- Present your ideas in clear written form to a specific audience

In addition, writing a case study allows you to discover some of the problems you will face if you become involved in an actual social situation that parallels your case study. For example, writing a case study like the example included at the end of this chapter can help you to understand the following:

- Some of the potentials and problems of society in general
- The operation of a particular cultural, ethnic, political, economic, or religious group
- The development of a particular problem, such as crime, alcoholism, or violence within a group
- The interrelationships—within a particular setting—of people, structures, rules, politics, relationship styles, and many other factors

Using Case Studies in Research

Isaac and Michael suggest that case studies offer several advantages to the investigator. For one thing, they provide useful background information for researchers planning a major investigation in the social sciences. Case studies often suggest fruitful hypotheses for further study, and they provide specific examples by which to test general theories.[5] Philliber et al. believe that by intensively investigating only one case the researcher can gain more depth and detail than might be possible by briefly examining many cases.[6] Also, the depth of focus in the study of a single case allows investigators to recognize certain aspects of the object being studied that might otherwise go unobserved. For example, Becker et al. noticed that medical students tend to develop a slang that Becker and his associates refer to as "native language." Only after observing the behavior of the students for several weeks were the researchers able to determine that the slang word "crocks" referred to those patients who were of no help to the students professionally because they did not have an observable disease. The medical students felt the "crocks" were robbing them of their important time.[7]

---

[4] Susan G. Philliber, Mary R. Schwab, and G. Sam Sloss. 1980. *Social Research*. Itasca, IL: F. E. Peacock, p. 64.

[5] Stephen Isaac and William B. Michael. 1981. *Handbook in Research and Evaluation*. 2d ed. San Diego: EdITS Publishers, p. 48.

[6] Susan G. Philliber, Mary R. Schwab, and G. Sam Sloss. 1980. *Social Research*. Itasca, IL: F. E. Peacock, p. 64.

[7] Becker, Blanche Geer, Everett C. Hughes, and Anselm L. Strauss. 1961. *Boys in White: Student Culture in Medical School*. Chicago: University of Chicago Press.

Bouma and Atkinson call attention to the exploratory nature of some case studies. Researchers, for example, may be interested in what is happening within a juvenile detention center. Before beginning the project, they may not know enough about what they will find to formulate testable hypotheses. The researchers' purpose in doing a case study may be to gather as much information as possible to help in the formulation of relevant hypotheses. Or the researchers may intend simply to observe and describe all that is happening within the case being studied.[8]

Limitations of the Case Study Method

Before writing a case study you should be aware of the limitations of the methods you will be using to avoid drawing conclusions that are not justified by the knowledge you acquire. First, case studies are relatively subjective exercises. When you write a case study, you select the facts and arrange them into patterns from which you may draw conclusions. The quality of the case study will depend largely on the quality of the facts you select and the way in which you interpret those facts.

A second potential liability to the case study method is that every case study, no matter how well written, is in some sense an oversimplification of the events that are described and the environment within which those events take place. To simplify an event or series of events makes it easier to understand but at the same time distorts its effect and importance. It can always be argued that the results of any case study are peculiar to that one case and, therefore, offer little as a rationale for a general explanation or prediction.[9] A third caution about case studies pertains strictly to their use as a learning tool in the classroom. Remember that any interpretations you come up with for a case study in your class, no matter how astute or sincere, are essentially parts of an academic exercise and therefore may not be applicable in an actual situation.

Types of Case Studies Written in Sociology

Sociology case studies usually take one of two basic forms. The first might be called a *didactic case study*, because it is written for use in a classroom. It describes a situation or a problem in a certain setting but performs no analysis and draws no conclusions. Instead, a didactic case study normally lists questions for the students to consider and then answer, either individually or in class discussion. This sort of case study allows the teacher to evaluate student analysis skills and, if the case is discussed in class, to give students an opportunity to compare ideas with other students.

The second form, an *analytical case study*, provides not only a description but an analysis of the case as well. This is the form of case study most often assigned in a sociology class, and the example at the end of this chapter models this type of qualitative research.

Sociologists conduct case studies for a variety of specific purposes. An *ethnographic case study*, for example, is an in-depth examination of people, an organization, or a

[8] Gary D. Bouma and G. B. J. Atkinson. 1995. *A Handbook of Social Science Research: A Comprehensive and Practical Guide for Students.* 2d ed. New York: Oxford University Press, pp. 110–114.
[9] Susan G. Philliber, Mary R. Schwab, and G. Sam Sloss. 1980. *Social Research.* Itasca, IL: F. E. Peacock, p. 65.

group over time. Its major purpose is to lead the researchers to a better understanding of human behavior through observations of the interweaving of people, events, conditions, and means in natural settings or subcultures.

Ethnographic case studies examine behavior in a community or, in the case of some technologically primitive societies, an entire society. The term ethnography means "a portrait of a people," and the ethnographic approach was historically an anthropological tool for describing societies whose cultural evolution was very primitive when compared to the "civilized" world.[10] Anthropologists would sometimes live within the society under scrutiny for several months or even years, interviewing and observing the people being studied.

The in-the-field nature of ethnographies has caused them to sometimes be referred to as field studies, and some social researchers classify studies of subcultural groups as small as gangs as ethnographies.

Read&Write 6.2 Write a Case Study

The subjective nature of case studies means that they are often written in the first person. The example included below is a student's qualitative research project in Professor David Ford's Sociology of Religion class at the University of Central Oklahoma. Students in this class were assigned a case study of some religious groups in the community with which they were not familiar. They were given this assignment as an introduction to qualitative research. Since most students had not been exposed to this type of research or the theoretical tools necessary for in-depth analysis, Professor Ford's requirements were more descriptive than analytical. Students were required to perform the following in their case studies:

- Conduct at least one interview with clergy of this religious group
- Conduct at least one interview with a layperson of this religious group
- Attend a minimum of two meetings of this religious group; these meetings could be two formal services or one formal service and one more informal service, such as a Bible study or prayer meeting
- Use interviews, participant observation, and information from official publications of this religious group to write this case study
- Write an in-depth description of this religious group

  Students were then required to address the following areas in writing their papers:

- A general description of the religion represented (introduction)
- The belief structure of this religious group
- The physical settings of the religious meetings
- A description of the worship or other services or meetings attended
- Observations about the roles of men and women in this religious group
- Observations about the roles of clergy and laypeople in this religious group
- Personal observations and feelings—What did you learn? (conclusions)

---

[10] David E. Hunter and Phillip Whitten, eds. 1976. *Encyclopedia of Anthropology*. New York: Harper & Row, p. 147.

The following paper is an example submitted by one of the students who was given Professor Ford's assignment.

Sample Analytical Case Study Paper

"The Refreshing: A Twenty-First-Century Experience":
An Analytical Case Study of a Nondenominational Evangelical Church

by

Michelle Thompson

for

Sociology of Religion 3573

Section 5237

Dr. David Ford

University of Central Oklahoma

November 7, 2000

Introduction

Coming from a varied religious background made the search for a new religious group more difficult. Friends had mentioned a charismatic church, the Refreshing, located in southwest Oklahoma City. This nondenominational evangelical church has beliefs that are founded in Christian fundamentalism. The Refreshing is in a covenant relationship with and accountable to the Christian Center in Lawton, Oklahoma, and the Bahamas Faith Ministries International in Nassau, Bahamas. In order to familiarize myself with this church I attended two services, gathered some general information, and interviewed a clergy member and a layperson. They provided insight into the group's religious doctrine and belief structure that would have taken multiple visits, if not months of observation, to obtain. The Refreshing church has a well-defined set of goals in the form of vision and mission statements.

The Belief Structure

Vision

In their vision statement, the Refreshing church is described as an evangelistic and disciple ministry focusing on responding to the environmental needs of the twenty-first century. Responding to this ever-changing environment requires a keen consciousness and obedience to biblical principles to make a significant impact on society. The church consists of a body of believers who provide a house full of God-kind-of-faith. God's Holy Spirit commits them to remaining fresh in their obedience to God according to his word. The church strives to remain fresh and sharp in its continued development of skills by renewing member's minds. One method to accomplish this is by proselytizing—compelling others to come into the kingdom of God and reach their destiny through Christ. The church provides the community with development training and life survival skills for the purpose of producing twenty-first century, destiny-filled leaders. This vision requires activity by all clergy members to make it a reality.

Mission

Their mission is to provide a place where all people (regardless of race, class, or socio-economic background) can experience a "refreshing" of mind, body, and spirit as well as love, hope, and purpose. They believe that members will receive a fresh start through godly principles and move effectively into their destiny.

Doctrine

According to the Refreshing doctrine, the Chief Cornerstone, Jesus Christ, governs the Refreshing. The pastors (willing vessels) of the Refreshing strive to maintain a strong commitment to both biblical principles and experiences. They have a sense of responsibility to aggressively teach God's word and welcome His Spirit. Great value is placed on the full range of gifts described in the scriptures; thus members are encouraged to exercise within the guidelines provided by the New Testament. The Refreshing is characterized by team preaching and pastoral care provided through a team of elders and appointed leaders, based upon scripture. Over the past few decades, the ministerial leaders have been created through various forms of education, training, and equipping (some formal and some informal). They have been "chosen" and put in place for this generation and generations to come.

According to doctrine, the church's beliefs are truths to be affirmed, boundaries to be observed, and principles to be practiced by all that represent the Refreshing. Scriptures are the inspired Words of God, without error. The writings comprise the complete revelations of God's will for salvation of men and the final authority for an all-Christian faith and life.

Beliefs

They believe in the Trinity, one God, creator of all things, infinitely perfect and eternally existing in three persons: the Father, the Son, and the Holy Spirit. God the Father is an infinite personal Spirit, perfect in holiness, wisdom, power, and love. A concrete belief of this religion is that God actively and mercifully intervenes in the affairs of men, that He hears and answers prayer, and that He saves from sin and death all that come to Him through His Son Jesus Christ. The Son, Jesus Christ, is God and man. He was conceived by the Holy Spirit and born of the Virgin Mary. He lived a sinless life and died on the cross as a sacrifice for human sins. He rose bodily from the dead and ascended into heaven. Jesus Christ is now the High Priest and advocate at the right hand of the Father. The Holy Spirit is fully God, equal with the Father and the Son. The Holy Spirit convinces nonbelievers of their need for Christ and gives new birth to believers. The Holy Spirit indwells, sanctifies, leads, teaches, and empowers believers for godly living and service. All biblical gifts of the Spirit continue to be distributed by the Spirit today, as these gifts are divine provisions central to spiritual growth and effective ministry. These gifts are to be eagerly desired, faithfully developed, and lovingly exercised according to biblical guidelines.

The creation of man was in God's own image. However, man is a sinner by nature and action, and is, therefore, spiritually dead. Those who repent sin and trust in Jesus Christ as Savior are spiritually born again to new life by the Holy Spirit. Salvation is a free gift of God and is received by man through faith in Jesus Christ apart from any human merit, works, or rituals. The shed blood of Jesus Christ and His resurrection provided forgiveness of sins.

The Second Coming of Christ is their future hope, and has vital bearing on the personal life and service of the believers. Following this coming is the resurrection from the dead of the believers to everlasting joy with the Lord and of the unbelievers to judgment and everlasting conscious punishment. Christ will also, at this time, bring about the ultimate defeat of Satan. The kingdom of God will be completely fulfilled in the heavens and the new earth, in which He will be worshipped forever.

Ordinances

The Refreshing ordinances are similar to other Christian churches—believer's baptism and the Lord's Supper. Baptism is a testimony to the death of sin and resurrection of new life in Christ. The Lord's Supper symbolizes the death of the Lord Jesus Christ and salvation through faith in Him. All believers should participate in the ordinances.

Responsibilities

The Christian responsibility is found in the great commandments: "Love the Lord your God with all your heart, soul, and mind. Love your neighbor as yourself." Glorifying God, enjoying Him, and fulfilling His great commission to go and make disciples of all nations fulfills these commands. These pursuits require personal commitments to live by the truth of God's word and to depend on the power of His Spirit. Both the Word and the Spirit call people to a life of Christ-like character, wholehearted worship, generous giving, unselfish service, and compassionate outreach to the lost. These beliefs are fundamental and unchanging.

The Setting

Two years ago the church began holding meetings in an urban shopping center. This sanctuary was located next door to a bar. The congregation was soon forced to look for a new location, as the bar patrons complained that the group's profession of faith disrupted their consumption of alcohol. They were fortunate to utilize a community center until finding their current location.

The church is now located at the corner of Southwest Fifty-Ninth and Walker, behind the Homeland grocery store. It sounds like this would be easy to locate, but finding the church proved very difficult. The church is actually located on a small side street. After driving in circles for 15 minutes, I asked a police officer for directions, but he was not sure of the street or the church location. Once I located the street, it appeared that I was lost again; all that I saw was an empty field ahead of me as the road began to curve. Suddenly a large sign appeared that stated: "The Refreshing: A Twenty-First-Century Experience."

Continuing to follow the road, I noticed a large metal building in the distance. I pulled into the parking lot and began looking for directions, but nothing was visible. The exterior of the building was a dull, yellow-colored wavy metal, with a small awning projecting off the front of the building. There were only two other cars in the parking lot. Upon entering the building, I found myself in a large foyer with dark wood paneling on the walls and gray commercial grade carpet on the floor. This area had very few furnishings—two love seats and a bulletin board, which displayed upcoming events for the church. To the right was a set of unlit stairs, and on the left doors were open to a large room full of metal chairs. This appeared to be the location of the worship service.

Upon entering the room a table with literature caught my eye. I gathered fliers on the church and familiarized myself with the surroundings. The room was unusual in its design. The walls were red brick for about the first ten feet, and then changed to a tan-colored sheet-rock material that spanned to the twenty-five foot ceiling. Gold exterior lights were mounted around the room on the brick part of the wall, every ten feet. The lights were the only items on the walls; there were no religious symbols. The upper section of the northern wall contained one five-by-twenty-foot tinted window and another opening the same size, as the window had been removed, which allowed sight of a projection machine.

A computer and some high-tech audio equipment—equalizers and synthesizers—were located on a folding table directly beneath these windows. Eight three-by-five-foot speakers, stacked two on top of each other, were placed in the southeast corner of the room. They were placed on either side of a semicircle-shaped stage. There were three steps up to the stage, which was covered with microphones on stands, drums, and an electric keyboard. The seating for this room was set up in the same format as church pews, but consisted of one hundred beige metal chairs. On the west wall was a small bookshelf that contained many Bibles. Completing my observation of the sanctuary, I was greeted by members of the congregation and invited to sit with a woman during the worship service.

The Worship Service

The worship service began with music, which was very edifying, charismatic, and loud. It continued for approximately 10 minutes without interruption. During the singing, members of the congregation were standing in front of their chairs, with their arms raised in the air, singing and swaying or dancing to the beat of the music. Those that were not singing were verbally praising God.

Following the music a layperson approached the front of the room, and explained that the pastor was ill and that he would be preaching. As he began his sermon, the projection machine came to life. As he spoke of scriptures they were displayed onto the painted portion of the wall above the bricks with the help of a PowerPoint presentation. His sermon was brief, but he spoke of praying or becoming prey. The congregation responded to questions posed and repeated the teachings as instructed. When the sermon ended, we began what is called intercession. This is best described as members individually praying and singing while moving about through the sanctuary.

The woman sitting with me said that "God had directed me to this church for a reason," and asked if she could pray with me. As she asked God to come into my life, she was holding my hands. As the prayer continued she moved her hands to the sides of my face and then placed one hand on my forehead and the other on my heart. During the prayer she spoke in both English and in tongues (glossolalia). Soon another member of the congregation walked up behind me and placed his hands on my shoulders while speaking in tongues. After praying, the woman asked me to accompany her to the altar (stage), which I agreed to do. We walked to the front of the sanctuary, kneeled at the steps, and began praying again.

When the intercession was over, the layperson minister asked for tithing. A small basket was placed at the center of the altar (stage), and members came forward to give money to the church. We prayed a closing prayer followed by announcements from the members of the congregation concerning upcoming events. As I was leaving, many members hugged me and expressed their happiness about my attendance. Since I had arrived before most of the members, they apologized that I was not hugged by all of the members of the welcoming committee upon my arrival.

My second meeting was very similar in structure to the first. However, it lasted three hours rather than one hour, like the first meeting. The pastor was in attendance for this service, which he commenced by singing and playing the electric keyboard for over 30 minutes. As he finished singing, the man who gave the sermon during my first meeting approached him to wipe the sweat from his head and face. During his sermon the PowerPoint presentation was again present. Again, the congregation repeated specific verses loudly, accentuating specific words as he commanded. He interpreted the scriptures for the congregation, even rephrasing them in modern-day slang. His sermon was very energetic, motivational, and directed. He spoke of those who live in the supernatural as opposed to those who live in the natural. He instructed the congregation that they should live in the supernatural as God instructed them and avoid individuals that only lived in the natural. Those "lost souls" would only drag down the members of the congregation.

We did not have an intercession during this worship service or collect the tithe. The pastor reminded members of the upcoming revival; it was described as "three nights of anointed preaching, teaching, miracles, and praise." He showed how to anoint individuals at the revival without them knowing, in an effort to invite the Holy Spirit into their life. Another announcement was a reminder of the forum to "identify, define, discuss, and provide solutions" to those who are involved with twenty-first century youth, education systems, the juvenile justice system, mental health providers, and the members of the legal system. The service ended with a prayer. As I was leaving, a member approached and asked how I found out about the church, what I thought of the service, and invited me back.

Sex Roles and Lay Ministry

I was not surprised by their position on the roles of men and women within the church. Unlike most fundamentalist religious groups, this church pays no attention to gender. The senior pastors of the church are a man and his wife. Both men and women fill the elected elder positions. If a member feels "moved" to speak to the congregation, all that the pastor asks is that the "individual be knowledgeable of scripture." The church expresses a realization for a greater freedom in the worship service. The layperson that I interviewed stated that the pastor feels that the message does not change but that the method of delivery must change with the times.

Conclusions

I was very impressed with the energy and commitment of these people. While this church is relatively new—it was created just two short years ago—it has gathered over 250 into its fold. The clergy member explained that their members are "burned out" from traditional church settings and seeking a "refreshing" experience. The clergy and elders strive to provide an inspirational setting where members can experience the "birthing" of God's Spirit.

The focus of the church is not on the exterior, which was the reason for the lack of religious symbols, but is directed toward assisting the members' spirits to connect with God. They believe that one way to accomplish this is by involving members with every aspect of the church, from preaching to prophesying and even having direct input on the direction the church will take.

The innovative ideas that are used in this church make the worship service exciting and energizing, while providing what they believe are the fundamental teachings of God. The Refreshing congregation has a goal they believe is determined by God, and they will let nothing stand in the way of accomplishing this goal. I believe they have found their niche in the religious realm.

Now that you have read the directions and a sample case study, write one of your own.

6.3   READ QUANTITATIVE SCHOLARLY ARTICLES IN SOCIOLOGY

The major goal of quantitative research is to *operationalize* (make measureable) the concepts being studied so that they can be described in a precise and objective manner. Because sociologists investigate a wide variety of issues and problems, their quantitative research can take many forms. Four of the most common quantitative research designs are:

- Surveys
- Experiments
- Direct observation
- Content analysis

Since survey research is the most widely used quantitative design in sociology, we will discuss it in the next section of this paper.

The processes of conducting experiments, performing scientific observation, and making content analysis studies require extensive additional knowledge and are normally only undertaken by students in upper division courses or at the graduate level. However, it is important for all sociology students to have some basic knowledge of these procedures. Therefore, we provide a brief introduction to them here.

Of all the forms of quantitative research, *experiments* give us the most confidence in supporting a cause-and-effect relationship; we are far more likely to detect the "smoking gun" if we follow the rules of experimental design. Experimentation is the fundamental method of acquiring knowledge in the physical sciences. As a research method, it has one primary and substantial benefit: Experimentation allows the researcher to control the variables, making it easier than it might otherwise be to determine the effect of the *independent variable* (the cause, sometimes referred to as the experimental treatment) upon the *dependent variable* (the effect). Experiments are more difficult to conduct in the social sciences than in the physical sciences because the research subjects are human beings and the number of causal variables is normally large. Despite these difficulties, social scientists are now successfully conducting more experiments than they have in the past.

Experiments in the social sciences are set up according to several different basic designs. The first is the simple *post-test measurement*. For example, a lecture on the social consequences of using marijuana may be followed by a test of the knowledge of the participants who heard the lecture. The *test-retest method* (pre/post method) is more accurate. A researcher using this method might measure the effects of a lecture upon the attitudes of the people in an audience by first having the members of the audience complete a survey, then listen to the lecture, and finally complete the survey again. The researcher could then measure the differences in opinion registered before and after the survey. Without the first survey, the researcher cannot be sure of the level of knowledge or the respondents' attitudes before the test was given, and the effects of the lecture or speech, then, are less certain.

The *alternative-form* type of experiment uses two different measures of the same concept. In a research project concerning the effects of peer pressure on adolescents, for example, the analyst could measure subjects' propensity to conform in one test and then their desire for acceptance in another test. The *split-halves* device is similar to the alternative-form measurement, except that two measures of the concept under study are applied at the same time.

All experimental designs confront the following problems:

- Control of variables: Can the environment be controlled to rule out other factors?
- Time passage: People get tired, or for some other reason take a different attitude.
- Varying acts of measurement: Different pollsters may record responses differently.
- Statistical regression: Someone who is on the high end of a test score range may register a high score only temporarily.
- Experimental mortality: Subjects drop out.
- Instrument decay: The instrument may not be used as carefully the second time.
- Selection error: Control and experimental groups may not be equivalent.

Researchers have developed a number of complex methodologies to overcome these problems. *Multi-group designs*, for example, test multiple independent variables against the same dependent variable. *Factorial designs* may test the effects of several independent variables in different combinations. A simple 2 × 2 factorial design, for example, might test combinations of four possible results from two different actions a researcher might take to test the social acceptability of her actions. Let's suppose that the researcher made an identical presentation of information on the health hazards of smoking to four different groups of people and later had the groups complete a questionnaire that would indicate their acceptance of her presentation. Normally the researcher would wear a traditional business suit when addressing a group, but since the experiment's goal is to study how socially acceptable her appearance is to her audiences, she decides to alter her customary dress in each group setting, using a straw hat and a pink leotard. The chart below illustrates the four possible variations in her appearance:

Wear Pink Leotard	(1) Both hat and leotard
Do Not Wear Pink Leotard	(2) Hat but no leotard
Wear a Straw Hat	(3) Leotard but not hat
Do Not Wear a Straw Hat	(4) Neither hat nor leotard

A factorial design based upon the choices set forth in the above chart would test the results of presentation participant acceptance according to each of the four situations.

Researchers conduct dozens of different types of experimental designs, using different combinations of strategies. The above factorial design is intended to be used as part of a *field experiment*—an experiment conducted within a natural setting—which in our example above would be four regular high school health classes.

In the following example the groups who participate in the experiment have not been left in their natural setting or randomly assigned but rather have been preselected by the researcher. Some researchers claim that this type of interference with subjects creates a quasi-experimental design and raises questions about the impact of the experimental treatment (independent variable) on the outcome measurement (dependent variable).

Let us suppose that we will design an experiment to test this research hypothesis: "Students who are anxious because they believe their instructor will have access to their evaluations of the instructor's effectiveness before the assignment of the students' final grades will give the instructor a higher evaluation than if they had no such anxiety."

For our experiment the teacher will use two course sections of his Introduction to Sociology class, the sections being similar in size and student makeup. Section 1, the control group, will be given the teacher evaluation form in the usual manner. The teacher will leave the room while a monitor—a student in the class—dispenses the forms, reads the instructions, collects the forms after they have been completed, seals them in an envelope, and then leaves the room, supposedly to take them where they will be kept from the teacher until final grades have been assigned to transcripts. As part of the instruction, the teacher emphasizes the fact that he does not have access to the results until final grades have been recorded.

Section 2, the experimental group, will follow the same procedure with one exception. The monitor is again a student in the class, but she is also a confidant of the experimenter whose role is to administer the experimental treatment. While distributing the evaluations forms she will disclose information to the students that she has been given about teachers being allowed to look at the evaluations prior to the final grades being assigned. She will state that this is something she has heard from several reliable sources, but that she is unwilling to disclose those sources. Everything else in the evaluation process will be carefully controlled to emulate the procedure used with the control group. The evaluations are then tallied to determine whether the experimental group's perception that the teacher might have access to their evaluations before the final grades are assigned caused them to give their teacher significantly higher evaluations than the control group.

Can you determine the dependent variable in this experiment? Independent variable? Is this a true experiment, or is it really a quasi-experiment? Why? Remember that to be a true experiment the control group and the experimental group cannot vary in any meaningful way. That allows us to be confident that any significant difference (a statistical concept) between the two groups on the dependent variable (student evaluations of the teacher) is caused by the independent variable (anxiety about the teacher knowing the evaluation before assigning final grades). Can you think of any other variables that might explain the difference between the two groups on the dependent variable? Do you see any ethical issues in this study? See if you can name some.

A number of techniques are used for data collection. *Direct observation* of social phenomena is conducted by trained observers who carefully record selected behaviors. Observation may be structured, which means that a definite list of phenomena is compiled and studied. Or observation may be unstructured, in which case observation attempts to take in every action in a certain setting that may possibly be significant. In either case, successful observation for purposes of social science research always follows clear guidelines and standard procedures.

Direct scientific observation is difficult to conduct for several reasons. First, researchers usually consider observation data to be qualitative and therefore subjective in nature. Although much of the data can be quantified, qualitative considerations are hard to avoid. Another problem is that social events can be difficult, time-consuming, and expensive to observe, and an entire event, such as an election, may require several observers whose activities are highly coordinated and regulated.

Content analysis, a method used in both qualitative and quantitative research, is used for analyzing written documents and allows researchers to transform nonquantitative data into quantitative data by counting and categorizing certain variables within the data set. Content analysts look for certain types of words or references in the texts and then categorize or count them. A content analyst of news articles on women, for example, might count the number of times the authors of the articles portray women in a positive manner.

Press reports, statistics, televised and radio reports, personal records, newspapers, and magazines provide inexhaustible mines of data for content analysts. Government documents are an especially rich source of material for political scientists. Different types of government documents include presidential papers; the Code of Federal Regulations; the Congressional Record; federal, state, and local election returns; historical records; judicial decisions; and legal records. The data analyzed in content analysis are most often the words contained in books, journals, magazines, newspapers, films, and radio or television broadcasts. But content analysis may also be conducted on photographs, cartoons, or music.

An example of content analysis design is found in the research of Levin, Arluke, and Mody-Desbareau, who coded 311 celebrity and noncelebrity profiles that appeared in the four most widely circulated gossip magazines—*National Enquirer, Star, Globe,* and *National Examiner*—from February through July of 1983. The researchers concluded that while the profiles of noncelebrities mostly emphasized extraordinary acts of heroism, strength, or charity, celebrities were usually featured for some mundane or minor event, such as a shopping spree or a quarrel with a spouse or lover.[11]

Read&Write 6.3   Evaluate Three Quantitative Scholarly Articles

Locate three recent sociology articles, one that describes an experiment, one that employs direct observation, and one that uses content analysis. Write an essay explaining how each study reveals both the strengths and weaknesses of the particular research method it employs.

6.4   OPINION SURVEY PAPERS

Survey design is the most commonly used research methodology in sociological research. A survey is simply a device for identifying and counting events, actions, perceptions, attitudes, or beliefs. Sociological surveys are the barometers of society. They describe a society's quality of life and the characteristics of its culture. They tell us who we are. There is little doubt that the skillful use of surveys dramatically increases the accuracy of our perceptions of ourselves.

[11] Jack Levin, Arnold Arluke, and AmitaMody-Desbareau. 1986. "The Gossip Tabloid as an Agent of Social Control." Presented at the annual meeting of the American Sociological Association, September 1, New York City.

As a student of sociology, you will find that writing your own sociological survey paper will serve two purposes. First, in learning how to construct, conduct, and interpret a sociological survey, you will add to your understanding of society and of one of the most basic processes of sociological research. By writing this paper you will gain a skill—if only at the introductory level—that you may actually use in your professional life. Public and private organizations often conduct surveys on attitudes and preferences in order to make their services more effective and desirable. Second, you will learn how to evaluate critically published surveys. Knowing the strengths and weaknesses of the surveying process will help you to obtain some of the fundamental knowledge necessary to appraise the validity of surveys you read about in books, journals, magazines, and newspapers.

Read&Write 6.4   Write a Public Opinion Analysis

A previous section of this chapter (6.1) explains how to read a qualitative scholarly article. Since the same principles apply to reading quantitative articles, you will find it most helpful to read Section 6.1 before proceeding. This chapter explains how to construct and conduct a simple sociological survey and how to apply to your survey results some elementary data analysis and evaluation techniques. Your instructor may want to add supplemental tasks, such as other statistical procedures, and your class text in sociology methods will explain much more about the process of sociological research. The following set of directions, however, will provide a general framework that will help you create and interpret a sociological survey; consider these as the essential steps for writing a sociological survey paper:

1. *Focus on a specific topic.* The first step in writing a sociological survey paper is to select a topic that is focused on one specific issue. While nationally conducted surveys sometimes cover a broad variety of topics, confining your inquiry to one narrowly focused issue will allow you to gain an appreciation for even a single topic's complexity and for the difficulties inherent in clearly identifying opinions. Precision is vital to the success of a sociological survey. Topics for sociological papers are nearly as numerous as the titles of articles in a daily newspaper. Sociological surveys are conducted on topics pertaining to local, state, national, or international politics. You will usually increase the interest of the audience of your paper if you select an issue that is being widely discussed in the news. Many issues of health and safety are publicized on a regular basis. General topic headings found almost daily in the news include the following: Drugs, Crime, Education, Abortion, Family life.

2. *Formulate a research question and hypothesis.* After you have selected a topic, your task is to determine what you would like to investigate about that topic. One student who was interested in family relationships, for example, wanted to try to identify the factors that contribute to and detract from marital satisfaction. The first thing you need to understand when conducting survey research is that you must phrase your questions carefully. If you simply ask, "What do you think makes for a happy marriage?" you will probably receive obvious replies from a substantial majority of your respondents, replies that may not have much to do with actual marital satisfaction. To find out what really makes for a good marriage, you have to design more specific questions. The following sections of this chapter will help you to do this.

However, to create these specific questions, you will first need to formulate a research question and a research hypothesis. A research question asks exactly what the researcher wants to know. Here are some examples of research questions posed by national surveys:

- What factors contribute to family stability?
- What social conditions contribute to violence?
- What are the social issues about which Americans are most concerned?

Research questions for papers for sociology classes, however, should be more specific and confined to a narrowly defined topic. Consider the following:

- What is the relationship, if any, between ethnicity and philanthropy?
- To what extent do the people surveyed believe that their own personal actions, such as working hard toward a goal, will actually make a difference in their lives?
- What is the relationship, if any, between sexual orientation and choice of vocation?

It is important to note that while you are formulating a hypothesis or hypotheses from your research question, hypotheses can only be accepted or rejected through the application of decision-making statistics. Techniques for making effective use of statistics require special skills that you may or may not have acquired. Since the statistical techniques outlined below are only descriptive, their application can only suggest direction and trends. Therefore, it would be inappropriate to make a decision about the correctness of your hypothesis in the absence of decision-making statistics.

3. *Select your sample.* Researchers usually conduct sociological surveys to find out how large groups of people—such as Americans in general, African Americans, women, or welfare recipients—behave in certain situations. It is normally unnecessary and too costly to obtain data on every member of the group under consideration, so most surveys question a small but representative percentage of the total group that is being studied. The individual units studied in a sociological survey are usually called *elements*. An element might be a group—such as an ethnic group, social organization, or church denomination—but it is most often an individual. The *population* is the total number of elements covered by the research question. If, as in our sample survey research design, the research question is "Are left-handed fifth-grade boys more likely than right-handed fifth-grade boys to identify with sports heroes?" then the population is all fifth-grade boys in the United States. The *sampling frame* consists of all fifth-grade boys who attend the school in which your survey will take place. The *sample* is the part of the population that is selected to respond to the survey. A *representative sample* includes numbers of elements in the same proportions as they occur in the general population. In other words, if 81 percent of the population of fifth-grade boys in the United States are right-handed and 19 percent are left-handed, then 81 percent of a representative sample of fifth-grade boys will also be right-handed and 19 percent will be left-handed. Conversely, *non-representative samples* do not include numbers of elements in the same proportions as they occur in the general population.

Sample Survey Research Design

Research question: Are left-handed fifth-grade boys more likely than right-handed fifth-grade boys to identify with sports heroes?

Research hypothesis: Left-handed fifth-grade boys are more likely than right-handed fifth-grade boys to identify with sports heroes.

Elements: Individual fifth-grade boys
Population: American fifth-grade boys
Sampling frame: Fifth-grade boys at Hoover Elementary School

Sample: 84 students in Mr. Smith's and Mrs. Baker's classes, out of the total
population of 420 fifth-grade boys at Hoover Elementary School

How large must a sample be to accurately represent the population? This question is difficult to answer, but two general principles apply. The first is that a large sample is more likely, simply by chance, to be more representative of a population than a small sample. The second is that the goal of a representative sample is to include representatives of all of the strata that are included in the whole population.

Let us consider the case of a student who has designed a research survey to determine the degree of marital satisfaction experienced by students at her college. The target population for the survey is the married students enrolled at the college. Now our student research must determine how to secure a representative sample, meaning one in which the percentages of student marital satisfaction are the same as the percentages in the much larger target population. Generalizing from a sample to a population always contains some error. The objective is to draw the most representative sample—one with the lowest error—from the population. A random sample has the lowest chance of error because every element in it has an equal opportunity of being selected. However, circumstances often do not allow the researcher to use this sampling technique.

Sometimes the researcher is able to control error from certain variables by stratifying the sample, or subdividing it into different layers based on prior knowledge of how these variables are distributed in the population. If, for example, before sampling a university population, we know that 58 percent of the student body is female, 13 percent are minorities, the average age is twenty-eight, and 54 percent of the students attend all or part of their program at night, we can stratify the sample according to these variables before making random selections. Again, obtaining a stratified sample, like a purely random sample, is very difficult, if not impossible, when the population in question is college students.

Faced with such problems, the most reasonable and economical question becomes: Can the survey be completed in select classes that represent the student body? For example, would sampling classes that are diversified by age, sex, ethnic background, major field, and so on lower the error enough to allow the researcher to feel comfortable generalizing to the target population as a whole? Our answer depends to some extent on the degree to which the makeup of the classes parallels the stratification of the university. While this is often the best sampling procedure available in such a complex environment as a university, the problem with the method lies in our inability to gauge the amount of error. When we read about a plus or minus 3 or 4 percent error in samples that have been taken for opinion polls and other scientific endeavors, it is important to understand that the researchers have applied controlled procedures to judge the error involved in generalizing to the population being sampled. So while we may have given careful thought to selecting classes that are stratified much like the student body of the university, the absence of random selection prevents us from accurately measuring the error involved in generalizing to the population.

As you begin to work on your own sociological survey, you will find it most convenient to select as your sample the class in which you are writing your paper. The disadvantage of this sample selection is that your class may not be representative of your college or university.

Even if this is the case, however, using the class will enable you to learn the procedures for conducting a survey, which is the primary objective of this exercise.

Sociological surveys are conducted with human subjects, and they often ask for personal information. The people whose responses are sought are then known as human subjects of the research. Most colleges and universities have policies concerning *research with human subjects*. Sometimes administrative offices, known as institutional review boards (IRBs), are established to review proposals for research to ensure that the rights of human subjects are protected. It may be necessary for you to obtain permission from your Institutional Review Board or college to conduct your survey. Be sure to comply with all policies of your college and university with respect to research with human subjects.

4. *Construct the survey questionnaire.* Your research question is your primary guide for constructing survey questions. As you begin to write your questions, ask yourself what it is that you really want to know about the topic. Suppose that your research question is: "What are the views of sociology students regarding the role of the government in regulating abortions?" If you ask as one of your survey questions, "Are you for abortion?" you may get a "no" answer from 70 percent of the respondents. If you then ask, "Are you for making abortion illegal?" you may get the answer "no" from 81 percent of your respondents. These answers seem to contradict each other. By asking additional questions, you may determine that, although a majority of the respondents finds abortion is regrettable, only a minority wants to make it illegal.

But even this may not be enough information to get a clear picture of people's opinions. The portion of the population that wants to make abortion illegal may be greater or smaller according to the strength of the legal penalty to be applied for having an abortion. In addition, some of the students who want no legal penalty for having an abortion may want strict medical requirements imposed on abortion clinics, while others may not. You will need to design additional specific questions to accurately determine respondents' views on these issues.

You must consider carefully the number of questions to include in your questionnaire. The first general rule, as mentioned, is to ask a sufficient number of questions to find out precisely what it is you want to know. A second principle, however, conflicts with this first rule. This second principle—which may not be a problem in your sociology class—is that people generally do not like to fill out surveys. Short surveys with a small number of questions are more likely to be answered completely than long questionnaires. The questionnaire for your paper in survey research methods should normally contain between ten and twenty-five questions.

Surveys consist of two types of questions—closed and open. *Closed questions* restrict the response of the respondent to a specific set of answers, normally two to six. Multiple-choice examination questions are typical closed questions. *Open questions* do not restrict respondents to preselected answers, but allow them to answer in any manner they choose. Therefore, open questions call for a more active and thoughtful response than do closed questions. The increased time and effort may be a disadvantage, though, because in general the more time and effort a survey demands, the fewer responses it is likely to get. However, open questions have the advantage of providing an opportunity for unusual views to be expressed. For example, you might get the following response to the question "What should be done about gun control?": "All firearms should be restricted to law enforcement agencies in populated areas. Special privately owned depositories should be established for hunters to be able to store rifles in hunting areas, where they can be used for target practice or outdoors during hunting season."

Open questions are preferable to closed questions when you want to expand a range of possible answers to find out how much diversity there is among opinions on an issue. For practice working with open questions, you should include at least one in your survey questionnaire. Where quantitative research is concerned, the greatest difficulty with open questions is quantifying the results. The researcher must examine each answer and then group responses according to their content. For example, it might be possible to differentiate responses that are clearly in favor, clearly opposed, and ambivalent to gun control. Open questions are of particular value to researchers who are doing continuing research; the responses they obtain help them to create better questions for the next survey they conduct.

In addition to the regular open and closed questions on your survey questionnaire, you will want to add what are often called *identifiers*—questions that ask for personal information about the respondents. If you ask questions about gun control, for example, you may want to know if men respond differently from women, if Caucasians respond differently from African Americans, or if young people respond differently from older people. Identifier questions, sometimes referred to as *demographic variables*, concern such things as the respondent's gender, age, political party, religion, income level, or other items that may be relevant to the particular survey topic. For an example of a questionnaire containing both closed and identifier questions, see Appendix A on paged 187.

5. *Collect data.* After you have written the survey questionnaire, you need to conduct the survey. You will need to distribute it to the class or other group of respondents. Be sure to provide on the survey form clear directions for completing it. If the students are to fill out the survey in class, read the directions out loud to the class and ask if there are any questions before the students begin.

6. *Tabulate data.* If your sample is only the size of a small sociology class, you will be able to tabulate the answers directly from the survey form. If you have a larger sample, however, you may want to use data collection forms such as those available from the Scantron Corporation (online at scantron.com). You may already be using Scantron forms when you take multiple-choice tests in some of your classes now. On Scantron forms—which are separate from your survey form—respondents use a number 2 pencil to mark multiple-choice answers. The advantage of Scantron forms is that they are processed through computers that tabulate the results and sometimes provide statistical measurements. If you use Scantron sheets, you will need access to computers that process the results, and you may need someone to program the computer to provide the specific statistical measurements that you need.

7. *Analyze data.* After you have collected and tabulated the completed questionnaires, you will need to analyze the data that they provide. There are many statistical procedures especially designed to describe data and to imply the correctness of hypotheses. Several useful types of statistics are easily processed with the aid of common computer programs. Ask your instructor for advice about which statistical methods to use and which software package to choose. Each software package will provide its own directions for entering data and determining results. The following example describes one way to collect, tabulate, and analyze data.

An example

Using the marital satisfaction questionnaire in Appendix A, suppose we survey a sample of 200 married students at Coweta State College. Taken together, the first 10 items on this questionnaire are an example of a summative scale—because they are all measuring some component of the same variable (marital satisfaction), they can be added to yield a score that represents this variable. Notice that respondents are asked to rate each of the 10 items on a scale that ranges from 1 (least degree) to 5 (greatest degree). After adding the ratings for the 10 items, the marital satisfaction scale yields a score that ranges from 10 (very unsatisfied) to 50 (very satisfied). Each individual in the sample receives a score on this scale that represents his or her level of marital satisfaction.

These scores allow us to associate each of the identifier variables on the questionnaire (sex, number of children, etc.) with marital satisfaction. For example, if we choose to describe how sex relates to marital satisfaction, we can compare the level of male marital satisfaction to that of female marital satisfaction. To do so, we must find some number that lies between the extremes of marital satisfaction (10–50) to represent each of the categories (male and female). Since we are dealing with scores, we can use the mean (arithmetic average) to represent each category. We can calculate the mean by simply adding all the male scores and dividing that sum by the number of males in the sample $(42 + 37 + 48 + 41 + 37+ . . . . / 94 = 42.35)$ Then we do the same for the females. This gives us a mean value for males (42.35) and a mean value for females (38.75). We now have a way to describe the difference between males and females in their level of marital satisfaction.

You've heard the saying that "a picture is worth a thousand words." That's also true with data analysis. If we describe our analysis with charts, graphs, or figures, the reader is more likely to see and understand what we are trying to communicate. The following figure is one way to visualize our results.

Marital Satisfaction Scale

Charts and graphs are helpful in visualizing how sex and marital satisfaction are related. While there are several types of charts or graphs (e.g., bar, pie, line) that visually describe data, the bar chart is a popular choice for a problem like ours. The bar chart that follows presents the same analysis as the preceding figure, but the visual presentation is more appealing to some people.

This chart was created in Microsoft Word by clicking on *insert*, then clicking on *chart*. There are many options in the chart selection. Both of the graphic displays above allow the reader to visualize the difference between males and females as it is depicted on the marital satisfaction scale.

While we have done a good job of *describing* the association between sex and marital satisfaction, it's important to understand that we cannot make an inference or decision about this association without the application of inferential or probability statistics. Both visual presentations clearly indicate that males scored higher than females in marital satisfaction, but without the application of probability to this difference, we cannot determine if it is really due to the sex of the respondents or to chance.

Our example shows that charts and figures are helpful tools in describing data. The remaining identifier variables on this questionnaire can be described in the same manner.

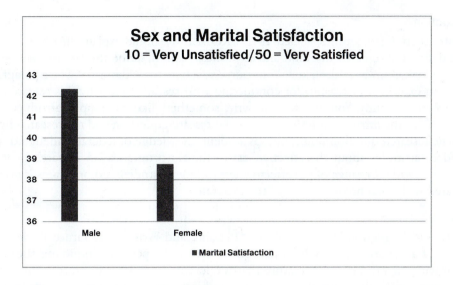

The Elements of a Sociological Survey Paper

A sociological survey paper is composed of five essential parts:

1. Title page
2. Abstract
3. Text
4. References
5. Appendices

1. *Title page*. The title page should follow the directions given in Chapter 3. The title of a sociological survey paper should provide the reader with two types of information: the subject matter of the survey and the population being surveyed. Examples of titles for papers based on in-class surveys are "University of South Carolina Student Opinions on Welfare Reform," "Middlebury College Student Attitudes about Sexual Harassment," and "The 2000 Presidential Election: Ohio University Student Opinions on a Recount in Florida."

2. *Abstract*. Abstracts for a sociological survey paper should follow the directions given in Chapter 3. In approximately 150–200 words, the abstract should summarize the subject, methodology, and results of the survey. An abstract for the example used in this chapter might be like the one presented in Chapter 3 on page 70.

3. *Text*. The text of the paper should include five sections:

1. Introduction
2. Literature review
3. Methodology
4. Results
5. Discussion

Introduction

The introduction (sometimes labeled THE PROBLEM) should explain the purpose of your paper, define the research question and hypothesis, and describe the circumstances under which the research was undertaken. Your purpose statement will normally be a paragraph in which you explain your reasons for conducting your research and why this research problem is worthy of study. You may want to write something like the sample introduction that follows. Next, the introduction should state the research question and the research hypotheses. The research question might be, "Is student knowledge of federal student aid related to student attitudes about the effectiveness of the aid programs?" A research hypothesis might be, "Student ratings of the effectiveness of federal student aid programs is positively correlated with student knowledge of the programs."

Literature Review

As stated in the section in this book on "Reading and Writing Literature Reviews," the purpose of a literature review is to demonstrate that the person conducting the study is familiar with the professional literature that is relevant to the survey and to summarize the content of that literature for the reader. The subject matter of the survey may be gender discrimination in secondary education programs. In this case, the purpose of the literature review would be to briefly inform your readers about (1) the history, content, and social implications of gender differences in secondary educational programs; and (2) the current status of discriminatory practices. In providing this information you should cite appropriate documents, such as previous studies on the subject. If the research paper is using inferential statistics to test certain hypotheses, then only professional sources from academic journals should be cited in the literature review.

Sample Introduction

University students often have problems discovering financial aid programs, and, once such programs are identified, accessing channels to apply for funds. The purpose of this paper is to define Howard University student attitudes toward federal student aid programs. In particular, this study seeks to understand how students view the criteria for aid eligibility and the efficiency of application procedures. Further, the survey is expected to indicate the amount of knowledge students have about the federal student aid process. The primary reason for conducting this study is that the results will provide a basis for identifying problems in the aid application and disbursement process, and facilitate discussion among administrative officers and students about solutions to problems that are identified.

Methodology

The methodology (sometimes labeled DESIGN) section of your paper describes how you designed and conducted your study. It should also briefly describe the format and content of the questionnaire: How many questions were asked? What kinds of questions (open, closed, etc.) were asked, and why these formats were selected? It should explain how each variable in the survey was *operationalized* or measured—how were the *instruments* or *scales* created? The methodology section should also briefly address the statistical procedures used in data analysis: What statistical methods are used? Why were they selected? What information are these procedures intended to provide? (Some studies include this information in the Results section.) Finally, the methodology section should explain how the *sample* was drawn and what *population* is being sampled—who are the *participants* and what *procedures* were utilized to obtain the sample?

Results

The results (sometimes labeled FINDINGS) section of your paper should present the findings of your study. Here, you report the results of your statistical calculations. Raw data should not be included. The descriptive statistics you create from the data should be presented in tables and/or charts like the examples above. Interpret the results as they relate to your hypotheses. Remember, hypotheses can only be accepted or rejected through the application of decision-making/inferential statistics. Allow your descriptive statistics to assist you in determining the accuracy of the hypothesis, but avoid statements that bring finality to your conclusion unless you are utilizing probability statistics to aid you in your decision making.

Discussion

In your discussion (sometimes labeled CONCLUSIONS) section, draw out the implications of your findings: What is the meaning of the results of your study? How do the results of your study relate to those you described in your review of literature section? What conclusions can you draw? What questions remain unanswered? At the end of this section, provide the reader with suggestions for further research that are derived from your research findings.

4. *References.* Your references and source citations in the text should be completed according to *ASA* guidelines, which were presented in a preceding section of this book. If your instructor is using the article format referred to in the Formats section presented in a preceding part of this book, you should double-space after the last line of the discussion section of your survey paper and type "REFERENCES" in all caps. Double-space again and begin listing your references. Some instructors prefer a separate page for the references. In this case, insert a page break and type "REFERENCES" at the top of the page, double-space, and list your sources. Remember that, as stated in the *ASA* guidelines section of this manual, only those sources cited in the paper can be included in the reference section, and all reference listings must be cited somewhere in the paper.

5. *Appendices.* See the Formats section of this book for further guidelines on including appendices at the end of the paper. The only thing that must be included in an appendix for a sociological survey paper is a copy of the questionnaire used in the study, like the example at the end of the Formats section. Other material that might be appropriate for inclusion in a survey paper appendix includes:

- Tables or charts of survey data not sufficiently important to be included in the text but helpful for reference.
- Summaries of survey data from national or regional surveys on the same subject, if such surveys are available and discussed in your text.

Now that you have learned about survey research design, find a sociological article that used this approach to quantitative research, maybe in a professional journal or a book of sociological articles, and see if what you have learned helps you read and understand the material. If questions arise while you are reading the article, refer back to sections above to help you find the answers. Remember that you probably won't be doing this type of research until your senior year, so don't be too hard on yourself if everything isn't clear and understandable. Becoming a sociology researcher takes time and practice. When you actually design and conduct a quantitative survey study of your own, the things you read above will make a lot more sense. So onward and upward, and remember that the pursuit of truth will set you free from the shackles of dogmatism.

6.5   CRITIQUE AN ACADEMIC ARTICLE

In sociology, we utilize articles from academic journals for many of the papers we write. Both quantitative and qualitative research usually review the available literature in the area they are researching. An *article critique* evaluates an article published in an academic journal. A good critique tells the reader what point the article is trying to make and how convincingly it makes this point. Writing an article critique achieves three purposes. First, it provides you with an understanding of the information contained in a scholarly article and a familiarity with other information written on the same topic. Second, it provides an opportunity to apply and develop your critical thinking skills as you attempt to critically evaluate the work of a sociologist. Third, it helps you to improve your own writing skills as you attempt to describe the selected article's strengths and weaknesses so that your readers can clearly understand them.

Read&Write 6.5   Critique a Recent Article from a Sociology Journal

The first step in writing an article critique is to select an appropriate article. Unless your instructor specifies otherwise, select an article from a scholarly sociological journal, e.g., *American Journal of Sociology*, *American Sociological Review*, *Sociological Quarterly*, *Social Forces*, or *Free Inquiry in Creative Sociology*, to mention a few, and not a popular or journalistic publication like *Time*, *Newsweek*, or the *National Review*. Your instructor may also accept appropriate articles from academic journals in other disciplines, such as history, political science, or criminal justice.

Three other considerations should guide your choice of an article. First, browse article titles until you find a topic that interests you. Writing a critique will be much more satisfying if you have an interest in the topic. Hundreds of interesting journal articles are published every year. The following is a list of the articles that appear in the November 2015 issue of the *American Journal of Sociology*:

- John-Paul Ferguson, "The Control of Managerial Discretion: Evidence from Unionization's Impact on Employment Segregation."
- Maria Abascal and Delia Baldassarri, "Love Thy Neighbor? Ethnoracial Diversity and Trust Reexamined."
- Bernice A. Pescosolido, Jack K. Martin, Sigrun Olafsdottir, J. Scott Long, Karen Kafadar, and Medina Tait, "The Theory of Industrial Society and Cultural Schemata: Does the 'Cultural Myth of Stigma' Underlie the WHO Schizophrenia Paradox?"

- Josh Pacewicz, "Playing the Neoliberal Game: Why Community Leaders Left Party Politics to Partisan Activists."
- Elizabeth H. Boyle, Wesley Longhofer, and Kim Minzee, "Abortion Liberalization in World Society, 1960–2009."
- Guang Guo, Yi Li, Hongyu Wang, Tianji Cai, and Greg J. Duncan, "Peer Influence, Genetic Propensity, and Binge Drinking: A Natural Experiment and a Replication."[12]

The second consideration in selecting an article is your current level of knowledge. Many sociology studies, for example, employ sophisticated statistical techniques. You may be better prepared to evaluate them if you have studied statistics.

The third consideration is to select a current article, one written within the 12 months prior to making your selection. Much of the material in sociology is quickly superseded by new studies. Selecting a recent study will help ensure that you will be engaged in an up-to-date discussion of your topic.

Once you have selected and carefully read your article, you may begin to write your critique, which should cover the following four areas:

1. Thesis

2. Methods

3. Evidence

4. Evaluation

Thesis

Your first task is to find and clearly state the thesis of the article. The thesis is the main point the article is trying to make. In a 1998 article in *Free Inquiry in Creative Sociology*, Professors Cynthia Y. A. Jacob-Chien of the University of Northern Iowa and Richard L. Dukes of the University of Colorado at Colorado Springs examine "Understanding Adolescent Work in Social and Behavioral Contexts." In this article, Jacob-Chien and Dukes state their thesis in the introduction:

Traditional explanations of crime and delinquency imply that adolescent work is a useful control mechanism. . . . [Some] theories appear to overlook the notion that the workplace can be an environment that displays significant sources of deviant activities. We expect that . . . *work intensity will have a negative effect on well-being and academics and a facilitating effect on delinquent and substance use behavior.*[13] (*Italics ours*)

Sometimes the thesis is more difficult to ascertain. Do you have to hunt for the thesis of the article? Comment about the clarity of the author's thesis presentation, and state the author's thesis in your own paper. Before proceeding with the remaining elements of your paper, consider the importance of the topic. Has the author of the article written something that is important for sociology students or professionals to read?

---

[12] "Table of Contents." 2015. *AJS: American Journal of Sociology* 121(3). Retrieved March 28, 2016 (https://www.jstor.org/stable/10.1086/681062).

[13] Cynthia Y. A. Jacob-Chien and Richard L. Dukes. 1998. "Understanding Adolescent Work in Social and Behavioral Contexts." *Free Inquiry in Creative Sociology* 26(1):23.

Methods

What methods did the author use to investigate the topic? In other words, how did the author go about supporting the thesis? In your critique, carefully answer the following two questions: First, were appropriate methods used? In other words, did the author's approach to supporting the thesis make sense? Second, did the author employ the selected methods correctly? Did you discover any errors in the way he conducted his research?

Evidence

In your critique, answer the following questions: What evidence did the author present in support of the thesis? What are the strengths of the evidence presented by the author? What are the weaknesses of the evidence presented? On balance, how well did the author support the thesis?

Evaluation

In this section, summarize your evaluation of the article. Tell your readers several things. Who will benefit from reading this article? What will the benefit be? How important and extensive is that benefit? What is your evaluation of the article? What suggestions do you have for repeating this study or one like it? Your evaluation might begin like this:

In their article on "Abortion Liberalization in World Society, 1960–2009," Elizabeth Boyle, Wesley Longhofer, and Minzee Kim examine the spread of abortion liberalization policies from 1960 to 2009 by conducting an event history analysis. They identify three dominant frames: a women's rights frame; a medical frame; and a religious, natural family frame. Among these competing frames, the indicators of a scientific, medical frame show the strongest consistent association with policy liberalization that specifies acceptable grounds for abortion. Their findings are very important in the quest to better understand what influences global abortion policies.[14]

6.6   WRITE A BOOK REVIEW

Successful book reviews answer three questions:

- What does the writer of the book try to communicate?
- How clearly and convincingly does he or she get this message across to the reader?
- Is the message worth reading?

Capable book reviewers of several centuries have answered these three questions well. People who read a book review want to know if a particular book is worth reading, for their own particular purposes, before buying or reading it. These potential readers want to know the book's subject and its strengths and weaknesses, and they want to gain this information as easily and quickly as possible. Your goal in writing a book review, therefore, is to help people efficiently decide whether to buy or read a book. Your immediate objectives may be to please your instructor and get a good grade, but you are most likely to meet these objectives if you focus on a book review's

---

[14] Elizabeth H. Boyle, Minzee Kim, and Wesley Longhofer. 2015. "Abortion Liberalization in World Society." *AJS: American Journal of Sociology* 121(3):882–913.

audience: people who want help in selecting books to buy or read. In the process of writing a book review that reaches this primary goal, you will also:

- Learn about the book you are reviewing
- Learn about professional standards for book reviews in sociology
- Learn the essential steps of book reviewing that apply to any academic discipline

This final objective, learning to review a book properly, has more applications than you may at first imagine. First, it helps you to focus quickly on the essential elements of a book, and to draw from a book its informational value for yourself and others. Some of the most successful people in government, business, and the professions speed-read several books a week, more for the knowledge they contain than for enjoyment. These readers then apply this knowledge to substantial advantage in their professions. It is normally not wise to speed-read a book you are reviewing because you are unlikely to gain enough information to evaluate it fairly from such a fast reading. Writing book reviews, however, helps you become proficient in quickly sorting out valuable information from material that is not. The ability to make such discriminations is a fundamental ingredient in management and professional success.

In addition, writing book reviews for publication allows you to participate in the discussions of the broader intellectual and professional community of which you are a part. People in law, medicine, teaching, engineering, administration, and other fields are frequently asked to write book reviews to help others assess newly released publications.

Before beginning your book review, read the following sample. It is Gregory M. Scott's review of *Political Islam: Revolution, Radicalism, or Reform?*, edited by John L. Esposito. The review appeared in volume 26 of the *Southeastern Political Science Review* (June 1998) and is reprinted here by permission. It is included in this chapter because the book contains both sociological and political topics, and because its topic, thesis, and findings are still highly salient.

Behold an epitaph for the specter of monolithically autocratic Islam. In its survey of Islamic political movements from Pakistan to Algeria, *Political Islam: Revolution, Radicalism, or Reform?* effectively lays to rest the popular notion that political expressions of Islam are inherently violent and authoritarian. For this accomplishment alone John L. Esposito and company's scholarly anthology merits the attention of serious students of religion and politics, and justifies the book's own claim to making a "seminal contribution." Although it fails to identify how Islam as religious faith and cultural tradition lends Muslim politics a distinctively Islamic flavor, this volume clearly answers the question posed by its title: yes, political Islam encompasses not only revolution and radicalism, but moderation and reform as well.

Although two of the eleven contributors are historians, *Political Islam* exhibits both the strengths and weaknesses of contemporary political science with respect to religion. It identifies connections between economics and politics, and between culture and politics, much better than it deciphers the nuances of the relationships between politics and religious belief. After a general introduction, the first three articles explore political Islam as illegal opposition, first with a summary of major movements and then with studies of Algeria and the Gulf states. In her chapter titled "Fulfilling Prophecies: State Policy and Islamist Radicalism," Lisa Anderson sets a methodological guideline for the entire volume when she writes:

Rather than look to the substance of Islam or the content of putatively Islamic political doctrines for a willingness to embrace violent means to desired ends, we might explore a different perspective and examine the political circumstances, or institutional environment, that breeds political radicalism, extremism, or violence independent of the content of the doctrine (18).

Therefore, rather than assessing how Islam as religion affects Muslim politics, all the subsequent chapters proceed to examine politics, economics, and culture in a variety of Muslim nations. This means that the title of the book is slightly misleading: it discusses Muslim politics rather than political Islam. Esposito provides the book's conclusion about the effects of Islamic belief on the political process when he maintains that "the appeal to religion is a two-edged sword. . . . It can provide or enhance self-legitimation, but it can also be used as a yardstick for judgment by opposition forces and delegitimation" (70).

The second part of the volume features analyses of the varieties of political processes in Iran, Sudan, Egypt, and Pakistan. These chapters clearly demonstrate not only that Islamic groups may be found in varied positions on normal economic and ideological spectrums, but also that Islam is not necessarily opposed to moderate, pluralist politics. The third section of the anthology examines the international relations of Hamas, Afghani Islamists, and Islamic groups involved in the Middle East peace process. These chapters are especially important for American students because they present impressive documentation for the conclusions that the motives and demands of many Islamic groups are considerably more moderate and reasonable than much Western political commentary would suggest.

The volume is essentially well written. All the articles with the exception of chapter two avoid unnecessarily dense political science jargon. As a collection of methodologically sound and analytically astute treatments of Muslim politics, *Political Islam: Revolution, Radicalism, or Reform?* is certainly appropriate for adoption as a supplemental text for courses in religion and politics. By way of noting what it does not cover, readers may consider that although it is sufficient for its purposes as it stands, the volume could be a primary text in a course on Islamic politics if it included four additional chapters:

1. An historical overview of the origins and varieties of Islam as religion
2. A summary of the global Islamic political–ideological spectrum (from liberal to fundamentalist)
3. An overview of the varieties of global Islamic cultures
4. An attempt to describe in what manner, if any, Islam, in all its varieties, gives politics a different flavor from the politics of other major religions.[15]

Elements of a Book Review

Your first sentence should entice people to read your review. A crisp summary of what the book is about entices your readers because it lets them know that you can quickly and clearly come to the point. They know that their time and effort will not be wasted

---

[15] Gregory M. Scott. 1998. Review of *Political Islam: Revolution, Radicalism, or Reform?* Ed. John L. Esposito. *Southeastern Political Review* 26(2):512–24.

in an attempt to wade through your vague prose in hopes of finding out something about the book. Notice Scott's opening line: "Behold an epitaph for the specter of monolithically autocratic Islam." It is a bit overburdened with large words, but it is engaging and precisely sums up the essence of the review. Your opening statement can be engaging and catchy, but be sure that it provides an accurate portrayal of the book in one crisp statement.

Your book review should allow the reader to join you in examining the book. Tell the reader what the book is about. One of the greatest strengths of Scott's review is that his first paragraph immediately tells you exactly what he thinks the book accomplishes.

When you review a book, write about what is actually in the book, not what you think is probably there or ought to be there. Do not explain how you would have written the book, but instead how the author wrote it. Describe the book in clear, objective terms. Tell enough about the content to identify the author's major points.

Clarify the book's value and contribution to sociology by defining (1) what the author is attempting to do and (2) how the author's work fits within current similar efforts in the discipline of sociology or scholarly inquiry in general. Notice how Scott immediately describes what Esposito is trying to do: "This volume clearly answers the question posed by its title." Scott precedes this definition of the author's purpose by placing his work within the context of current similar writing in his field by stating that "for this accomplishment alone John L. Esposito and company's scholarly anthology merits the attention of serious students of religion and politics, and justifies the book's own claim to making a 'seminal contribution.'"

The elucidation portion of book reviews often provides additional information about the author. Scott has not included such information about Esposito in his review, but it would be helpful to know, for example, if Esposito has written other books on the subject, has developed a reputation for exceptional expertise on a certain issue, or is known to have a particular ideological bias. How would your understanding of this book be changed, for example, if you knew that its author were a leader of ISIS or the Taliban? (He isn't.) Include information in your book review about the author that helps the reader understand how this book fits within the broader concerns of the discipline.

Once you explain what the book is attempting to do, you should tell the reader the extent to which this goal has been met. To evaluate a book effectively, you will need to establish evaluation criteria and then compare the book's content to those criteria. You do not need to define your criteria specifically in your review, but they should be evident to the reader. Your criteria will vary according to the book you are reviewing, and you may discuss them in any order that is helpful to the reader. Consider, however, including the following among the criteria that you establish for your book review:

- How important is the subject to the field of study, which is the book's focus?
- How complete and thorough is the author's coverage of the subject?
- How carefully is the author's analysis conducted?
- What are the strengths and limitations of the author's methodology?
- What is the quality of the writing? Is it clear, precise, and interesting?
- How does this book compare with others on the subject?
- What contribution does this book make to its discipline (its field of study)?
- Who will enjoy or benefit from this book?

When giving your evaluations according to these criteria, be specific. If you write, "This is a good book; I liked it very much," you say nothing of interest or value to the reader. Notice, however, how Scott's review helps to clearly define the content and the limitations of the book by contrasting the volume with what he describes as an ideal primary text for a course in Islamic politics: "By way of noting what it does not cover, readers may consider that although it is sufficient for its purposes as it stands, the volume could be a primary text in a course on Islamic politics if it included four additional chapters."

Read&Write 6.6 Review a New Sociology Book

Format and Content
The directions for writing papers provided in Chapters 1 through 3 apply to book reviews as well. Some further instructions specific to book reviews are needed, however. First, list on the title page, along with the standard information required for sociology papers, data on the book being reviewed: title, author, place and name of publisher, date, and number of pages. As the sample that follows shows, the title of the book should be in italics or underlined, but not both:

Reflective or Analytical Book Reviews
Instructors in the humanities and social sciences normally assign two types of book reviews: the *reflective* and the *analytical*. Ask your instructor which type of book review you are to write. The purpose of a reflective book review is for the student reviewer to exercise creative analytical judgment without being influenced by the reviews of others. Reflective book reviews contain all the elements covered in this chapter—enticement, examination, elucidation, and evaluation—but they do not include the views of others who have also read the book.

Analytical book reviews contain all the information provided by reflective reviews but add an analysis of the comments of other reviewers. The purpose is, thus, to review not only the book itself but also its reception in the professional community.

To write an analytical book review, insert a review analysis section immediately after your summary of the book. To prepare this section, use the *Book Review Digest* and *Book Review Index* in the library to locate other reviews of the book that have been published in journals and other periodicals. As you read these reviews:

1. List the criticisms of the book's strengths and weaknesses that are made in the reviews.
2. Develop a concise summary of these criticisms, indicate the overall positive or negative tone of the reviews, and mention some of the most commonly found comments.
3. Evaluate the criticisms found in these reviews. Are they basically accurate in their assessment of the book?
4. Write a review analysis of two pages or less that states and evaluates *steps* 2 and 3 above, and place it in your book review immediately after your summary of the book.

The following is a list of analytical book reviews (done by professional sociologists) that appear in the November 2015 issue of the *American Journal of Sociology*.

- Sassen, Saskia, *Expulsions: Brutality and Complexity of the Global Economy*. Reviewed by Michele Lamont.
- Robinson, William I., *Global Capitalism and the Crisis of Humanity*. Reviewed by Christopher Taylor.

- Ruef, Martin, *Between Slavery and Capitalism: The Legacy of Emancipation in the American South*. Reviewed by Joseph O. Jewell.

Concerning issues of format and length, the directions for writing papers provided in Part I of this manual apply to book reviews as well. Unless your instructor gives you other specifications, a reflective book review should be three to five pages in length, and an analytical book review should be from five to seven pages. In either case, a brief, specific, concise book review is almost always preferred over one of greater length.

6.7   WRITE A LITERATURE REVIEW

When sociologists write research papers, one of their goals is to provide readers an opportunity to increase their understanding of the subject that is being addressed. They want the most current and precise information available. Whether you are writing a traditional library research paper, conducting an experiment or survey, doing an observational study, or preparing an analysis of a policy enforced by a social service agency, you need to know what has already been learned about the subject you are studying. This is a basic necessity to give your readers comprehensive and up-to-date information or to add something new to what is already known about the subject. For example, if your topic is how marital satisfaction is influenced by sex, you will need to survey the professional journals to discover what is already known about this subject. When you seek this information, you will be conducting a *literature review*, a thoughtful collection and analysis of available information on the topic you have selected for study. It tells you, before you begin your experiments or analyses, what is already known in this area.

Why do you need to conduct a literature review? It would be embarrassing to spend a lot of time and effort preparing a study only to find that the information you are seeking has already been discovered by someone else. Also, a properly conducted literature review will tell you many things about a particular subject. It will tell you the extent of current knowledge, sources of data for your research, examples of what is not known about the subject (which generates ideas for formulating hypotheses), methods that have been used for research, and clear definitions of concepts relevant to your own research.

Let's consider an example. Suppose you are enrolled in a political sociology class and have been assigned to research the question: "How are voter attitudes affected by negative advertising?" First, you will need to establish a clear definition of "negative advertising," then find a way to measure attitudes of voters, and finally use or develop a method of discerning how attitudes are affected by advertising. Using research techniques explained in this and other chapters of this manual, you should begin your research by looking for studies that address your research question or similar questions at the library, on the Internet, and through other resources. You will discover that many studies have been written on voters' attitudes and the effects of advertising. As you read these studies, certain patterns will appear. Some research methods will appear to have produced better results than others. Some studies will be quoted in others many times—some confirming and others refuting what previous studies have done. You will constantly be making choices as you examine these studies, reading very carefully ones that are highly relevant to your purposes, and skimming those of only marginal interest. As you read, constantly ask yourself the following questions:

- How much is known about this subject?
- What is the best available information, and why is it better than other information?
- What research methods have been used successfully in relevant studies?
- What are the possible sources of data for further investigation of this topic?
- What important information is still unknown, despite previous research?
- Of the methods that have been used for research, which are the most effective for making new discoveries? Are new methods needed?
- How can the concepts being researched be more precisely defined?

You will find that this process, like the research process as a whole, is recursive: Insights related to one of the above questions will spark new investigations into other insights, which will, in turn, bring up new sets of questions, and so on.

Read&Write 6.7 Write a Sociological Literature Review

Literature reviews can be either a complete product or part of a larger, more comprehensive creation. For example, your instructor may request that you include a literature review as a section of the paper you are writing. Your written literature review may be from one to several pages in length. It should tell the reader:

- The best available information on the selected topic from previously compiled or published studies, articles, or other documents.
- Conclusions reached by these studies about the topic.
- The apparent methodological strengths and weaknesses of these studies.
- A list of any discoveries yet to be made about the topic.
- The most effective methods for developing new information on the topic.

Your literature review should consist of a written narrative that answers, not necessarily consecutively, the above questions. The success of your own research project depends in large part on the extent to which you have carefully and thoughtfully answered these questions.

6.8   ANNOTATED BIBLIOGRAPHIES

What Is an Annotated Bibliography?

A bibliography is, simply, a listing of written items—essays, reviews, books—that share one or more important characteristics: they were all written by the same author, perhaps, or they all deal with the work of a particular author or else focus on a particular field of study. The sort of annotated bibliography we will be dealing within this chapter is a listing and brief description of articles, books, or other sources on a given topic. Depending on the uses for which it is intended, the annotated bibliography may be organized in various ways. For example, if the purpose of the bibliography is to chart the growth and development of critical interest in its topic, then the listed items may appear in chronological order according to the dates when they were first published. Most frequently, however, the items listed in an annotated bibliography are simply organized alphabetically, each one placed either by the last name of its author or, if no author's name is available, by the first important word in its title.

There are usually two components to each item in an annotated bibliography:

- The bibliographical citation, using one of the standard citation systems, such as the MLA system or the ASA system described in Chapter 4.
- The annotation, a brief description or summary (usually 100 to 250 words) of the contents of the source.

Sometimes the annotation attempts to be strictly objective in nature, meaning that it only describes the contents and purpose of the source without offering an opinion as to its quality. Scholars in some disciplines refer to this type of objective annotation as an *abstract*. Another type of annotation offers a brief assessment or appraisal of the source in addition to a description. We'll call this type an *evaluative annotation*.

Annotated bibliographies are usually limited to a specific theme, area, topic, or discipline. Taken together, the annotations provide a lucid and balanced account or synopsis of the state of research on its subject.

Why Write an Annotated Bibliography?

The purpose for writing an annotated bibliography can differ with the audience and the assignment. It might be a project in a course you are taking or a requirement for research in the organization or agency for which you work. (Your supervisor or colleagues may wish to know more about a particular topic.) Depending on the assignment, the annotated bibliography may serve a number of purposes, such as:

To review the literature on a particular subject

- To illustrate the quality of your research
- To give your research historical perspective
- To illustrate the types of sources available in a given area
- To describe other items relating to a topic of interest to the reader
- To explore a particular subject for further research

Who Uses Annotated Bibliographies?

One of the great benefits of an annotated bibliography is that it saves time for those who consult it. Since extensive and scholarly annotated bibliographies provide a comprehensive overview of material published on a topic, they can give both researchers and practitioners a swift impression of the types of research already conducted on that topic, as well as a notion of the types of research left to do. An annotated bibliography can make researchers aware of articles or books they should read to advance their own research. Practitioners can scrutinize annotated bibliographies rapidly to see what new research their colleagues have conducted or what new practices have been developed in their fields and whether it would be worth their time to locate and read the entire article or book annotated.

But there is another important use for annotated bibliographies written by students. There are few ways of developing the descriptive and analytical skills needed in most scholarly disciplines more effectively than by compiling and writing an annotated bibliography. By summarizing and evaluating articles on a particular topic you are both learning valuable information about that topic and gaining confidence in assimilating and connecting facts the way scholars do. You are gaining mastery of the material and the mental processes that comprise your discipline.

Read&Write 6.8   Write an Annotated Bibliography

What Is the Content of an Annotated Bibliography?

The specific structure and approach to writing an annotated bibliography may vary with the professional community for which you are writing it. For example, in some situations an annotated bibliography may have an introductory paragraph or two in order to define its audience, purpose, rationale, and topic. In other situations, it may not. Here are a list and description of the most commonly found elements of an annotated bibliography:

Introduction. In addition to defining your audience and expressing your purpose, your introduction should also describe the scope of your bibliography (the specific areas or types of works upon which you are focusing) and explain the reasons why you have limited your exploration to these parameters. It is also important to let your reader know clearly what kind of annotations you are providing, whether objective or evaluative. If you say your annotations are objective, then you are telling your reader that every opinion or theory expressed in each annotation belongs to the source and its author. If, however, the annotation is evaluative, then at least some of the material in it expresses *your* opinion about the quality of the source, an opinion that the writer might not share. You must not let your reader think that every opinion or theory expressed in the annotation belongs to the source when, in fact, that is not the case.

Citations. Like a regular (unannotated) bibliography or a works cited page at the end of a research paper, an annotated bibliography provides a full bibliographic entry for each source it lists. Make sure you follow a bibliographical format approved by your instructor or by the publication for which you are writing. Chapter 4 of this manual gives guidelines for the ASA system of bibliography.

Annotations. For most annotated bibliographies, the annotations should be one or two paragraphs that together range from about 100 to 250 words. To some extent, the conventions of the professional community in which you are writing will dictate the contents of your annotations, as well as your specific purpose and audience. If you are writing your annotated bibliography for a course, your instructor will provide guidelines. It can be helpful to your reader for you to establish a consistent form for your annotations, perhaps beginning each time with a clear statement of the source's thesis, then a brief description of the argument used to prove or justify that thesis, followed, if required, by your evaluation of the work's value and achievement.

To quote or not to quote? How much of your annotation should be direct quoting as opposed to your own wording? This is an important question to address, and one whose answer depends to a large extent on the uses you project for your bibliography. Importing the thesis sentence directly from the source, for example, may help you to be accurate about the source's purpose—but it may also establish a tone or a level of complex reasoning that the rest of a brief annotation cannot sustain. You do not want to give the impression that you are merely pasting together passages from the source without having thoroughly understood them yourself. Remember: while the style and tone of the source belong to the source's author, the style and tone of the annotation belong to you. You want your annotation, though it is small, to have the coherence and confidence of a well-made paragraph.

Depending on your project or assignment, your annotations may provide one or more of the following:

Summation: As stated above, while *some* annotations offer evaluative comments, *most* annotations summarize the source. Here is a tip about summarizing: Although it is logical, when summarizing, to ask yourself what the source is about, it is rarely a good gambit to begin a brief annotation with the phrase, "This source is about . . . ." Why not? Because a sentence beginning with these words cannot help but end with a generalization about the source's subject that will be vaguer than a simple restatement of the source's thesis.

Here are introductory sentences from two objective annotations of the same source. Which sentence more effectively sets up the rest of the annotation?

Wilson's article is about racial profiling and how it is misused in school counseling programs.

Wilson argues that racial profiling should be prohibited in school counseling programs because it results in preferential treatment for certain minorities at the expense of others.

Sentence one establishes the *topic* of the source, but sentence two establishes the *thesis*, which is a more comprehensive and necessary task.

After relating the thesis of the source, you might describe such elements as methodology, results, and conclusions. The required length of the annotations will determine how detailed your summary should be.

Evaluation: Your assignment may require you to include a brief critique or appraisal in each annotation. If you are writing evaluative annotations, ask yourself the following questions: What is the overall goal of this source? Does the source achieve its goal? Do you find the contents of the source useful in relation to your own research? How does the source compare with other sources in your bibliography? Is the information reliable? How biased is it?

Reflection. If you are compiling this annotated bibliography to facilitate your own research project, you will probably want to examine the perspective taken in each source to ascertain how it fits into your research on the topic. The perspective could be a political one (liberal or conservative), a subject-matter perspective (sociological, psychological, medical, etc.), or some other perspective. It might help to point out similarities or contradictions between sources. For example, you might say, "Like Monroe, Jones approaches racial profiling from a sociological perspective. However, while Monroe focuses on how law enforcement has used racial profiling to increase the probability of arrests, Jones analyzes the practice of businesses profiling Blacks to apprehend shoplifters." You might then want to reflect on how this source has changed how you think about your topic and how it fits into your research project.

The following sample short-version annotated bibliography is fictitious. It describes articles that might be written on racial profiling. The annotations in this example are like abstracts, since they are summative and contain no evaluative component.

Annotated Bibliography

Racial Profiling

Arnold, Eugene H. 2015. "Terrorism and Racial Profiling." *Journal of International Terrorism* 17(3): 510–518.

    Arnold believes that the use of racial profiling to help control terrorist activities is both justified and necessary. Applying a random intervention policy wastes precious time investigating those with little potential for terrorism, while allowing those most likely to put others in harms way—middle eastern, Muslim males between 15 and 29 years of age—to avoid careful examination.

Jones, William B. 2015. "Targeting Blacks in Shoplifting Surveillance: Unjust and Inaccurate." *Social Issues* 26(2): 37–45.

    Jones argues that while racial profiling of shoplifters by major department stores is an unjust practice, the process also fails to target those most likely to shoplift. No data exists that supports the probability that blacks are more likely to shoplift than other racial groups. Targeting blacks in surveillance procedures only increases the opportunity to catch those blacks that shoplift and improves the chances of success for whites that shoplift.

Monroe, Victor G. 2015. "Using Racial Profiling to Impede the Trafficking of Illicit Drugs." *Drug Enforcement Bulletin*, August 14, 42–45.

    Using racial profiling to impede drug trafficking, contends Monroe, is not a good way to decrease the flow of illicit drugs in the United States. Race should never be a factor in probable cause, and the harm done from this practice far outweighs any perceived benefit. He supports applying legal sanctions to those practicing racial profiling to catch drug traffickers.

    Here are longer, abstract-type annotations for the same sample articles.

Annotated Bibliography

Racial Profiling

Arnold, Eugene H. 2015. "Terrorism and Racial Profiling." *Journal of International Terrorism* 17(3): 510–518.

    Arnold believes that the use of racial profiling to help control terrorist activities is both justified and necessary. Applying a random intervention policy wastes precious time by focusing on those with little potential for terrorism, while allowing those most likely to put others in harm's way—middle eastern, Muslim males between 15 and 29 years of age—to avoid careful examination. Arnold constructs a three-part defense of his position, establishing first the legal argument for racially geared anti-terrorist policies, then the economic argument and, finally, what he calls the moral argument. Borrowing heavily on scripture from both the Old Testament and the Koran in the last third of the article, Arnold defines a religious imperative for racial profiling that, he admits, will not be to everyone's taste but that may provide direction and control for a problem that threatens to spiral out of control.

Jones, William B. 2015. "Targeting Blacks in Shoplifting Surveillance: Unjust and Inaccurate." *Social Issues* 26(2): 37–45.

    Jones argues that while racial profiling of shoplifters by major department stores is an unjust practice, the process also fails to target those most likely to shoplift. No data exists that supports the probability that blacks are more likely to shoplift than other racial groups. Targeting blacks in surveillance procedures only increases the opportunity to catch those blacks that shoplift and improves the chances of success for whites that shoplift. Jones takes issue with Elsner and Squires, whose study published in the June 2002 *Journal of Crime and Criminology* supports racial profiling on the basis of its cost effectiveness. While Jones concedes that targeting a single race reduces the cost to businesses by allowing them to streamline their security operations, he argues that this cost-effectiveness is offset by the increase in white shoplifting. Instead of using racial profiling, Jones recommends that businesses invest in more extensive human relations training for security personnel.

Monroe, Victor G. 2015. "Using Racial Profiling to Impede the Trafficking of Illicit Drugs." *Drug Enforcement Bulletin*, August 14, 42–45.

Using racial profiling to impede drug trafficking, contends Monroe, is not a good way to decrease the flow of illicit drugs in the United States. Race should never be a factor in probable cause, and the harm done from this practice far outweighs any perceived benefit. Monroe supports this argument by discussing recent, disastrous attempts of government agencies in six different countries to base a drug interdiction policy on data regarding race. While two of the six countries, the Netherlands and Luxembourg, reported a slight drop in the importation of marijuana and cocaine during their interdiction campaigns, all six of the countries eventually abandoned racial profiling for two reasons: the legal tangle it caused in the courts and the negative effect such profiling had on race relations within each country. Monroe provides information charting the effects of racially based drug policing programs on morale and social and economic development among minority populations in the United States. A former state attorney-general, Monroe concludes with an argument supporting the application of legal sanctions against those practicing racial profiling to catch drug traffickers.

7

PRELIMINARY SCHOLARSHIP
Research Effectively

7.1 INSTITUTE AN EFFECTIVE RESEARCH PROCESS

Your skills as an interpreter of details, an organizer of facts and theories, and a writer of prose come together in a research paper. Building logical arguments on the basis of fact and hypothesis is a way of achieving things in sociology, and mastering the art of research makes one a successful sociologist.

Students new to the writing of research papers are sometimes intimidated by the job ahead of them. After all, writing a research paper is adding an extra set of complexities to the writing process. Just like an expository or persuasive paper, a research paper must present an original thesis that has a carefully organized and logical argument. The writer sometimes has to write on a topic that is extrinsic to his or her own experience. This means that writers must locate and evaluate information that is new and in the process educate themselves as they explore their topics. Sometimes, a budding researcher may be overwhelmed by the basic requirements of the assignment or by the authority of the source material being investigated.

Initially, it may be difficult to establish control over the different tasks that you are undertaking in a research project. You may have little notion of where to search for a thesis or even for the most helpful information. If you do not carefully monitor your work habits, you may end up being irresponsible with your paper's argument by borrowing it wholesale from one or more sources.

Who is in control of your paper? The answer must be "you"—not the instructor who assigned you the paper, and certainly not the published writers and interviewees whose opinions you solicit. Your paper has little use if all it presents is the opinions of others. You must synthesize an original idea by judiciously evaluating your source material. Initially, you will, of course, be unsure of the elements of your paper. For example, you may not yet have a definitive thesis sentence or a clear understanding of the shape of your argument. But you can establish control over the process involved in completing the paper. Your sense of control grows if you work regularly and systematically, welcoming new ideas as they present themselves. Some suggestions to help you establish and maintain control of your paper:

1. **Understand your assignment**. A research assignment can sometimes go bad just because the writer did not read the assignment carefully. Considering the time and effort you are investing in your project, you must ensure that you have a clear understanding of what your instructor wants you to do. Ask your instructor about any aspect of the assignment that is unclear to you—but only after reading it carefully. Recopying the assignment in your own handwriting is a good way to start, even though your instructor has given it to you in writing. Before diving into the project, consider the following questions:

2. **What is your topic?** The assignment may give you a great deal of specific information about your topic, or you may be allowed considerable freedom in establishing one for yourself. In a government class in which you are studying issues affecting American foreign policy, your professor might give you a very specific assignment—a paper, for example, examining the difficulties of establishing a viable foreign policy in the wake of the collapse of international communism—or he or she may allow you to choose for yourself the issue that your paper will address. You need to understand the terms, as set up in the assignment, by which you will design your project.

3. **What is your purpose?** Irrespective of the freedom you have about your topic, pay close attention to the way your instructor has phrased the assignment. Ask if your primary job is to *describe* a current political situation or to *take a stand* on it. Must you *compare* political systems, and if so, to what extent? Must you *classify*, *persuade*, *survey*, or *analyze*? Look for such descriptive terms in the assignment to determine the purpose of your project.

4. **Who is your audience?** Your orientation to the paper is profoundly affected by your conception of the audience for whom you are writing. Of course your main reader is your instructor but check who else would be interested in your paper. Are you writing for the voters of a community, a governor, or a city council? For example, a paper that describes the proposed renovation of city buildings may justifiably contain much more technical jargon for an audience of contractors than for a council of local business and civic leaders.

5. **What kind of research are you doing?** You will be doing one, if not both, of the following kinds of research:

   - *Primary research*, which requires you to discover information firsthand, often by conducting interviews, surveys, or polls. Here, you collect and sift through raw data—not already interpreted by researchers—that you will later study, select, arrange, and speculate on. These raw data may be the opinions of experts or laypersons, historical documents, published letters of a famous politician, or material collected from other researchers. It is important to set up carefully the methods used to collect your data. Your aim must be to gather credible information, from which sound observations may be made later, either by you or by other writers using the material you have uncovered.

- *Secondary research*, which uses published accounts of primary materials. If a primary researcher polls a community for its opinion on the outcome of a recent bond election, the secondary researcher uses the information from the poll to support a particular thesis. In other words, secondary research focuses on interpretations of raw data. Most of your college papers will be based on your use of secondary sources.

Primary Source	Secondary Source
A published collection of Thurgood Marshall's Letters	A journal article arguing that the volume of letters illustrates Marshall's attitude toward the media
An interview with the Mayor	A character study of the mayor based on the interview
Material from a Questionnaire	A paper basing its thesis on the results of the questionnaire

6. **Keep your perspective**. Whichever type of research you perform, you must keep your results in perspective. As a primary researcher, you cannot be completely objective in your findings. It is not possible to design a questionnaire that will net you absolute truth, and it is unsure if the opinions of the people questioned during interviews are accurate and unchanging. Likewise, if you are conducting secondary research, you must remember that the articles and journals you are using are shaped by the aims of their writers, who are interpreting primary materials for their own ends. The farther you are removed from a primary source, the greater the possibility for distortion. As a researcher you must be as accurate as possible, which means keeping in view the limitations of your methods and their ends.

In any research project, there will be moments of confusion; by establishing an effective research procedure, you can prevent the confusion from overwhelming you. Design a schedule that is as systematic as possible, yet flexible enough so that you do not feel trapped by it. By always showing you what to do next, a schedule will help keep you from running into dead ends. At the same time, the schedule helps in retaining the focus necessary to spot new ideas and strategies as you work.

Give Yourself Plenty of Time

You may feel like delaying your research for various reasons: unfamiliarity with the library, the press of other tasks, or a deadline that seems comfortably far away. Never allow such factors to deter you. Research takes time. Working in a library seems to speed up the clock, so that the time you expected it would take you to find a certain source may double. You must allow yourself the time needed not only to find material but also to read it, assimilate it, and set it in the context of your own thoughts. If you delay starting, you may be distracted by the deadline, having to keep an eye on the clock while trying to make sense of a writer's complicated argument.

The following schedule lists the steps of a research project in the order in which they are generally accomplished. Remember that each step is dependent on the others and you may have to revise earlier decisions in light of new discoveries. After some background reading, for example, your notion of the paper's purpose may change, a fact that may in turn alter other steps. One of the strengths of a good schedule is its flexibility. Note that this schedule lists tasks for both primary and secondary research; you must use only those steps that are relevant to your project.

Read&Write 7.1   Write a Research Proposal

Do you aspire to a professional career? entrepreneur? doctor? lawyer? engineer? school principal? professor? nurse? architect? marketing director? Executive Director, nonprofit organization? research director? The ability to write a high-quality research proposal may well be one of the most useful, and profitable skills you acquire on route to your B.A. or B.S. Research proposals are written by the hundreds in public and private agencies and by innovators and entrepreneurs every day. A long-standing motto of entrepreneurs of all sorts is a simple guide to commercial success: "Find a need and fill it." From the light bulb to the iPhone, this principle has been a guiding motivation for thousands of successful inventors, entrepreneurs, CEOs, volunteers, and medical missionaries. Remember that a *need* is both a problem that someone wants to solve and an opportunity for you to make a contribution by solving it.

How does writing a research proposal foster success in this process? Simple. Most new ventures require *funding*. Most sources of funding (government agencies, nonprofit organizations, investors) require you to submit a *plan or feasibility study* that demonstrates: (1) the need for a particular project, (2) the economic viability of the project, and (3) the inclusion of the talent, expertise, and experience needed to successfully undertake the project.

The first step in acquiring funding is a *research proposal* to acquire funds and/or authorization to conduct the research necessary to affirm the need for and feasibility of the project.

Research proposals, therefore, are sales jobs. Their purpose is to "sell" the belief that a research study needs to be done. Before conducting a research study for a government agency, you must convince someone in authority that a study is necessary, by accomplishing the following tasks:

1. Prove that the study is necessary.
2. Describe the objectives of the study.
3. Explain how the study will be done.
4. Describe the resources (time, people, equipment, facilities, etc.) that will be needed to do the job.
5. Construct a schedule that states when the project will begin and end, and gives important dates in between.
6. Prepare a project budget that specifies the financial costs and the amount to be billed (if any) to the government agency.
7. Carefully define what the research project will produce, what kind of study will be conducted, how long it will be, and what it will contain.

The Content of Research Proposals

An Overview

In form, research proposals contain the following four parts:

1. Title page
2. Outline page
3. Text
4. Reference page

An outline of the content of research proposals appears as shown below:

  I. Need for a study

    A. An initial description of the current problem

       1. A definition of the problem
       2. A brief history of problem
       3. The legal framework and institutional setting of the problem
       4. The character of the problem, including its size, extent, and importance

    B. Imperatives

       1. The probable costs of taking no action
       2. The expected benefits of study

  II. Methodology of the proposed study

    A. Project management methods to be used
    B. Research methods to be used
    C. Data analysis methods to be used

 III. Resources necessary to conduct the study

    A. Material resources
    B. Human resources
    C. Financial resources

 IV. Schedule for the study

  V. Budget for the study

 VI. Product of the study

A Note on Research Process and Methods. Your research proposal will briefly describe the steps you will take to find, evaluate, and draw conclusions from the information that is pertinent to your study. The research process normally proceeds in these steps:

1. Data (information) collection: Gathering the appropriate information
2. Data analysis: Organizing the data and determining its meaning or implications
3. Data evaluation: Determining what conclusions may be drawn from the data
4. Recommendation: A concise description of the study that needs to be undertaken

Note on the Anticipated Product of the Study. In the final section of the proposal, you will describe the anticipated product of your study. In other words, you will tell the persons for whom you are writing the proposal exactly what they will receive when the project is done. If you are writing this paper for a class in public, you will probably write something like the following:

> The final product will be a research study from 25 to 30 pages in length, which will provide an analysis of the problem and an evaluation of alternative new policies that may solve the problem.

7.2 ~ EVALUATE THE QUALITY OF ONLINE AND PRINTED INFORMATION

The quote "Winning isn't everything, it's the only thing" may not have originated with Vince Lombardi, famous coach of the Green Bay Packers, but he certainly popularized it. In terms of academic scholarship, it is a bit of an exaggeration to say "Credibility isn't everything; it's the only thing" because the importance of what is written cannot be underestimated. Similarly, as you write sociology scholarship, assume that your work has no value if it lacks credibility. With this in mind, understand that the credibility of your writing depends, more than anything else, on the credibility of your sources. Here, therefore, are some guidelines to assess the credibility of the sources you employ in your paper.

You may have already read the news article appraisal checklist in Section 1.3 of this manual. Almost the same principles apply to both reading other sources of information and reading news articles, but for more complex information sources, the following additional suggestions would be helpful.

Reputation

In general, reputation of information conforms to a clear hierarchy, described here in descending order of credibility. Here is a list of high-quality sources:

- *Articles in academic journals*, though not foolproof, have a huge credibility advantage. They conform to the research and writing standards explained throughout this manual. They often require months, if not years, to write, allowing for revision and refinement. They often employ a team of several authors, each of whom can assess the quality and accuracy of the others' work. Once submitted to a journal for publication, they are distributed (blind) to experts in the articles' topics for review and comment. Once published, they are exposed to widespread readership, providing an additional quality filter.

- *Research studies by recognized think tanks* (research institutes) are often of exceptionally high quality. They are not exposed to the same extent of external review before publication as academic journals, and the institutions that produce them often have a known ideological perspective. Yet whether they are conservative, liberal, or libertarian in orientation, their writers know that the credibility of their work depends on maintaining high-quality consistently.

- *Research studies by government agencies* are much like think tank papers but are likely to be controversial because their findings will always annoy people who are unhappy with their conclusions. They can be very powerful, however, if they are used by presidents or by Congress to adopt particular public policies.

- Reports in high-quality nonpartisan magazines and television journalism are often highly reliable in both research and reporting. Some examples are periodicals such as *The Economist, The Atlantic Monthly, The New Yorker, The American Scholar, Foreign Affairs, Foreign Policy*, and Public Broadcasting Service (PBS) journalism in features such as *Frontline* and *The American Experience*.
- Articles in high-quality newspapers, such as the *New York Times, Wall Street Journal, Washington Post*, and the *Christian Science Monitor* cite authoritative sources.
- Pieces in high-quality partisan magazines such as *The Nation* and *The National Review* can provide relatively reliable, if slanted and selective information.

Low-quality sources are of several sorts, and all are to be read for quickly secured unverified "facts" and amusement rather than education. Here are some low-quality sources:

- *Wikipedia* provides much information quickly, and some tolerable overviews of topics, but is notoriously vulnerable to people who provide unverified and even false information.
- Partisan blogs, such as the *Huffington Post* are fun and provide an interesting array of perspectives and insights, but any information you find on them must be verified by more credible sources.
- Commercial TV news sources, such as CNN and especially Fox News are so sensational and clearly biased that their value is little more than entertainment.

As with newspapers, the following elements of information sources are essential to assessing content quality:

- *Author*. What are the credentials and reputation of the author of the publication?
- *Information sources*. What sources of information are used by the author of a particular article? Are they recognized individuals or institutions?
- *Writing quality*. Is the article well written? Is it clear and cogent? Does it use a lot of jargon? Can you understand it?
- *Quantity of information*. Is the article sufficiently comprehensive to substantiate its thesis?
- *Unsupported assumptions*. Beware of statements like this: "Statistics prove that hospitals in urban areas provide better care than rural facilities." What statistics? Does the article identify them?
- *Balance*. Does the article cover all relevant aspects of a subject?

Develop a Working Bibliography

As you begin your research, you will look for published sources—essays, books, or interviews with experts—that may help you. This list of potentially useful sources is your *working bibliography*. There are many ways to develop this bibliography. The cataloging system in your library gives you sources, as will the published bibliographies in your field. (Some of these bibliographies are listed below.) The general references used for your background reading may also list such works, and each specialized book or essay will have a bibliography that its writer used, which may be helpful to you.

It is from your working bibliography that you will select the items for the bibliography that will appear in the final draft of your paper. Early in your research, you will not know which of the sources will help you and which will not; therefore, it is important to keep an accurate description of each entry in your working bibliography so that you can tell clearly which items you have investigated and which you will need to consult again. Establish your working bibliography in the bibliographical format you are required to follow in your final draft. Ensure that all the information about each of your potential sources is in the proper format and punctuation. (Chapter 3 describes in detail the bibliographical formats most often required for sociology papers.)

Request Needed Information

In the course of your research, you may need to consult a source that is not immediately available to you. For example, while working on a textbook censorship paper, you might find that a packet of potentially useful information may be obtained from a government agency or public-interest group in Washington, DC. Or you may discover that a needed book is not owned by your university library or by any other local library, or that a successful antidrug program has been implemented in the school system of a city of comparable size in another state. In such situations, it may be tempting to disregard potential sources because of the difficulty of consulting them. If you ignore this material, however, you are not doing your job.

It is vital that you take steps to acquire the needed data. In the first case mentioned above, you can simply write to the Washington, DC, agency or interest group; in the second, you may use your library's interlibrary loan procedure to obtain the book; in the third, you can track down the council that manages the antidrug campaign by e-mail, phone, or Internet, and ask for information. Remember that many businesses and government agencies want to share their information with interested citizens; some have employees or entire departments whose job is to facilitate communication with the public. Be as specific as possible when asking for such information. It is a good idea to outline your own project briefly—in no more than a few sentences—to help the respondent determine the types of information that will be useful to you.

Never let the immediate unavailability of a source stop you from trying to consult it. And be sure to begin the job of locating and acquiring such long-distance material as soon as possible, to allow for the various delays that often occur.

Read&Write 7.2   Write a Bibliography with a Dozen High-Quality Sources

Assume you are going to write a 10-page paper on a topic of your choice. Locate and list, in ASA bibliographical format, a dozen high-quality sources for your paper.

PART

3

PRACTICE SOCIOLOGY IN ADVANCED COURSES

8 Analyze a Government Policy

9 Observe Culture

8

ANALYZE A GOVERNMENT POLICY

8.1 LEARN THE BASICS OF POLICY ANALYSIS

What Is Policy Analysis?

When President Obama took office, he faced a long list of problems, some of which seemed almost overpowering. The nation was in the trough of its deepest recession since the Great Depression of the 1930s. America was fighting wars in both Iraq and Afghanistan. The health care system was the worst among the world's great powers. Hundreds of medical bankruptcies, gaps in health insurance coverage, and soaring medical costs added to the many challenges to be faced. Governments solve problems by formulating *policies*, which are sets of principles or rules that guide government agencies in creating and running programs aimed at dealing with the problems. Confronted with a vast array of serious national predicaments, President Obama's administration developed and proposed to Congress a set of policies, some of which were eventually passed and became law.

Domestic policies include matters *within* nations, such as issues related to highways, hospitals, schools, water treatment plants, law enforcement, public safety, and many others. International policies related to trade, war, educational exchanges, disaster relief efforts, and so on, affect relations *between or among* nations.

Policy analysis is the examination of a policy (domestic or international) to determine its *effectiveness* (how well it solves the problem it was designed to solve) and its *efficiency* (the extent to which the cost of implementing the policy is reasonable, considering the size and nature of the problem to be solved).

Every day, analysts, sometimes called policy wonks, at all levels of government are writing policy analysis papers. Legislators, at the state and national levels, hire staff people who continually investigate public policy issues and seek ways to improve legislated policy. At the national level, the Congressional Research Service continually finds information for representatives and senators. Each committee of Congress employs staff members who help in reviewing current laws and defining options for making new ones. State legislatures also employ their own research agencies and committee staff. Legislators and other policymakers are also given policy information by hundreds of public interest groups and research organizations.

Public officials constantly face challenges to initiate new policies or change old ones. If they have a current formal policy at all, they want to know how effective it is. They then want to know the available options, the changes they might make to improve the current policy, and the possible consequences of those changes. Policies are reviewed under a number of circumstances. Policy analyses are sometimes conducted as part of the normal agency budgeting processes. They help decision makers in determining the policies that must be continued or discontinued. These policies that are under scrutiny may be very narrow in scope, such as deciding the hours of operation of facilities at city parks. Or they may be very broad, such as deciding how the nation will provide health care or defense for its citizens.

A good example of an organization that conducts policy analysis is the U.S. *Office of Management and Budget* (OMB), an agency within the White House that provides information to the President and public servants in his administration. Within the OMB is the *Office of Information and Regulatory Affairs* (OIRA), which conducts policy analyses on many subjects. On the OIRA web page (https://www.whitehouse.gov/omb/policy_analyst/), you will find the following explanation of what OIRA analysts do:

Policy Analyst
Office of Information and Regulatory Affairs

Policy analysts oversee the Federal regulatory system so that agencies' regulatory actions are consistent with economic principles, sound public policy, and the goals of the President. They also review requests by agencies for approval of collections of information [including surveys, program evaluations, and applications for benefits] under the Paperwork Reduction Act of 1995. In addition, policy analysts review and analyze other Administration and Congressional policy initiatives. Policy analysts in OIRA work directly with high-level policy officials and have a great deal of responsibility in a wide array of policy areas. Major topic areas include virtually every domestic policy area including environment, natural resources, agriculture, rural development, energy, labor, education, immigration, health, welfare, housing, finance, criminal justice, information technology, and other related domestic policy issues.

Specifically, an OIRA policy analyst:

Oversees and evaluates the regulatory, information policies, and other policy initiatives of one or more government agencies, applying economics, statistics, and risk assessment.

Analyzes agency regulations prior to publication to ensure that the regulations adhere to sound analytical principles, and that agencies evaluate the need for, societal costs and benefits of, and alternatives to new regulations.

Reviews and approves agency collections of information in accordance with the Paperwork Reduction Act [PRA] of 1995. Ensures that agency collections reduce, minimize and control paperwork burdens and maximize the practical utility and public benefit of the information created, collected, disclosed, maintained, used, shared and disseminated by or for the Federal government.

Coordinates the review of regulations and collections of information within OMB and the Executive Office of the President, as well as among other relevant Federal agencies. Monitors and analyzes legislative and policy proposals and testimony for conformance with the policies and priorities of the President. Performs special analyses and advises senior policy officials on specific issues.[1]

Become Familiar with Policy Analysis Institutions

In general, policy analysis institutions are of two sorts: public (government) and private (mostly nonprofit). Virtually every federal government agency conducts some sort of policy analysis, and there are many that specialize in this activity. The most important *federal* policy analysis organizations are:

- Congressional Budget Office (CBO)
- Congressional Research Service (CRS)
- National Council for Science and the Environment (NCSE)
- U.S. Department of State Office of Economic Policy Analysis & Public Diplomacy
- Office of Management and Budget (OMB)
- U.S. General Accountability Office (U.S. GAO)

Every state also has its own policy analysis offices. California's agencies, for example, include:

- California Senate Office of Research (SOR)
- California Office of the Governor, Legislative Analyst's Office

Private research institutes (think tanks) provide a great deal of often-influential policy analysis and research upon which policy analysis can be conducted. Some of the most important are:

- American Enterprise Institute
- American Foreign Policy Council
- Battelle Memorial Institute
- Brookings Institution
- Carnegie Endowment for International Peace
- Cato Institute
- Center for Strategic and International Studies
- Claremont Institute

Read&Write 8.1   Write a Brief Domestic Policy Analysis

In writing a policy analysis paper, you should:

1. Select and clearly define a specific government policy.
2. Carefully define the social, governmental, economic, or other problem that the policy is designed to solve.

---

[1] "Office of Information and Regulatory Affairs." N.d. Office of Management and Budget. Retrieved March 28, 2016 (https://www.whitehouse.gov/omb/policy_analyst/).

3. Describe the economic, social, and political environments in which the problem arose and in which the existing policy for solving the problem was developed.

4. Evaluate the effectiveness of the current policy or lack of policy in dealing with the problem.

5. Identify alternative policies that could be adopted to solve the selected problem, and estimate the economic, social, environmental, and political costs and benefits of each alternative.

6. Provide a summary comparison of all policies examined.

Successful policy analysis papers all share the same general purpose: to inform policymakers about how public policy may be improved in a specific area. A policy analysis paper, like a position paper, is an entirely practical exercise. It is neither theoretical nor general. Its objective is to identify and evaluate the policy options that are available for a specific topic.

The Contents of a Policy Analysis Paper

Policy analysis papers contain six basic elements:

1. Title page
2. Executive summary
3. Table of contents, including a list of tables and illustrations
4. Text (or body)
5. References to sources of information
6. Appendices

Parameters of the Text

Ask your instructor for the number of pages required for the policy analysis paper assigned for your course. Such papers, at the undergraduate level, often range from 20 to 50 typed, double-spaced pages in length.

Two general rules govern the amount of information presented in the body of the paper. First, the content must be adequate to make a good policy evaluation. You must include all the facts necessary to understand the significant strengths and weaknesses of a policy and its alternatives. If your paper omits a fact that is critical to the decision, a poor decision will likely be made.

Never omit important facts merely because they tend to support a perspective other than your own. It is your responsibility to present the facts as clearly as possible, not to bias the evaluation in a particular direction.

The second guideline for determining the length of a policy analysis paper is to omit extraneous material. Include only the information that is helpful in making the particular decision at hand. If, for example, you are analyzing the policy by which a municipal government funds a museum dedicated to the history of fishing in area lakes, how much information do you need to include about the specific exhibits in the museum?

The Format of a Policy Analysis Paper

Title Page

The title page for a policy analysis paper should follow the format provided for title pages in Chapter 3.

Executive Summary

A one-page, single-spaced executive summary immediately follows the title page. The carefully written sentences of the executive summary express the central concepts to be explained more fully in the text of the paper. The purpose of the summary is to allow the decision maker to understand, as quickly as possible, the major facts and issues under consideration. The decision maker should be able to get a clear and thorough overview of the entire policy problem and the value and costs of available policy options by reading the one-page summary.

Table of Contents

The table of contents of a policy analysis paper must follow the organization of the paper's text and should conform to the format shown in Chapter 3.

Text

The structure of a policy analysis paper's text may be outlined as follows:

  I. **Description of the policy currently in force**

  A. A clear, concise statement of the policy currently in force
  B. A brief history of the policy currently in force
  C. A description of the problem the current policy was aimed at resolving, including an estimate of its extent and importance

 II. **Environments of the policy currently in force**

  A. A description of the *physical* factors affecting the origin, development, and implementation of the current policy
  B. A description of the *social* factors affecting the origin, development, and implementation of the current policy
  C. A description of the *economic* factors affecting the origin, development, and implementation of the current policy
  D. A description of the *political* factors affecting the origin, development, and implementation of the current policy

III. **Effectiveness and efficiency of the current policy**

  A. How well the existing policy does what it was designed to do
  B. How well the policy performs in relation to the effort and resources committed to it

 IV. **Policy alternatives**

  A. Possible alterations of the present policy, with the estimated costs and benefits of each
  B. Alternatives to the present policy, with the estimated costs and benefits of each

  V. **Summary comparison of policy options**

  Most public policy analysis textbooks describe in detail each of the policy analysis components listed in the above outline. The following sections of this chapter, however, provide further information with respect to section II of this outline. Be sure to discuss the outline with your instructor to ensure that you understand what each entails.

References

You must be sure to cite properly all sources of information in a policy analysis paper. Follow the directions for proper citation in Chapter 3.

Appendices

Appendices can provide the reader of policy analysis papers with information that supplements the important facts contained in the text. For many local development and public works projects, a map and a diagram are often very helpful appendices. You should attach them to the end of the paper, after the reference page. You should not append entire government reports, journal articles, or other publications, but feel free to include selected charts, graphs, or other pages. The source of the information should always be evident on the appended pages.

9

OBSERVE CULTURE

9.1   CULTURAL ANALYSIS

Finn Squires, an older student in an advanced undergraduate sociology course entitled *Cultural Perspectives*, was asked to produce a brief reflection on an environment that contributed to his sense of his family's identity. He came up with the following paragraph:

> Aroostook County Maine's heyday—the first half of the twentieth century—produced a culture seemingly as foreign to us now as some present day cultures of India or Peru. Potato capital of America until eclipsed by Idaho, Aroostook's production required pine potato barrels, which my grandfather's industrial-revolution-age cooperage was eager to provide. With forty or so coopers and sawyers in his employ, my grandfather Ransford ran the premier enterprise in his small Canadian border town. When he drove his '49 Dodge pickup to town for supplies he never used cash or checks, he merely walked out of the stores with nails, hammers, saws, and more and paid the bill at the end of the month. On his way home he would stop at a couple of "Mom and Pop" small grocers instead of bringing his business to the A&P. After the harvest he was likely to have his crews restore an old dilapidated house, which, when completed, he simply gave to a family in need. I loved it when he bought a new car. He would call a couple of dealers and tell them what he was looking for. They would each deliver three cars to his house, and tell him, "Let us know when you have made a choice, Ransford." Relationships ran on integrity and a deep knowledge of and concern for neighbors. With isolated exceptions, it's a lost world.

When sociologists write about culture, they usually mean the material (technology, buildings, neighborhoods, utensils, clothes, etc.) and nonmaterial (symbols, language, values, norms, beliefs, etc.) aspects of any society. All these things together make up the culture of a given people. If you're a citizen of the United States, you have probably been socialized into the culture of the region, generation, religion, and so on of your particular time and place. Because the United States is made up of many subcultures, you most likely embrace the values and beliefs that were given to you by the most significant others in your life. This can range from your preference in music, clothes, speech, activities, and personalities to a wide variety of other factors. For example, a girl raised in rural Oklahoma may prefer country music, cowboy boots, tight blue jeans, line dancing, honky-tonks, and cowboys. She may like the wide-open spaces more than the city life. All this would be due to the influence of rural Oklahoma culture on her personality.

As you can see, culture is one of the most complex aspects of a sociologist's bag of tools. Even with the description of the above example, our "cowgirl" is much more complex than the cultural influences listed—maybe she can't wait to denounce those values and beliefs or maybe the last thing she wants is to embrace the "cowgirl" she was raised to be. And because she is human, not a programmed machine, she can choose the life she wants to live. She may decide to abandon the "cowgirl" life and become a city girl. Experiencing new cultures can be very exciting and seductive. They offer new interests in music, dress, entertainment, and people.

However, nothing is more important in our lives than the meaning and purpose that we give it. The culture that we internalize during our formative years always remains a part of who we are. To some extent, it always defines us. So maybe our cowgirl will do well with her new life in the city with all its glitter and glam. Or maybe she finds that it's not what she fantasized and longs to return to her former self and the cultural surroundings she once knew and loved. Whatever happens, she is both experiencing and creating "culture" at every moment in her life. She symbolically interacts with others and herself using the tools that her culture has given her: symbols, language, beliefs, values, and, of course, her iPhone.

Cultural change is also an important part of how sociologists access the impact of culture on the citizens of a particular society. When Margaret Mead, the famous anthropologist, studied the Samoan culture, she was dealing with a society that had experienced little to no change in its material culture. Therefore, when the elders narrated stories to the young people, those stories were very meaningful because all the members of that society, young and old, were living within the same overall culture. But when older people in American society attempt to relate their experiences to their grandchildren, technological advancements place them in two separate worlds. Sociologists refer to this as "cultural lag," which means that attitudes and beliefs tend to lag behind the changes in technology and material culture. Older people find it hard to change their beliefs and attitudes to align with advancing technology.

For example, when the two daughters of Finn Squires, the older student who wrote, in the paragraph reproduced above, of his family background in Maine, grew up and went to college, Finn was hurt that they wouldn't answer his phone calls or return his voice mails. He had to accept that they were spreading their wings and wanted less of his influence on their new lives. But they would text their mother, Finn's wife, with short, choppy lines that didn't tie them down to a prolonged conversation on the phone. It became clear to Finn that if he wanted to communicate with them, he must learn to text. He had resisted this cultural innovation in the same manner that, years earlier, he had resisted the TV remote control, the remote garage door opener, the microwave oven, and many other technological advances. You could say, as Finn often did, that he was "set in his ways"—his beliefs and attitudes. At the time of his daughters' move to college, Finn actually had a

flip phone and believed that was the final step in his need for telephone technological advancement. He firmly resisted the iPhone and went so far as to say that
he would never own one. But it's important to be careful with the word "never."
Finn had professed the same "never" with the TV remote, garage door remote, and
microwave oven. In his attempt to stay connected to his daughters, Finn discovered
just how difficult and time consuming it can be to try to text with a flip phone. So
now Finn has an iPhone and texts his daughters regularly. And they text him back.

Around the world cultures vary in the things they value and the norms they ask
their citizens to follow. The way they treat various groups within their societies sexually, racially, ethnically, religiously, or in terms of age also varies. Comparing these
differences between two societies would be an interesting project for you to read
and write about.

Read&Write 9.1   Compare the Cultures of Aging in Two Nations

Your sociology text will provide you with much more information about culture. After
reading it, you will be prepared to read more about this topic and write a cross-cultural
analysis of the similarities and differences between these two cultures on the subject of aging.
As you produce your paper, follow these three steps:

1. Research the sociological/anthropological material on cross-cultural analysis. That
   way you will know how these scholars go about comparing two cultures on a given
   entity.
2. Select several articles (six or seven) that show how each of these cultures deals with
   the aging population in its society.
3. Now write a paper using the cross-cultural approach you learned in Step 1 with the
   information you gained in Step 2.

Ask your professor about his or her desired length for your paper. Lacking further
direction, it will probably require eight to ten pages.

9.2   SOCIALIZATION

Socialization is called a complex process in textbooks, and so it is, but—because an
illustration can simplify complexity—we offer one here:

> I was a fat kid but they let me join in. They didn't seem to know my name, and little
> did they care, so I was always "Porky." My excessive weight and lack of athletic abil-
> ity, however, never excluded me from our seasonal round of preteen neighborhood
> backlot games: baseball, football, basketball, hockey, and baseball again. Outfielder,
> tackle, bench warmer, or goalie, I was peripheral, but I was there. They liked me.
> I had a sweet disposition. I learned to enjoy inclusion, action, participation, making
> a contribution. The older guys were even a bit paternal, so that in their company
> I never feared being picked on. I learned the course of team life and how to flow with
> it. In school I was even elected to Student Council and served as French Club President.
> It was a good life. It still is.

Most simply, socialization is progressive enculturation. More formally, it is "the process by which a human being beginning at infancy acquires the habits, beliefs, and accumulated knowledge of society through education and training for adult status" (Merriam Webster medical definition). It is our communal identity. Our individual socialization experiences are affected by many factors, including

biology	ethnicity
cognitive development	religion
emotional development	community
family	country
schools	events (wars, disease, tornadoes)
peers	social media
economic class	news media

Imagine for a moment what it would be like if we, as a species, were fully communicative on the day we are born. As we open our eyes, Mom gently cradles us, and Dad asks us, "Well, now, youngster, what do you want from life?"

We respond casually, "Naturally, I want it all. I want to be warmly included—unified in family and social life with those I love. Of course, I also want to be viewed as unique, special, and independent, someone who has never lived before."

So we grow, live, and learn, and we conform to our communities and societies in ways we hesitate to admit, at the same time subtly transforming the modes of the populations around us. We internalize values, habits, modes of expression, aggression, condescension, affirmation, toleration, and appreciation. The evolving mutual interaction that results is *socialization*.

Read&Write 9.2 Analyze the Effects of Social Media on Personal and Cultural Socialization

Your sociology text will provide you with much more information about socialization. After reading it, you will be prepared to tell your own story and then discover its effects and significance in your life more precisely and profoundly. Your paper will proceed in three sections:

1. Write an essay in which you relate a seminal experience or set of experiences in your life that epitomize your own socialization *with respect to your experience with social media*. Your story will describe the interaction of your internal cognitive and emotive states within the context of people and places in which they transpired.

2. Review the last decade of sociological scholarship on the subject of socialization and social media in the last decade. Select six or seven articles that deepen your understanding of the process, and prepare a long-version annotated bibliography. (Review Section 6.7 of this text.)

3. In an analytical essay, apply the insights gleaned from the scholarship to the experiences described in your personal experience essay. What have you learned about yourself? What have you learned about your society?

Ask your professor about his or her desired length for your paper. Lacking further direction, it will probably require at least 10 pages.

9.3 INEQUALITY

Extreme social inequality can bring extreme reactions. On October 16, 1793, Marie Antoinette, an Austrian princess and wife of France's King Louis XVI, mounted a platform in the *Place de la Révolution*, one of the great public squares of Paris, to face a jeering crowd and the guillotine. Her husband had been executed nine months earlier, and thousands of other nobles had met the same fate. Why? The French Revolution was a virtually inevitable remedy to an extreme division of wealth. During his reign, Louis IV, the previous king, had built France into the world's reigning empire. He had also gathered 2,000 of his nobles at his Versailles estate where, together, the nobility accumulated one-half of the entire country's wealth. While millions led lives of cruelest poverty, life at Versailles was lavish. Mark Twin, in his travelogue, *The Innocents Abroad*, notes an example. On one warm July day, to fulfill a whim, Antoinette had the streets of the town filled with snow and proceeded to happily cruise them in her royal sleigh.

The French and Russian revolutions are only the two most famous of many wealth-distribution-caused political explosions. Today's American billionaires are more discreet than French royalty, but America's richest 1% now controls 37% of the nation's wealth.

When sociologists analyze inequality in a society, they are concerned with how individuals and groups are ranked or stratified; they look at how *power*, *status*, and *prestige* are distributed. They usually construct a hierarchy, placing individuals, groups, and social classes in rank order according to several criteria: occupation, income, education, dwelling area, and other cultural considerations. Sometimes, this is referred to as *socioeconomic status*. When we are socialized into a culture, these hierarchies already exist, and they become part of our own psyche; we develop an intuitive understanding of their reality.

Although several elements comprise our status in society, our *wealth* is the leading single factor. Over the past half century, the distribution of wealth in the United States has changed to favor substantially the very wealthy. Credit Suisse tracks world wealth distribution trends. The following three charts indicate the distribution of

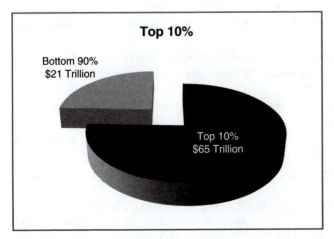

Top 10%

Bottom 90%
$21 Trillion

Top 10%
$65 Trillion

FIGURE 9.1 Top 10 percent of wealth in the United States in 2015

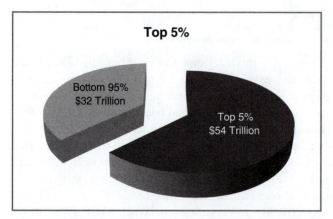

FIGURE 9.2 Top 5 percent of wealth in the United States in 2015

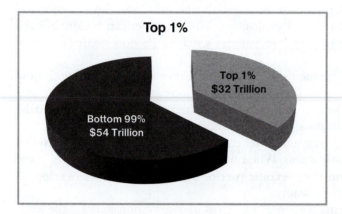

FIGURE 9.3 Top 1 percent of wealth in the United States in 2015

wealth in the United States in 2015. The first chart indicates that the wealthiest 10% of the U.S. population controls 75% of the nation's wealth.

The next chart indicates that the top 5% of the population controls more than half of the country's wealth.

The third chart shows that 1% of the population enjoys 36% of the nation's wealth.

For the most part, the gap in wealth between the very poor and the very rich is widening each year.[1]

American society struggles with the differences in power and prestige, which are given to some simply because they are male, white, or wealthy through inheritance. Because we are a country founded on a Constitution that is designed to enhance freedom for all, and our laws are based on the tenants of that Constitution, the differential access to power and prestige, which stems from *acquired status*, is constantly

[1] Credit Suisse. 2015. "Wealth Shares and Minimal Wealth of Deciles and Top Percentiles for Regions and Selected Countries, 2015." *Global Wealth Databook 2015*, October, table 6.5, p. 149. Retrieved March 29, 2016 (http://publications.credit-suisse.com/tasks/render/file/index.cfm?fileid=C26E3824-E868-56E0-CCA04D4BB9B9ADD5).

being challenged. Thanks to these challenges, doors that were once closed to minorities because of their acquired status are now opening.

Therefore, while social inequality is a reality in any society, in an *open-class system*, similar to the one we have in the United States, *social mobility*—the ability to move up and down the class structure—is legally, if not actually, available to everyone. This is not the case in a closed-class or *caste* system, in which social mobility is unattainable and citizens are fixed into a social caste for life. However, it doesn't mean that in an open-class system all people have equal access to raise their social status. It only means that there are opportunities for social advancement. But in a caste system, those opportunities are missing. However, as mentioned above, laws that once made upward mobility very difficult—like Jim Crow laws, which enforced racial segregation in America through much of the twentieth century—are constantly being challenged in U.S. courts.

This growing opportunity for change has opened doors for those at the bottom of the social hierarchy to seek advancement through education, job training, and other means of upper social mobility that were once unavailable. Women and racial minorities are now moving into occupations that were once reserved for White males. For example, in recent years, women have exceeded men in admissions to medical schools and law schools—two occupations that are always ranked toward the top of the occupational prestige scale. And more and more blacks, especially black women, are attaining college degrees and advanced degrees, which open doors to prestigious occupations.

Social inequality permeates almost every aspect of our lives. While it's clear that upper social mobility in the United States is available today to more and more people, things are far from perfect, and the struggle to seek freedom of opportunity for all citizens, regardless of gender, race, ethnicity, religion, or sexual orientation continues.

During the Clinton administration, United States enjoyed one of the most prosperous periods in its history, and a wide variety of people benefited from these good economic times. However, since that time the gap between the very rich and the very poor has actually widened, which somewhat contradicts the notion that more people are experiencing upward mobility. This would make a very interesting topic for you to read and write about in this class, so let's look at how you might explore that.

Read&Write 9.3 Describe the Extent and Effects of the Increasing Economic Inequality in the United States

Your sociology text will provide you with much more information about social inequality. Reading it will help prepare you to write a paper on the increasing gap between the very rich and the very poor in the United States. You should proceed through the following steps:

1. Write an essay in which you relate your own experience or set of experiences with social inequality, especially as it relates to the gap in wealth in your own life. It can be something that occurred when you were growing up or something very recent. Your story should describe the interaction of your internal cognitive and emotive states within the context of people and places in which the experiences transpired.

2. Review the last decade of sociological scholarship on the subject of the gap between the very poor and the very rich. Select five or six articles that help you understand how and why this gap occurred and continues to widen, and prepare a short-version annotated bibliography. (Review Section 6.7 of this text.)

3. In an analytical essay, apply the insights gleaned from the scholarship (Step 2) to the experiences described in your personal experience essay (Step 1). What have you learned about the gap in wealth that you can relate to your life? And what have you learned about your society and the gap between the very rich and the very poor?

Ask your professor about his or her desired length for your analytical essay. Lacking further direction, it will probably require about eight to ten pages.

9.4   ETHNICITY AND RACE

Racial animosities can be blatant and even violent, but they can also be insidiously embedded in daily life activities, as the following paragraph written by an older white citizen of the American South illustrates:

> Among my childhood memories of Georgia are "Whites Only" signs on gas station rest rooms and restaurant doors. As late as the autumn of 1987 I was taught a vital lesson on how black people experience discrimination that is strangely invisible to whites. On a train from Charlottesville, Virginia, to Washington DC I noticed a young man reading a book with which I was familiar, so I decided to strike up a conversation. His name was David. He was wonderfully articulate, and I learned that he had recently graduated from the University of Virginia and was in route to Cambridge, Massachusetts, to attend Harvard Divinity School. Before we arrived in Washington, he asked if I had noticed some things on the trip. He asked if I had noticed how the conductor asked to see his ticket but not mine. He asked if I had noticed that, while we were buying soft drinks in the club car, the attendant, placing a Coke on the counter for my travel companion, had said to him, "Now don't you give me a pocket full of pennies." He had in fact no pennies. David pointed out how, in the course of less than two hours, he, a black man, and I, a white man, had been treated differently in this mode at least four more times. Looking back, I knew instantly that David had accurately reported every incident. I had been oblivious to the entire insidious process. I owe David much for this experience. I will never forget it.

It is no wonder that, among many sensitive areas in American culture, none conjure up more emotional fervor than race and ethnic relations. With the recent rash of white police officers killing young black males and the rise of the Islamic State of Iraq and Syria (ISIS), these racial and ethnic/religious conflicts are front and center in the news almost every day. So it might be very helpful to understand what is meant by race and ethnicity.

The term *race* is used quite often with little understanding of what it really means. While many people hold the belief that race is a biological reality, most sociologists and biologists do not embrace this position for the human species. They are more apt to see race as an isolated gene pool, created from geographical natural selection. While sociologists are quite certain of the *social* reality of race, they base their definition of race on people's belief that race is a *biological* reality. If we believe something is real, it becomes real to us. With these subtle distinctions in mind, we could define a race as *a category of people that most individuals believe share important traits that are genetically transmitted.* If most members of a population distinguish between groups of people on the basis of *presumed* biological differences, then the social reality of race becomes real. And the consequences of that social reality can be positive or negative, depending on the assumptions people make about the innate or cultural differences among the racial groups.

On the other hand, *ethnicity* derives from *a shared historical and cultural heritage,* which gives its member a sense of group identity. These groups often share a common language, religion, and national origin. Because so many different ethnic groups have immigrated to the United States at various moments in history, our culture is one of the most diverse in the world. If you just consider your options for dinner tonight, for example, and you live in a large urban city, you will realize how many cuisines are available to you based on ethnicity: Mexican, German, Italian, French, Chinese, Thai, Japanese, and many more.

When these different ethnic groups immigrated to the United States, they arrived with physical and cultural characteristics that were either somewhat similar to or vastly different from those of the dominant white, Anglo-Saxon, English-speaking majority population. The more similar these characteristics of the immigrants—skin color, language, religion, and so on—the easier their assimilation into the existing culture. Throughout the nation's history, racial beliefs have made it very difficult for people of color—blacks, Asians, Hispanics, American Indians, and others—to find acceptance from the majority population. Exclusionary laws were passed by white males, many of whom believed that people of color were inherently inferior. The so-called *melting pot* of American culture was really a crock restricted to white Eastern European immigrants.

While there has been some advancement in racial and ethnic equality since the earlier days of American culture, one has to only watch the news or read about current events to see that many problems still exist. Can it be said today that, finally, the American Dream is alive for those minority populations who have experienced harsh discrimination for many years? That would be an interesting subject to read and write about in this class. So let's proceed with learning more about it and writing a sociological paper on this topic.

Read&Write 9.4 Describe Current Trends in Ethnic and Race Relations

Your sociology text will provide you with much more information about race and ethnicity. Reading it will help prepare you to write a paper about the current state of the American Dream for racial and ethnic minorities in the United States. Follow these steps to produce your paper:

1. Write an essay in which you relate a seminal experience or set of experiences in your life in which race or ethnicity played a role in what happened to you. This can be very personal and subjective in nature.

2. Review the latest sociological scholarship on the subject of race and ethnicity in the United States. Select six or seven articles that deepen your understanding of this topic and prepare a long-version annotated bibliography on the articles that you have reviewed. (Review Section 6.7 of this manual.)

3. In an analytical essay, apply the insights gleaned from the scholarship (Step 2) to the experiences described in your personal experience essay (Step 1). What have you learned about how race and ethnicity have affected your life? What have you learned about your society?

Ask your professor about his or her desired length for your analytical essay. Lacking further direction, it will probably require eight to ten pages.

QUESTIONNAIRE

The following statements are concerned with your feelings about your marriage. To the left of each question, please put the number that indicates the degree to which your marriage possesses each of the following qualities. Number 1 represents the least degree and 5 represents the greatest degree.

Least Degree 1 2 3 4 5 Greatest Degree

_____ 1. Spend time doing things together.

_____ 2. Are very committed to each other.

_____ 3. Have good communication (talking, sharing feelings).

_____ 4. Deal with crises in a positive manner.

_____ 5. Express appreciation to each other.

_____ 6. Have a very close relationship.

_____ 7. Have a very happy relationship.

_____ 8. My spouse makes me feel good about myself.

_____ 9. I make my spouse feel good about himself or herself.

_____ 10. If I could, I would marry my current spouse again.

Please give the following information:

AGE ____ SEX ____ male ____ female

Number of years married to current spouse ____

Number of children ____

Have you ever had an extramarital affair? ____yes ____no

THANKS FOR YOUR HELP!

Source: Modified from Stinnett and DeFrain (1985)

GLOSSARY

achieved status A social position within a stratification system that a person assumes voluntarily and that reflects a significant measure of personal ability and choice—for example, educational attainment.

ageism Prejudice and discrimination against the elderly.

age–sex pyramid A graphic representation of the age and sex of a population.

alienation The experience of powerlessness in social life in which the individual feels disassociated from the surrounding society.

animism The belief that natural objects—such as winds, clouds, rocks, and the like—are conscious forms of life that affect humanity.

anomie A state of normlessness in which social control of individual behavior has become ineffective and society provides little moral guidance to individuals.

ascribed status A social position a person inherits at birth or assumes involuntarily later in life on the basis of characteristics over which he or she has no control.

assimilation The process by which minorities gradually take on the values of the dominant culture.

authoritarian personality A personality pattern believed by social psychologists to be associated with a psychological need to be prejudiced.

authoritarianism A political system that denies popular participation in government, or a personality syndrome that finds comfort in such structure.

authority Power people perceive to be legitimate rather than coercive.

autosystem A system or institution whose major purpose is the perpetuation of itself.

beliefs Specific statements that people hold to be true; a community-held set of convictions related to a supernatural order.

blue-collar occupation Lower prestige work that involves mostly manual labor, including production, maintenance, and service work.

bureaucracy Formal organization designed to perform tasks efficiently by explicit procedural rules.

bureaucratic inertia The tendency of bureaucratic organizations to perpetuate themselves. Bureaucracies become autosystems that exist to maintain their existence.

bureaucratic ritualism A preoccupation with rules and regulations to the point of obstructing organizational goals. Associated individuals are said to have "trained incapacity" or bureaucratic personality.

capitalism An economic system in which natural resources and the means of producing goods and services are in private hands and are used to create more wealth for its owners.

capitalist	One who owns a factory or other productive enterprise and embraces the economic system of capitalism.
case studies	Observational studies of a given social unit, such as an individual, organization, neighborhood, community, or culture. Ethnographic or field research often describes a single unit or case.
caste system	Social stratification based on ascription.
cause and effect	A relationship between two variables in which change in one (the independent variable) causes change in another (the dependent variable).
charisma	Extraordinary personal qualities that can turn members of an audience into followers without the necessity of formal authority.
church	A formal religious organization well integrated into the larger society; a shared place of moral and ethical concerns.
cohabitation	The sharing of a household by an unmarried couple committed to a long-term relationship.
cohort	A category of people with a common characteristic, usually their age—for example, all persons born during the Great Depression (1929–1939).
colonialism	The process by which some nations enrich themselves through political and economic control of other nations.
concept	An abstract idea that represents some aspect of the world, such as descriptive properties or relations, inevitably in a somewhat simplified form.
constant	A characteristic of a sample or population that does not take on different values and is the same from one element to the next. For example, if a sample contained all males, gender would be a constant because it does not vary.
corporation	An organization with a legal existence, including rights and liabilities, apart from those of its members.
correlation	The measured strength of an association between two or more variables.
correlation coefficient	A number whose magnitude shows how strongly two or more variables are correlated, or related to one another. Values range from +1.00 to −1.00, with strength of association increasing as the value approaches either extreme.
counterculture	Cultural patterns that strongly oppose conventional culture. The individual member will usually experience alienation from the values and expectations of the dominant culture.
credentialism	Evaluating people on the basis of their credentials, especially educational degrees.
crime	The violation of a norm formally enacted into criminal law.
crimes against property (property crimes)	Crimes involving theft of property belonging to others.

crimes against the person (violent crimes)	Crimes against people that involve violence or the threat of violence.
criminal justice system	The lawful response to alleged crimes using police, courts, and state-sanctioned punishment.
criminal recidivism	A tendency by people previously convicted of crimes to commit subsequent offenses.
crude birth rate	The number of live births in a given year for every 1,000 people in a population.
crude death rate	The number of deaths in a given year for every 1,000 people in a population.
cult	A religious organization that is substantially outside the cultural traditions of a society.
cultural lag	The observation that some cultural elements (material culture and technology) change more quickly than others (values and norms), with potentially disruptive consequences.
cultural relativism	The practice of evaluating any culture by its own standards.
cultural transmission	The formal and informal learning process by which culture is passed from one generation to the next.
cultural universals	Traits found in every culture.
culture shock	The individual disorientation accompanying sudden exposure to an unfamiliar way of life.
culture	The beliefs, values, behavior, and material objects shared by a particular people.
democracy	Rule by the people.
democratic socialism	An economic and political system that combines significant government control of the economy with free elections.
demography	The scientific study of human population.
denomination	A religious group, not linked to the state, that claims doctrinal autonomy.
dependent samples	Two random samples whose elements are not mutually exclusive. An example would be when the same subjects are measured on some variable before (pre-) and after (post-) experimental manipulation, and the two samples were not independently selected.
dependent variable	The variable that is being affected or influenced by another variable. In a causal analysis, the dependent variable is caused by the independent variable; it is the effect.
descent	The system by which members of a society trace kinship over generations.
descriptive statistics	Statistics (numbers) used only to describe the data—in other words, percentages, charts, graphs, and so on; no hypotheses are tested.

deterrence	The attempt to discourage criminality through fear of punishment.
deviance	The recognized violation of cultural norms.
discrimination	Treating groups of people unfavorably based on categorical, rather than individual, grounds.
distribution	A listing of all the values or outcomes for a particular variable. It often takes the form of a frequency distribution or a percentile distribution.
division of labor	Specialized economic activity separating work into distinct parts.
dramaturgical analysis	The investigation of social interaction in terms of theatrical performance.
dyad	A social group with two members involving the presentation of selves.
ecology	The study of the interaction of living organisms and their natural environment; the spatial distribution of people and activities and the resulting interdependence, as in a community.
economy	The social institution that organizes a society's production, distribution, and consumption of goods and services.
ecosystem	A physical environment composed of the interaction of all living plants and animals in it.
education	The social institution through which society provides its members with important knowledge, including facts, skills, and values.
ego	Freud's designation of a person's conscious attempts to balance the pleasure-seeking drives of the human organism and the demands of society.
element	A single member of a population.
empirical distribution	A list of the different values for a variable and the number of times each value appears in the sample. It is also referred to as a frequency distribution.
endogamy	Marriage between people of the same social category.
ethnocentrism	The practice of judging another culture or group by the standards of one's own culture; usually involves taking the position that one's own culture or group is best.
ethnomethodology	The study of the way people make sense of their everyday surroundings. Sometimes referred to as ethnography, it is widely utilized in case studies.
euthanasia (mercy killing)	Assisting in the death of a person suffering from an incurable illness.
exogamy	Marriage between people of different social categories.
experiment	A research method that investigates cause-and-effect relationships under very controlled conditions.
extended family (consanguine family)	A social unit including parents, children, and other kin.

faith	Belief anchored in conviction rather than scientific evidence.
family	A set of persons who are related to each other by blood, marriage, or adoption, and who usually live together.
feminism	A social movement that advocates social equality for men and women, in opposition to patriarchy and sexism.
feminization of poverty	The trend by which women represent an increasing proportion of the poor.
fertility	The incidence of childbearing in a society's population.
folkways	Patterns of behavior common in and typical of a group.
formal organization	A large-scale, special-purpose group that is organized to achieve specific goals.
frequency distribution	A distribution of the values of a variable and the number of times each value occurs in the data; sometimes called an empirical distribution.
functional illiteracy	Reading, writing, and problem-solving skills that are judged to be inadequate for everyday living.
Gemeinschaft	A type of social organization (community) in which people are bound together by kinship and tradition.
gender	The significance a society attaches to the biological categories of female and male, sometimes labeled feminine and masculine.
gender roles	Attitudes and activities that a society links to each sex; often referred to as sex roles.
gender stratification	The differential ranking of males and females in societies where sex determines access to scarce resources.
genocide	The systematic killing of an entire race or people.
gerontocracy	A form of social organization in which the elderly have the most wealth, power, and privileges.
gerontology	The study of aging and the elderly.
Gesellschaft	A type of social organization in which relationships are contractual, impersonal, voluntary, and limited.
global economy	Economic activity across national borders.
global perspective	A view of the larger world and one's society's place in it.
government	A formal organization that directs the political life of a nation.
greenhouse effect	A rise in the Earth's average temperature (global warming) due to an increasing concentration of carbon dioxide in the atmosphere.
groupthink	Group conformity that limits individual understanding of an issue.
hate crime	A crime motivated by racial, ethical, or other bias.

hermaphrodite	A human being with a combination of female and male internal and external genitalia.
high culture	Cultural patterns that distinguish a society's elite.
holistic medicine	An approach to health care that emphasizes prevention of illness and takes account of a person's entire physical and social environment.
homogamy	Marriage between people with the same social characteristics.
horticulture	The use of hand tools to raise crops.
hunting and gathering	A stage of cultural evolution in which simple tools were used to hunt animals and gather vegetation.
id	Freud's designation of the human being's basic drives.
ideology	Cultural beliefs that justify particular social arrangements.
incest taboo	A norm forbidding sexual relations or marriage between closely related family members.
income	Wages or salary from work and earnings from investments.
independent variable	In a causal analysis, the cause of the dependent variable (the effect).
industry	The production of goods using sophisticated fuels and machinery.
infant mortality rate	The number of children per 1,000 live births who die during their first year of life.
inferential statistics	The type of statistics used to make inferences from sample data to populations through hypothesis testing. Probability is used to make a decision about the association between two or more variables; a null hypothesis is accepted or rejected based on the probability of an event occurring by chance.
in-group	An esteemed social group commanding a member's loyalty.
institutional discrimination	Discrimination against an individual or group that is supported by the values and organizations of a society.
intergenerational social mobility	The social standing of children in relation to their parents.
intragenerational social mobility	A change in social position occurring during a person's lifetime.
kinship	A social bond, based on blood, marriage, or adoption, that joins people into families.
labeling theory	The assertion that deviance and conformity result not so much from what people do as from the response of others to those actions.
language	A system of symbols that allows people to communicate with one another.
latent functions	The unrecognized and unintended effect of social action.

level of measurement   The mathematical properties of a variable. Different levels of measurement (data) include nominal (numbers are used to label mutually exclusive categories); ordinal (numbers are used to rank a variable on some criterion); interval (the distance between values is both known and constant—a unit of measurement that allows one to add, subtract, divide, and multiply without accumulating error); and ratio (has all the properties of interval data as well as a fixed meaningful zero point).

level of significance   The probability level (usually 0.05) used to determine the acceptance of a hypothesis or rejection of the null hypothesis. Sometimes referred to as rejection level or alpha level.

life expectancy   The average expectation of life at a given age, or the average number of years of life remaining for persons of a particular age.

looking-glass self   Cooley's term referring to a conception of self-derived from the responses of others: We see ourselves as we think others see us.

macro-level orientation   A concern with large-scale patterns that characterize society as a whole.

manifest functions   The recognized and intended consequences of social action.

marriage   A legally sanctioned relationship, involving economic cooperation as well as normative sexual activity and childbearing, that people expect to be enduring.

mass media   Impersonal communications directed to a vast audience by means of a technological medium.

mass society   A society in which industry and bureaucracy erode traditional social ties.

master status   A social position with exceptional importance for identity, often shaping a person's entire life.

matriarchy   A form of family organization in which power and authority are vested in the hands of the females.

mean   A measure of central tendency. The mean is the arithmetic average of a group of interval-level numbers (scores). Because it takes into account every score, it is affected by extremely low and extremely high scores.

mean deviation   A measure of dispersion for continuous data. In a distribution of scores, the mean deviation is the average absolute difference of each score from the mean of the scores. It measures, then, the average distance of each score from the mean. It is calculated by summing the absolute value of the difference between each score and the mean, and then dividing by the total number of scores.

measure of association   A statistic that indicates the strength of the relationship between two or more variables. The appropriate measure of association depends on the level of measurement of the variables involved.

measure of central tendency   Descriptive statistics that represent the most typical or representative score in a distribution of scores. The appropriate measure of central tendency depends on both the level of measurement and the dispersion of the data.

measure of dispersion	Descriptive statistics that reflect the amount of variability in a distribution of scores. These measures reveal how different the scores are from one another. The appropriate measure of dispersion depends on both the level of measurement and whether there are extreme scores in the data. When the magnitude of the measure of dispersion is large, it means that the scores are very different from one another and that there is a substantial amount of variability in the data.
measurement	The process of determining the value of a variable in a specific case.
mechanical solidarity	Social bonds based on collective conformity to tradition.
median	The score that is the exact middle score in a distribution of ranked scores. It is, therefore, the score at the 50th percentile. In a rank-ordered distribution of scores, the position of the median can be found using the formula $(n + 1)/2$, where n is the number of scores.
medicalization of deviance	The transformation of moral and legal issues into medical matters.
medicine	The social institution that focuses on combating disease and improving health.
meritocracy	Social stratification based on personal merit.
micro-level orientation	A concern with small-scale patterns of social interaction in specific settings.
midpoint of a class interval	In a grouped frequency distribution, the midpoint is exactly midway between the lower and upper class limits and is determined by adding the upper and lower limits (stated or true limits) and dividing by 2. The midpoint of the class interval 100–200 would be $(100 + 200)/2 = 150$.
migration	The movement of people into and out of a specified territory.
military-industrial complex	A close association among the government, the military, and defense industries.
minority	A category of people, distinguished by physical or cultural traits, that is socially disadvantaged.
miscegenation	The biological process of interbreeding among racial groups.
mode	A measure of central tendency. The mode is the most frequently occurring score in a distribution of scores or the most frequently occurring interval in a grouped frequency distribution.
modernity	Social patterns linked to industrialization.
modernization	The process of social change in a society or a social institution initiated by industrialization.
modernization theory	A model of economic development that explains global inequality in terms of technological and cultural differences among societies.
monarchy	A type of political system that transfers power from generation to generation within a single family.

monogamy	Marriage involving two partners.
monopoly	Control of a market by a single producer.
mores	Norms that are widely observed and have compelling moral significance.
mortality	The incidence of death in a society's population.
multiculturalism	An educational program recognizing the cultural diversity of a population and promoting the equality of all cultural traditions.
multinational corporation	A large business that operates in many countries.
natural environment	The earth's surface and atmosphere, including various living organisms as well as the air, water, soil, and other resources necessary to sustain life.
negative correlation	A correlation or association between two variables wherein the scores co-vary in opposite directions. High scores on one variable are related to low scores on the second variable, and low scores on one variable are related to high scores on the other.
neocolonialism	The economic and/or political policies by which a nation indirectly maintains its influence over other areas.
nonverbal communication	Communication using body movements, gestures, and facial expressions rather than speech.
norms	Rules by which a society guides the behavior of its members.
nuclear family (conjugal family)	A social unit containing one, or—more commonly—two adults and any children.
null hypothesis	The hypothesis of no difference or no association that is the object of a hypothesis test. The null hypothesis is tested against the alternative or research hypothesis, and it is the one that is rejected or not rejected in favor of the alternative.
oligarchy	The rule of the many by the few.
oligopoly	Domination of a market by a few producers.
organic solidarity	Social bonds based on specialization and interdependence.
outgroup	Social group toward which one feels competition or opposition.
participant observation	A research technique in which investigators systematically observe people while joining in their routine activities.
pastoralism	The domestication of animals.
patriarchy	A form of family organization in which power and authority are vested in the hands of the males.
peer group	A group whose members have interests, social position, and age in common.
percent	A descriptive statistic obtained by dividing the frequency of a subset of events by the total number of events and dividing by 100. For example, if there are 50 property crimes out of a total of 75 crimes, the percent of property crimes is 50/75, or 66.7 percent, of the total.

personal space	The surrounding area over which a person makes a claim to privacy.
personality	An individual's pattern of thoughts, motives, and self-conceptions.
perspective	A particular theoretical model or school of thought.
pluralism	A state in which people of all races and ethnicities are distinct but have social parity.
pluralist model	An analysis of politics that views power as dispersed among many competing interest groups.
political revolution	The overthrow of one political system in order to establish another.
politics	The actual act of distributing power and making decisions.
polity	The social institution that distributes power and makes decisions.
polygamy	Plural marriage, or marriage that involves more than one spouse simultaneously.
popular culture	Cultural patterns widespread among a society's people, usually limited to the arts and entertainment.
population	The entire collection or universe of objects, events, or people that a researcher is actually interested in and from which a sample is drawn. The population is often referred to as the universe of cases.
positive correlation	A correlation or association between two variables wherein the attributes co-vary in the same direction. For example, as religiosity increases, faith in people increases, and vice versa.
positivism	A path to understanding based on science, not on philosophic presuppositions or metaphysics.
postindustrial economy	A productive system based on service work and high technology.
postmodernity	Social patterns typical of a postindustrial society.
power	The ability to achieve desired ends despite opposition.
power-elite model	An analysis of social life that views power as concentrated among the rich.
prejudice	A rigid and problematic generalization about a category of people.
prescribe	To set down as a rule or direction to be followed.
presentation of self	Goffman's term for the ways in which individuals, in various settings, try to create specific impressions in the minds of others.
primary group	A small social group in which relationships are close, personal, and enduring.
prioritize	The condition of ranking items in the order of their importance.
profane	That which people define as an ordinary element of everyday life.
profession	A prestigious, white-collar occupation that requires extensive formal education.

proletariat	People who sell their productive labor; Marxian term for the "masses".
public opinion	The attitudes of people throughout a society about one or more controversial issues.
puppet government	A government in one country that is under complete control of a government of another country.
qualitative variable	A variable whose values differ in quality and kind rather than quantity. With a qualitative variable, one value is different from another, but numerical expressions such as "more than" or "less than" are meaningless. An example of a qualitative variable would be gender. Males are different from females, but we cannot say that males have "more gender" than females.
quantitative variable	A variable whose values differ in quantity. With a quantitative variable, you can make distinctions based on numerical properties, such as "more than" or "less than." An example of a quantitative variable would be the number of prior arrests a convicted offender has. A person with one prior arrest has less than a person with three prior arrests.
race	A category composed of men and women who share biologically transmitted traits that members of a society deem socially significant.
racism	The belief that one racial category is innately superior or inferior to another.
random selection	A way of ensuring that the sample selected is representative of the population from which it was drawn. In random selection, each element of the population has a known, nonzero, independent, and equal chance of being selected.
range	A measure of dispersion. With continuous data, the range is the difference between the highest score and the lowest score. With rank-ordered categorical data, the range is defined as the difference between the midpoints of the highest and lowest class intervals.
ratio-level variable	A continuous, quantitative variable in which the distance between values is both known and equal. Unlike an interval-level variable, a ratio-level variable has an absolute or true zero point, which implies the complete absence of the characteristic. An example of a ratio-level variable would be a robbery victimization rate per 100,000 for persons between the ages of 20 and 40.
rationality	Deliberate calculation of efficient means to accomplish any particular task.
rationalization	Weber's term for the change from tradition to rationality as the dominant mode of human thought.
recycling	Reuse of resources that we would otherwise discard as waste.
reference group	A social group that becomes a point of reference for making evaluations and decisions.
refugees	Persons who flee their native country seeking safety from persecution.
rehabilitation	Reforming the offender to forgo further offenses.

relative deprivation	A perceived disadvantage relative to some standard of comparison.
relative poverty	The deprivation of some people in relation to others.
reliability	The quality of consistency in measurement attained through repetition.
religion	A social institution involving beliefs and practices that distinguish the sacred from the profane.
religiosity	The importance of religion in social life.
religious fundamentalism	A conservative religious doctrine that opposes intellectuals and worldly accommodation in favor of the restoration of traditional religious systems.
replicate	To reproduce, model, or simulate. In science, studies are replicated to increase or decrease confidence in their findings.
research method	A strategy for systematically carrying out research. Sometimes referred to as the design of a study.
resocialization	Formal or informal socialization intended to radically alter an individual's personality.
retrospective labeling	The interpretation of someone's past consistent with present deviance.
robotics	The field of research and development of robots.
role	Normative patterns of behavior for those holding a particular status.
role conflict	Incompatibility among roles corresponding to two or more statuses.
role model	Someone who sets the example.
role set	A number of roles attached to a single status.
role strain	Incompatibility among roles corresponding to a single status.
routinization of charisma	Weber's term for the development of charismatic authority into some combination of traditional and bureaucratic authority.
sacred	That which people define as extraordinary, inspiring a sense of awe and reverence.
sample	A subset of objects, events, or people selected from a population. A sample is selected to estimate values or characteristics (parameters) of the population or to test hypotheses about the population.
satellite country	A country that is controlled by another, more powerful country.
scapegoat	A person or category of people, typically with little power, whom others unfairly blame for their own troubles.
schooling	Formal instruction under the direction of specially trained teachers.
science	A logical system that derives knowledge from direct, systematic observation.
secondary group	A large and impersonal social group based on some special interest or activity, usually of limited duration.
sect	A type of religious organization that stands apart from the larger society.

secularization	The historical decline in the influence of religion.
segregation	The physical and social separation of categories of people.
self	Mead's term for the dimension of personality composed of an individual's self-awareness and self-image.
sex	The biological distinction between females and males.
sex ratio	The number of males for every hundred females in a given population.
sexism	The belief that one sex is innately superior to the other.
sexual harassment	Comments, gestures, or physical contact of a sexual nature that are deliberate, repeated, and unwelcome.
sexual orientation	The manner in which people experience sexual arousal and achieve sexual pleasure.
sick role	Patterns of behavior defined as appropriate for those who are ill.
significance level	The probability of rejecting a null hypothesis when in reality it is true.
simple random sample	A type of probability sample in which each element of the population has a known and equal probability of being included in the sample.
social change	Any significant alteration in the structure of society.
social character	Personality characteristics common to members of a society.
social construction of reality	The process by which individuals creatively build reality through social interaction.
social control	The process by which society regulates the thoughts and behaviors of individuals.
social dysfunction	The undesirable consequences of any social pattern for the operation of society.
social epidemiology	The study of how and why health and disease are distributed throughout a society's population.
social function	The consequences of any social pattern for the operation of society as a whole or in part.
social group	Two or more people who identify and interact with one another.
social institution	An organized sphere of social life such as education or the family.
social interaction	The process by which people act and react in relation to others.
social mobility	Capability of change of position in a stratification system.
social movement	An organized effort to encourage or oppose some dimension of change.
social stratification	A system by which a society ranks categories of people in a hierarchy.
social structure	Any relatively stable pattern of social behavior.

social-conflict paradigm   A framework for building theory based on the assumption that society is a complex system characterized by inequality and conflict that generate social change.

socialism   An economic system in which the government owns the means of production.

socialized medicine   A medical care system in which the government owns most medical facilities and employs most physicians.

society   A social grouping within a limited territory guided by the culture.

sociobiology   A theoretical paradigm that explains cultural patterns in terms of biological forces.

socioeconomic status (SES)   A composite social ranking based on various dimensions of inequality or inequity.

sociology   A social science concerned with the systematic study of society.

standard deviation   The square root of the variance; a commonly used measure that indicates the degree of deviation or dispersion from the mean of all the scores in the distribution. Sometimes referred to as the standard error of the mean.

status   A general designation of social standing as measured by income or wealth.

status consistency   The degree of consistency in a person's social standing across various dimensions of inequality.

status set   All the statuses a person holds at a particular time.

stereotype   An exaggerated belief associated with a category; a prejudiced description of a category of people.

stigma   A powerfully negative label that radically changes a person's self-concept and social identity.

structural social mobility   Capability of shift in the social position of large numbers of people due less to individual efforts than to changes in society itself.

structural-functional paradigm   A framework for building theory based on the assumption that society is a complex system whose parts work together to promote stability.

subculture   Cultural patterns that distinguish some group of a society's population.

suburbs   Urban areas beyond the political boundaries of a city but usually containing more than half the population of such areas.

superego   Freud's designation of the presence of culture within the individual in the form of internalized values and norms.

survey   A research method in which subjects selected (sampled) from a larger population respond to a series of statements or questions in a questionnaire or interview.

sustainable ecosystem — The human use of the natural environment to meet the needs of the present generation without threatening the prospects of future generations.

symbol — Anything that stands for or represents something else—for example, symbolic words, phrases, and images associated with a social movement.

symbolic-interaction perspective — A framework for building theory based on the view that society is the product of the everyday interactions of individuals and how they define the situations they are in.

technology — The body of knowledge applied to the practical tasks of living.

terrorism — Violence or the threat of violence by an individual or a group as a political strategy.

tertiary sector — The part of the economy involving services rather than goods.

theoretical paradigm — A set of fundamental assumptions that guides thinking and research; a perspective from which reality is defined.

total institution — A setting in which individuals are isolated from the rest of society and manipulated by an administrative staff.

totalitarianism — A highly centralized political system that extensively regulates people's lives.

totem — An object collectively defined as sacred or as emblematic of a clan.

tracking — The division of a school's students into different educational programs based on their achievement level.

tradition sentiments — Beliefs about the world that are passed from generation to generation.

tradition-directedness — Rigid conformity to time-honored ways of living.

transsexual — A person who feels he or she is one sex though biologically the other.

triad — A social group with three members.

urban ecology — Study of the link between the physical and social dimensions of cities.

urbanization — The concentration of humanity into cities.

validity — The quality of measurement gained by measuring exactly what one intends to measure; pertains to the accuracy of the measurement instrument.

values — Culturally defined standards of desirability, goodness, and beauty that serve as broad guidelines for social life.

variable — A concept whose value changes from case to case.

variance — A way of measuring the deviation of the scores from the mean; the amount of error involved in using the mean to represent all other scores in the distribution.

victimless crime   Violation of law in which there is assumed to be no readily apparent victim—for example, prostitution or gambling.

wealth   An individual's or family's total financial assets.

white-collar crime   Crimes committed by people of high social position in the course of their occupations.

white-collar occupation   Higher prestige work that involves mostly mental activity.

"About ASA." N.d. American Sociological Association. Retrieved March 25, 2016 (http://www.asanet.org/about/about_asa.cfm).

"About CRL." N.d. Center for Research Libraries: Global Resources Network. Retrieved March 28, 2016 (http://www.crl.edu/about).

"AFC Concerts, Lectures, and Symposia with Webcasts, Photographs, and Essays." N.d. The American Folklife Center. Retrieved March 28, 2016 (https://www.loc.gov/folklife/events/pasteventsmenu.html).

Aristotle. N.d. *Politics.* 1.1253a. Retrieved March 7, 2016 (http://data.perseus.org/citations/urn:cts:greekLit:tlg0086.tlg035.perseus-eng1:1.1253a).

Babb, Drew. 2014. "LBJ's 1964 Attack Ad 'Daisy' Leaves a Legacy for Modern Campaigns." *Washington Post*, 5 September. Retrieved February 23, 2016 (https://www.washingtonpost.com/opinions/lbjs-1964-attack-ad-daisy-leaves-a-legacy-for-modern-campaigns/2014/09/05/d00e66b0-33b4-11e4-9e92-0899b306b-bea_story.html).

Becker, Howard. 1953. "Becoming a Marijuana User." *AJS: American Journal of Sociology* 59(3):235–42.

Becker, Howard S., Blanche Geer, Everett C. Hughes and Anselm L. Strauss. 1961. *Boys in White: Student Culture in Medical School.* Chicago: University of Chicago Press.

Bouma, Gary D. and G. B. J. Atkinson. 1995. *A Handbook of Social Science Research: A Comprehensive and Practical Guide for Students.* 2d ed, pp. 110–14. New York: Oxford University Press.

Boyle, Elizabeth H., Minzee Kim and Wesley Longhofer. 2015. "Abortion Liberalization in World Society." *AJS: American Journal of Sociology* 121(3):882–913.

Brooks, David. 2015. "The Minimum-Wage Muddle." *New York Times*, July 24. Retrieved March 7, 2016 (http://www.nytimes.com/2015/07/24/opinion/david-brooks-the-minimum-wage-muddle.html?_r=0).

Bulwer-Lytton, Edward. 1839. *Richelieu: Or, the Conspiracy, a Plan in Five Acts.* II, ii, p. 39. New York: Samuel French, [186–?]. *Making of America.* Ann Arbor: University of Michigan Library, 2005. Retrieved February 23, 2016 (http://name.umdl.umich.edu/AAX 3994.0001.001).

"Collections with Manuscripts." N.d. Library of Congress. Retrieved March 7, 2016 (https://www.loc.gov/manuscripts/collections/).

Credit Suisse. 2015. "Wealth Shares and Minimal Wealth of Deciles and Top Percentiles for Regions and Selected Countries, 2015." *Global Wealth Databook 2015*, October, table 6.5, p. 149. Retrieved March 29, 2016 (http://publications.creditsuisse.com/tasks/render/file/index.cfm?fileid=C26E3824-E868-56E0-CCA04D4BB9B9ADD5).

"Data and Statistics about the United States." N.d. USA.gov. Retrieved March 28, 2016 (https://www.usa.gov/statistics).

Forster, E. M. [1927] 1956. *Aspects of the Novel.* New York: Harvest.

Hartwell, Patrick. 1985. "Grammar, Grammars, and the Teaching of Grammar." *College English* 47(2):105–27.

"History of the Library." N.d. Library of Congress. Retrieved March 7, 2016 (https://www.loc.gov/about/history-of-the-library/).

Hunter, David E. and Phillip Whitten, eds. 1976. *Encyclopedia of Anthropology.* New York: Harper & Row.

Isaac, Stephen and William B. Michael. 1981. *Handbook in Research and Evaluation.* 2d ed. San Diego: EdITS Publishers.

Jacob-Chien, Cynthia Y. A. and Richard L. Dukes. 1998. "Understanding Adolescent Work in Social and Behavioral Contexts." *Free Inquiry in Creative Sociology* 26(1):23.

Krugman, Paul. 2015. "Liberals and Wages." *New York Times*, July 17. Retrieved March 7, 2016 (http://www.nytimes.com/2015/07/17/opinion/paul-krugman-liberals-and-wages.html).

Kübler-Ross, Elizabeth. N.d. "Quotes." Elizabeth Kübler-Ross Foundation. Retrieved March 25, 2016 (http://www.ekrfoundation.org/quotes/).om/2015/12/30/business/economy/for-the-wealthiest-private-tax-system-saves-them-billions.html).

Levin, Jack, Arnold Arluke and Amita Mody-Desbareau. 1986. "The Gossip Tabloid as an Agent of Social Control." Presented at the annual meeting of the American Sociological Association, September 1, New York City.

Lincoln, Abraham. [1863] N.d. "The Gettysburg Address." Abraham Lincoln Online. Retrieved March 25, 2016 (http://www.abrahamlincolnonline.org/lincoln/speeches/gettysburg.htm).

Lincoln, Abraham. N.d. "Letter to Horace Greeley" (August 22, 1862). Abraham Lincoln Online. Retrieved March 25, 2016 (http://www.abrahamlincolnonline.org/lincoln/speeches/greeley.htm).

Mead, Margaret. 1928. *Coming of Age in Samoa: A Psychological Study of Primitive Youth for Western Civilization*. New York: William Morrow.

Obama, Barack. 2016. "Weekly Address: Making America Safer for Our Children." The White House, 1 January. Retrieved February 23, 2016 (https://www.whitehouse.gov/the-press-office/2016/01/01/weekly-address-making-america-safer-our-children).

"Office of Information and Regulatory Affairs." N.d. Office of Management and Budget. Retrieved March 28, 2016 (https://www.whitehouse.gov/omb/policy_analyst/).

Partlow, Joshua. 2016. "Actor Sean Penn Secretly Interviewed Mexico's 'El Chapo' in Hideout." *Washington Post*, 10 January. Retrieved February 23, 2016 (https://www.washingtonpost.com/world/actor-sean-penn-secretly-interviewed-el-chapo-in-hideout-before-capture/2016/01/09/4cce48db-1dc5-40b2-9b21-aa412c87e7bc_story.html).

Pearce, Catherine Owens. 1958. *A Scientist of Two Worlds: Louis Agassiz*. Philadelphia: Lippincott.

Philliber, Susan G., Mary R. Schwab and G. Sam Sloss. 1980. *Social Research*. Itasca, IL: F. E. Peacock.

"Population of Cities (1920–2005)," "Historical Statistics of Japan: Chapter 2 Populations and Households." In *Statistics Japan*. Retrieved March 8, 2016 (http://www.stat.go.jp/english/data/chouki/02.htm).

Roosevelt, Franklin D. 1941. "'Four Freedoms Speech': Annual Message to Congress on the State of the Union." Franklin D. Roosevelt Presidential Library and Museum. January 6. Retrieved March 8, 2016 (http://www.fdrlibrary.marist.edu/pdfs/fftext.pd).

Scheiber, Noam and Patricia Cohen. 2015. "For the Wealthiest, a Private Tax System That Saves Them Billions: The Very Richest Are Able to Quietly Shape Tax Policy that will Allow Them to Shield Billions in Income." *New York Times*, 29 December. Retrieved March 25, 2016 (http://www.nytimes).

Scott, Gregory M. 1998. "Review of Political Islam: Revolution, Radicalism, or Reform?" Ed. John L. Esposito. *Southeastern Political Review* 26(2):512–24.

"Section on Aging and the Life Course." N.d. American Sociological Association. Retrieved March 25, 2016 (http://www.asanet.org/sections/aging.cfm).

Stinnett, Nick, and John DeFrain. 1985. *Secrets of Strong Families*. Boston: Little, Brown.

"Stray Bullet That Killed Long Island Girl Was Fired in Retaliation for Hoverboard Theft, Police Say." 2016. *New York Times*, January 11. Retrieved March 7, 2016 (http://www. nytimes.com/2016/01/12/nyregion/stray-bullet-that-killed-long-island-girl-was-fired-in-retaliation-for-theft-police-say.html?_r=0).

"Table of Contents." 2015. *AJS: American Journal of Sociology* 121(3). Retrieved March 28, 2016 (https://www.jstor.org/stable/10.1086/681062).

"U.S. Army Corps of Engineers Releases Report on Coastal Storm and Flood Risk in the North Atlantic Region of the United States." 2015. US Army Corps of Engineers, January 28. Retrieved March 28, 2016. (http://www.usace.army.mil/Media/NewsReleases/NewsRelease ArticleView/tabid/231/Article/562301/us-army-corps-of-engineers-releases-report-on-coastal-storm-and-flood-risk-in-t.aspx).

Warner, William Lloyd. 1947. *Social Class in America: A Manual of Procedure for the Measurement of Social Status*. Chicago: Science Research Associates.